AGAINST
ALL TIDES

AGAINST ALL TIDES

★ ★ ★ ★ ★

THE UNTOLD STORY OF THE USS *KITTY HAWK* RACE RIOT

MARV TRUHE

Lawrence Hill Books

Chicago

First hardcover edition published in 2023
First paperback edition published in 2024
Published by Chicago Review Press Incorporated
814 North Franklin Street
Chicago, Illinois 60610
ISBN 978-0-913705-57-5

The Library of Congress has cataloged the hardcover edition
under the following Control Number: 2022941136

Cover design: Jonathan Hahn
Cover photo: AV8 Collection 2 / Alamy Stock Photo
Interior design: Nord Compo
Interior photos are from the author's collection.

Printed in the United States of America

This book is dedicated to the loving memory of our dear son Jason who took great pleasure in reading and was often seen curled up with a favorite book in his lap. It is also dedicated to our unfailingly kind and precious grandchildren, Blythe and Blake, who are the center of our universe.

CONTENTS

Part IV: Trial Outcomes and Beyond

PREFACE

The date was October 12, 1972, during the latest escalation of the Vietnam War. The place was the Gulf of Tonkin in the South China Sea. The attack carrier USS *Kitty Hawk* was launching bombing runs onto North Vietnamese targets. At the same time, below her flight deck and through her labyrinth of passageways, numerous interracial confrontations erupted. It began with white marines assaulting Black sailors and then white and Black sailors assaulting each other, sometimes armed with makeshift weapons, including wrenches and broken-off broom handles. When the tumult finally ended several hours later, fifty-one crew members had suffered injuries for which medical reports were issued.

By the time *Kitty Hawk* disengaged from Yankee Station and headed back to port in the Philippines, twenty-five Black sailors were charged with rioting and with committing assaults on white sailors. Not a single white crew member was charged at that time.

A few weeks later, my life became inextricably linked with those Black sailors. My naval officer's uniform bore the military rank and insignia of a lieutenant in the Judge Advocate General's Corps. I was a JAG lawyer assigned to defend six of the accused in a series of special courts-martial trials at the Navy Station Law Center in San Diego, California.

The unofficial Navy record of the *Kitty Hawk* incident, as well as virtually all other published accounts, would lead you to the likely conclusion that the sole perpetrators of the disturbance were Black sailors, and all white sailors aboard that night were innocent victims and bystanders.

I wrote this book to examine the veracity of those accounts. I did so by reviewing the critical events of that evening aboard *Kitty Hawk*, probing the Navy investigations that followed, and chronicling the ensuing courts-martial trials. My credentials for this endeavor are the five months of my life spent in intense preparation for, and engaging in, those trials.

Since this is a first-person account, it necessarily includes my personal recollections. I am aided by my original case files, interview notes with clients and witnesses, and dozens of cassette tape recordings I dictated at the time. I also drew upon my personal copies of voluminous official *Kitty Hawk* documents including witness statements, investigative reports, and trial and hearing transcripts. Finally, and importantly, you will hear from former *Kitty Hawk* defendants and *Kitty Hawk* lawyers who shared their stories with me for this account.

During and after the trials, I assembled all the documents so someday I could bring to light the full *Kitty Hawk* story. That time is now, because even fifty years later, no publications or other accounts have captured the complete story, and too many have gotten it completely wrong.

Almost none have included the perspectives of the Black sailors aboard the *Kitty Hawk* that night, let alone the viewpoints of the twenty-five accused. The *New York Times* did cover some of the perspective of defense counsel, often using me as a source.

The trials in early 1973 garnered national attention for months, and local television stations carried virtually nonstop reports. Print reporters set up camp outside the Navy law center, vying for a seat in the overflowing spectator section of the courtroom. Articles flowed from newspapers and newsmagazines throughout the country. More often than not, their headlines trumpeted USS KITTY HAWK RACE RIOT! When the trials began, a group of picketers were marching outside the gates of the San Diego Naval Station with banners proclaiming, "Free the Kitty Hawk 21!"[1]

Politicians even joined in. A United States Congress subcommittee conducted daily hearings to investigate the *Kitty Hawk* incident. On January 3, 1973, just before I walked into a military courtroom to defend the first of my clients, the congressional subcommittee released its report to the national press:

> The subcommittee is of the position that the riot on Kitty Hawk consisted of unprovoked assaults by a very few men, most of whom were below-average mental capacity, most of whom had been aboard for less than one year, and all of whom were black. This group, as a whole, acted as "thugs" which raises doubt as to whether they should ever have been accepted into military service in the first place.[2]

As you will see in this narrative, virtually every assertion in that statement is pure fiction.

I was honored to wear the uniform of a US Navy officer and am proud of and eternally grateful for those who have worn military uniforms in defense of our country. You will read about some of them here. There are others, however, whom I have less respect for, and you will read about them also.

I witnessed racial injustice up close and personal while representing the *Kitty Hawk* sailors. My defense of those sailors remains to this day the most challenging and emotionally charged experience of my entire legal career.

This, then, is the untold story of the *Kitty Hawk* incident and the trials that followed.

ACKNOWLEDGMENTS

I began this book in 1973 after the *Kitty Hawk* trials concluded and during the time I was serving as a military judge in the same courtroom that hosted most of those trials. When I left the Navy, I retained all the original source documents and records, as I intended to complete the book within a few years. Life intervened, however, and I did not take up the effort again until 2021. I want to first of all thank Colorado author, John W. Anderson, who encouraged me to complete my *Kitty Hawk* narrative.

This book became a reality thanks to my literary agent Greg Johnson of WordServe Literary, who patiently guided this first-time author through a huge learning experience. I couldn't have asked for a better agent than Greg, who showed an immediate interest in my story and was always in my corner offering his encouragement and sage advice. Thank you, Greg.

I want to especially thank my publisher, Chicago Review Press, and its editors for agreeing to publish a story that very much needed to be told, and also Independent Publishers Group for promoting and marketing my book throughout the United States and internationally.

Special thanks go out to former *Kitty Hawk* sailors Perry Pettus, Durward Davis, and Vernell Robinson. They graciously agreed to share their memories of the October incident, their Navy service, and their lives before and after. Durward Davis and Vernell Robinson were *Kitty*

Hawk defendants and so were also able to offer that unique perspective. Sincere thanks also to Donna Mallory Coleman, the sister of *Kitty Hawk* sailor Cleveland Mallory, for sharing memories of her brother "Butch" who passed away in 2017.

I owe a sincere debt of gratitude to thirteen of the lawyers who served as counsel in the *Kitty Hawk* trials and shared their memories of those events. They are former JAG officers Paul Black, Jim Bradley, Harry Carter, Bruce Locke, Bob Pearson, Tom Phillips, Mike Sheehy, and Dick Smith, and civilian attorneys Clifton Blevins, Dennis Kelly, Alex Landon, Mike Pancer, and Milt Silverman. They offered fresh insight into the trials and the events preceding them. Sincere thanks also to Gayle Lash, the sister of JAG officer Glenn Haase, for sharing memories of Glenn, who passed away in 2013.

When I again took up writing the book last year, I began sharing excerpts with those former *Kitty Hawk* sailors and attorneys, asking for their comments and corrections. Several others read my ongoing work product and offered their input and candid reviews. First and foremost is my wife Nicki, a former high school English teacher, who spent countless hours patiently reading through and correcting and improving my manuscript. I also want to give special thanks to our son Eric Truhe and his wife Leigh, my brother Larry Truhe and his wife Carol, my sister Joann Condie, who recently had her own book published, and her husband Dave, and good friends Ron Blackwelder, Chuck and Carol Jansch, Walt Jones, an Army Vietnam veteran, and Rudy Swenson, a former US Navy line officer in WestPac. Each of them had a unique insight into the story, and all contributed immensely to the finished narrative.

The research for the book was entirely my own, so I alone am responsible for any errors within its pages. It contains more than one thousand endnote citations, taken primarily from my original source documents and personal records. That is a large number of endnotes, but I felt them necessary to ensure the accuracy and credibility of the narrative and to fulfill my goal of delivering a complete and evenly balanced account of the *Kitty Hawk* incident and its aftermath.

PART I

KITTY HAWK AT SEA

1

IN THE BEGINNING

Date: 12 October 1972
Time: 1530H
Location: US Naval Station Law Center, San Diego

I was in my office reviewing witness statements for a desertion trial when the law center director dropped by. Captain Newsome wasn't stopping just to visit as he sometimes did; he handed me a new case file.[1]

"I thought you'd like this one, Marv," he said. "Your guy is charged with sniffing jet fuel."

"Seriously?"

"Afraid so," he said. "He was on the Ticonderoga when the carrier's drug supply apparently dried up. They found him passed out next to a barrel of jet fuel with its lid pried off."

"Sniffing jet fuel? Is that even an offense?"

"I know," he said, with a hint of a smile. "I thought you'd find it interesting."[2]

After almost two years as a JAG lawyer, I was no longer surprised at the files that crossed my desk. I had arrived at the Naval Station Law Center in January of the previous year, fresh out of Naval Justice School and a newlywed of just over a week.

San Diego was sunny that morning, just like most mornings, when I drove up to the law center in my 1962 blue-and-white Chevrolet Impala.

The law center was a quiet, nondescript one-deck structure that looked over the San Diego harbor. As I pulled up, I noticed a large steel-gray Navy vessel at the pier just beyond the palm trees on the front lawn.

Although I was a US Navy officer, I didn't have a clue what kind of vessel it was. It was probably because I hadn't paid much attention to such things during Naval Officer Indoctrination School. Every ship has a hull classification code: *DE* is a destroyer escort, *LST* a landing ship tank, and so on for more than a hundred codes. We were supposed to memorize them, but for a bunch of soon-to-be Navy lawyers, we didn't see much point. An OIS classmate simplified it for us all by calling them *GBB*s and *LBB*s—Great Big Boats and Little Bitty Boats. After looking again at the vessel berthed across from the law center, I figured it must be a GBB.

Now, almost two years later, I had learned one ship designator, in particular: *CVA*—aircraft carrier attack. In 1972, and throughout the Vietnam War, San Diego was home port for several of the Seventh Fleet's eight carriers, the Navy's largest warships. The Eleventh Naval District's facilities were sprawled over more than four square miles in and around the San Diego harbor, a natural deepwater anchorage.

We judge advocates at the law center always had our hands full, usually juggling more than a dozen courts-martial cases at a time and having daily trials and other hearings. But when the "fleet was in," it sometimes got a little crazy. With deployments to Vietnam lasting up to ten months, crew members of the fleet often found time to get in trouble.

Drugs flowing out of Southeast Asia were cheap and plentiful, and liberty hours in the away ports sometimes led to alcohol-fueled barroom brawls. Aboard, disciplinary issues ran the gamut from simple disrespect to petty officers to the occasional altercation between a couple of sailors.

While at sea, ships' captains handled relatively minor infractions with "captain's masts" conducted onboard, but more serious cases were left for us JAGs in San Diego, when the ships returned home. On their arrival, especially carriers with up to five thousand crew members each, our case dockets sometimes doubled overnight.

I remember the carrier USS *Kitty Hawk* the most personally and unforgettably. It all started the same day the law center director stopped by my office, but halfway around the world.

Date: 12 October 1972
Time: 1930H
Location: Gulf of Tonkin, South China Sea

US Navy Carrier Group 77.7 was night steaming on a course of 335 degrees at a speed of fifteen knots on Yankee Station off the coast of North Vietnam.[3] The guided-missile cruiser USS *Gridley* (*DLG-21*) led the convoy, and a thousand yards off her starboard quarter churned the colossal attack carrier USS *Kitty Hawk* (*CVA-63*), the task group flagship.[4]

Displacing eighty-two thousand tons fully loaded with aircraft and armaments, and almost a quarter mile long, *Kitty Hawk* was one of the largest warships ever built. With an onboard air wing, she carried a complement of 4,483 officers and enlisted men.[5] *Kitty Hawk* was quite literally a floating city.

Kitty Hawk's credentials and statistics matched her massive size. Launched in May 1960, she could steam at thirty-two knots into a stiff headwind while launching and recovering jet attack aircraft on her huge four-acre flight deck. The ship's onboard Carrier Air Wing Eleven had 107 aircraft, an air wing world record.[6] That afternoon and evening, 12 October 1972, those aircraft were conducting nonstop bombing runs into North Vietnam, from just seventy-five miles off the coast of Haiphong Harbor. Those operations continued until 2030 that evening and resumed at 0800 the next morning.[7]

Before dawn broke on Friday the thirteenth, *Kitty Hawk* added yet another statistic to her credentials, and not a good one. She experienced an outbreak of confrontations and assaults between Black and white crew members that lasted several hours. From that time to the present, that incident is known as the *Kitty Hawk* Race Riot. Some even call it the only shipboard mutiny in US Navy history.

That uproar did not arise suddenly out of the ocean depths like Poseidon, the Greek god of the sea. It had its origins in the too-long history of racial segregation and discrimination in the US military that preceded it. That history is important in giving context to the *Kitty Hawk* story.

During the Revolutionary War, more than five thousand free Black men fought for the colonists, despite General Washington's initial opposition. After the war, however, virtually all Black men were excluded from the military. During the Civil War and after the Emancipation Proclamation, the Union began widespread enlistment of Black men. They proved to be excellent soldiers but were discriminated against in pay, pensions, and equipment. Of particular interest is that Black men also served honorably in the Union Navy, making up fully one-fourth of its fleet. That ratio was double the Black population of the country at the time. By the close of the Civil War, more than thirty-eight thousand Black men had given their lives fighting for the Union cause.[8]

About 370,000 Black Americans served in the US military during World War I, although most were not allowed to serve in combat units. Those who were allowed in combat fought well and earned many honors. None who served, however, were exempt from racial discrimination. Toward the end of the war, French military personnel were directed not to treat Black Americans equally, stating the official French desire not to offend white Americans in uniform.[9]

More than one million Black men and women served in uniform during World War II. Initially, the Army was segregated into separate Black units, always led by white officers. Later, the military began integrating, primarily due to military necessity. Even then, a large percentage of Black personnel were relegated to driving trucks and performing menial tasks, such as laundry and kitchen duty.

Some did find a way to get into combat. The exploits of the Tuske-
gee Airmen in North Africa and Europe, and the Ninety-Second Infantry
Division in Italy, are a lasting testament to the proud history of Black
men in uniform. Five Black soldiers received the Army's Distinguished
Service Cross during the war, and eighty-two Black pilots were awarded
the Army Air Corps' Distinguished Flying Cross.[10]

But what does the history of Black men and women in the military
have to do with a racial confrontation on board *Kitty Hawk* a quarter
of a century after World War II? Quite a lot, in fact.

The *Kitty Hawk* story is centered in WestPac, the western Pacific,
and more specifically in the Vietnam theater. In the summer and fall
of 1972 Vietnam was the Navy's hottest spot on the planet, and the
hottest spot for a young seagoing sailor was serving as a crew member
on an attack carrier on Yankee Station off the coast of North Vietnam.
Fleet Task Force 77's carrier battle groups conducted operations from
the Gulf of Tonkin in the South China Sea.

Eight years earlier, in August 1964, the Gulf of Tonkin was the
setting for America's full-scale commitment to the Vietnam War[11] and
its first insertion of combat troops into South Vietnam. As the war
escalated, so too did America's ground troop commitment, until it had
over half a million military personnel in Vietnam by 1968. By then,
however, antiwar sentiment back in the States was becoming a political
force that could not be ignored. Troop levels began to be scaled back,
and by early 1972 it appeared America finally was on its way out of
the quagmire it had gotten itself into.

But in April of that year, the North Vietnamese launched a full-
scale invasion into South Vietnam, later referred to as the Easter Offensive.[12] In response, President Nixon ordered the institution of a dramatic
increase in the air and naval campaigns against North Vietnam aimed at
convincing its leaders of the futility of continuing the war. Those orders
committed the US Pacific Fleet Naval forces to a level of combat not
seen before in the entire war. In 1971 the Navy's gunfire support ships
averaged two thousand rounds fired weekly, but following the 1972

Easter Offensive, those ships fired an average of twenty-six thousand rounds weekly.[13]

That escalation also had a dramatic impact on the operational schedule of *Kitty Hawk* and its sister carriers of Task Force 77. During the 1968 Tet Offensive, the previous largest escalation of the war, the carrier fleet's daily aircraft sortie rate into North Vietnam averaged 218, but after the 1972 escalation, that increased to 337.[14]

Kitty Hawk's crew felt the impact of that escalation in more ways than one. Before that time they could look forward to visits every six to eight weeks in desirable liberty ports like Hong Kong and Yokosuka, Japan. That was not possible after the escalation. Except for one brief visit to Hong Kong, her crew's only port of call for nearly a year was the Subic Bay Naval Base and Olongapo City in the Philippines.[15]

Kitty Hawk had departed San Diego, its home port, eight months earlier on 17 February, and on 12 October was beginning its seventh "line period" of the war.[16] Each deployment to Vietnam was broken up by several line periods, which are those times spent in a combat zone conducting daily air strikes, and not in port or steaming to and from the combat zone. *Kitty Hawk* had a total of seven such line periods in 1972, the longest lasting fifty days,[17] an inordinate amount of time.

During its current line period, the task group was engaged in Operation Linebacker, an air interdiction campaign conducted into North Vietnam. Along with the shore-based US Seventh Air Force, the task force launched bombing runs at North Vietnamese targets in an attempt to interrupt the flow of supplies and enemy soldiers into South Vietnam.

Since leaving San Diego, *Kitty Hawk's* 264 days of active deployment set a record for the longest of any attack carrier in the entire war. That time included 186 days actively engaged in air strikes on North Vietnamese targets.[18] Those combat sorties, often averaging 120 a day for sustained periods,[19] were carried out by jet aircraft crews of the Naval air squadrons attached to *Kitty Hawk* during the deployment.

Kitty Hawk returned periodically to the Subic Bay Naval Base in the Philippines, nine hundred miles eastward across the South China Sea, for replenishment of supplies and munitions. Those short periods of time spent away from the grueling line periods were too few and far between for the young sailors. The ship's infrequent time in foreign ports typically lasted six days, but for most sailors their liberty days were cut short by shipboard duty while in port.[20] The stress of the extended line periods was heightened by *Kitty Hawk's* increasingly unpredictable schedule. That unpredictability began with *Kitty Hawk* departing its home port of San Diego twenty-six days earlier than originally scheduled.[21] The crew was originally told the carrier would depart 14 March; however, in early February they were told they would be leaving port almost a full month earlier. That created considerable hardship on the carrier's crew whose home port schedules, travel plans, leave status, and shore housing were all geared to leaving a month later.

A Marine officer on board talked about how those initial hardships were exacerbated by an ever-changing return date. "We obviously deployed a month early, so as a result many family-type problems or situations weren't able to be resolved. . . [and] because of the nature of the offensive in April, the ship's schedule itself was literally thrown out the window. So there was hope that perhaps the ship would return in August, September, or possibly as late as October, but no one really knew. There was an uncertainty in the air about the ship's schedule. and that uncertainty started from the day we left San Diego."[22]

A Marine corporal presented an enlisted man's perspective: "There was no mail, half the time we didn't get the mail, our schedule was always messed up, they say you will be in PI [Philippines] on the 15th, we don't pull in, get overscheduled on the line another 10 days, that is just the morale, way low, sir. The guys are working for something and we never get to do it. . . . We would be out at sea for 30 days, and the guys want to go in and see the town and just don't get to see it, because the schedules are all messed up. Townsend, the CO of the boat, tries to inform the troops that I am trying to get this, trying to get that, but he just can't. I guess he doesn't have enough pull."[23]

Personnel on board a carrier are assigned either to the permanent ship's company, or to an onboard air wing. On 12 October, *Kitty Hawk's* company numbered 2,689 personnel, including its Marine Detachment, and 1,794 personnel in the air wing.[24]

What about the enlisted crew of this attack carrier and its attack air squadrons? If you picture them as seasoned and battle-hardened veterans, a closer look may surprise. When a recruit entered Navy boot camp it often was his first time away from home. In addition, many received shipboard assignments right out of boot camp.

Of the 4,135 enlisted men aboard *Kitty Hawk*, almost half made up the three lowest ranks.[25] Of that group, 100 were fresh out of basic training, in pay grade E-1.[26] Those in pay grade E-2 numbered 530, and E-3s numbered 1,196.[27] Since E-3s were at that level, were they seasoned veterans? Not necessarily. They could have attained that rank less than a year out of basic training. In short, the 1,826 men in the lowest three pay grades could hardly be considered battle-hardened veterans.

How did these young sailors and airmen end up in the Navy aboard *Kitty Hawk*? A major factor was the Army draft during the Vietnam War, which began in the sixties and continued until the summer of 1973. How many of them, almost all teenagers at the time, had simply enlisted to avoid the Army draft? We have no way of knowing.[28] However, living on a Navy base, or on a ship at sea, must have appeared decidedly preferable to slogging through the Vietnamese jungles, waiting for who knows what.

In lieu of the Army draft, an eighteen-year-old could fulfill his service obligation in the Navy, Air Force, or Coast Guard. In opting for the Navy, perhaps an impressionable teenager had been lured by a friendly Navy recruiter's siren call. See the world, visit exotic ports, and all on the Navy's dime. If he ended up aboard an attack carrier like *Kitty Hawk*, however, he would quickly discover that his promised world would be limited to, and confined within, a massive steel vessel occupied by more than four thousand men.

Security forces on *Kitty Hawk* included a master-at-arms (MAA) contingent and a Marine Detachment (MARDET). The MAAs were the ship's police force, typically petty officers, responsible for maintaining onboard discipline and order. Their counterparts in other service branches are military police (MPs). The carrier had an MAA force of thirty men when an air wing was onboard.[29]

The onboard contingent of marines numbered sixty-three, which included two officers.[30] MARDET's duties included backing up the MAA force. If the MAAs asked for help, the marines could be ordered out by their commanding officer or someone at a higher command level. The marines guarded high-security areas of the ship, including its nuclear weapons, oversaw the ship's six brig confinement cells, and provided extra pier security while in port.[31] The marines lived apart in their own berthing area and, unlike the MAAs, did not have a regular presence throughout the ship.

The commanding officer of *Kitty Hawk*, Captain Marland Townsend, acknowledged the heavy workload of his crew, but from his lofty perch he saw things primarily in terms of the ship's overall mission. As a result, he seems to have overlooked how his crew's morale might be impacted by the stress of those mission demands and unpredictable schedule, and how that might have contributed to the later onboard tumult.

When questioned about his crew's morale, he immediately shifted the focus to his pride in the carrier's combat missions. He conceded the crew's morale was "flat" when the 12 October incident erupted but boasted how *Kitty Hawk* consistently flew a third again as many strike sorties as any other carrier with up to eight cyclic launches each day.[32]

Captain Townsend claimed his ship was far and away the best operator, the "best in everything. We did those things; I knew we could. I set it up that way, and we did it."[33] That responsibility, of course, fell to his crew members. Air operations were typically conducted twelve hours a day, which meant flight quarters of sixteen hours a day. Flight deck crew members, for example, worked twelve-hour daily shifts during the weeks-long online periods.[34] The ship had about six hundred personnel assigned to the engineering department, and they often worked six hours on and six off, around the clock.[35]

The captain said it was safest to fly bombing runs at night, made possible because squadrons had Grumman A-6E Intruder twinjet all-weather attack aircraft.[36] They could cross into North Vietnam at five hundred feet altitude in pitch-black weather and pouring rain. They could then drop down to two hundred feet on their runs to avoid the radars of surface-to-air missile sites and anti-aircraft batteries. Nighttime sorties, however, meant many crew members had to work from dusk until midmorning the next day for weeks in a row.

It was not just the unrelenting hours that contributed to the tension and stress. During the day and nighttime bombing runs, the steel bulkheads reverberated from shrieking jet engines and steam turbines driving its flight deck steam catapults and massive propulsion shafts. Sailors often took weeks, sometimes never, to acclimate to the cacophony before they got any useful sleep. And how about zero privacy around the clock, even when not on duty? Eating elbow to elbow and sleeping on a row of racks[37] stacked three high next to another row and another.[38] Shore-based sailors can go on liberty to get away from it all, but seagoing sailors have no such escape.

Why don't we bring thousands of young men of different ethnicities and backgrounds together under these conditions, most away from home and family for the first time, and see what happens? What could possibly go wrong? Plenty, as it turns out.

2

NEW COMMANDING
OFFICER

Date: 5 June 1972
Time: 1130H
Location: USS *Kitty Hawk*, off coast of North Vietnam

A change of command on any seagoing vessel can give rise to both anticipation and concern among the ship's crew. What is the new captain like? Will life go on as usual, or will he shake things up? The *Kitty Hawk* crew, and in particular the young Black sailors, wanted to know how they would be treated by their new commanding officer (CO).

Captain Townsend took official command of the *Kitty Hawk* on 5 June 1972, four months before the October incident. As with all officers holding top carrier command positions, he was a former Navy aviator. He entered Navy flight training as a teenager just two months after the end of World War II. During the Korean War, he flew F9F Panthers off the flight deck of the USS *Valley Forge*. He later served as a Navy test pilot and commanded Fighter Squadron 121 in Miramar, California, later known as the TOPGUN school. He was awarded the Bronze Star, Air Medal, and Distinguished Flying Cross.[1] After command assignments on two other carriers, he was selected commanding officer ("captain")[2] of the *Kitty Hawk*. His illustrious career was to be severely tested in the days and weeks to come.

Commander Benjamin Cloud, the executive officer (XO), was second in command and had come aboard just two months before the October incident. Of Black and Native American descent, he had an exemplary career as a Navy aviator before assuming command positions on carriers. Originally from San Diego, he began pilot training in 1952 at the onset of the Korean War. Upon receiving his wings, he was assigned to the VC-61 fighter reconnaissance squadron in San Diego, which he later commanded. He was with that squadron when it deployed to WestPac in 1963.[3] He flew recon missions into Vietnam in an RF-8 Crusader, taking photos of troop and transport movements on the Ho Chi Minh Trail while dodging anti-aircraft fire.[4] After serving as protocol officer in the White House for two presidents,[5] followed by more aviation duty, Cloud was deep selected[6] to become the *Kitty Hawk*'s number two. Among his other flying honors, he was awarded the Distinguished Flying Cross.

Marine Captain Nicholas Carlucci, the commanding officer of the ship's Marine Detachment, said Captain Townsend's replacement of the previous *Kitty Hawk* captain came as a sudden and unexpected shock to all.[7] Carlucci reported aboard two years before the incident, by which time he had already distinguished himself in uniform. He enlisted in the Marines after college in 1968 during the Vietnam buildup and earned his commission in Officer Candidate School. He later served a combat tour in Vietnam followed by two years as an artilleryman instructor stateside.[8]

Commander Cloud had the impression that minority crew members felt the outgoing captain was not very sympathetic to their needs.[9] He said minority sailors had hoped for a change, or reprieve, with the new captain. They soon found out as shortly after Townsend came aboard they witnessed how he handled disciplinary matters, including interracial incidents, at captain's masts.[10]

Masts are a ship commanding officer's principal means for dealing with onboard disciplinary issues, and are typically reserved for minor offenses. Masts are the lowest level of disciplinary proceeding available under the *Uniform Code of Military Justice (UCMJ)*.[11] Masts are also referred to as nonjudicial, or Article 15, proceedings.[12] If the ship's commanding officer determines the disciplinary incident is too serious to be handled at his mast level, he can send the case up one or more levels to be dealt with before a court-martial tribunal.

In a mast procedure, the accused appears in person before the commanding officer and his charges are read to him. If he acknowledges his guilt, the hearing proceeds to sentencing. If he pleads not guilty, however, the ship's investigators provide details of the charged offense, and that is followed by witness testimony. The accused can also testify and bring out witnesses on his own behalf. If the commanding officer finds the accused guilty, he proceeds to the sentencing, with those potential punishments being substantially less than those possible at the higher courts-martial level.[13]

On 8 June, just three days after Townsend assumed command, he was presented with an interracial disciplinary matter. His handling of that incident, and all other interracial disciplinary matters after that, loomed large in the shipboard upheaval that followed.

Date: 8 June 1972
Time: 1630H
Location: Second deck, USS *Kitty Hawk*

The first interracial incident occurred when a white sailor was walking along the second deck and passed through a berthing compartment where several Black sailors were sitting. He said one of the Black sailors threw some popcorn kernels at him.[14] Although not mentioned by the white sailor, Captain Townsend said the sailor responded by giving them the "universal Italian sign"[15]—that is, the gesture of punching a fist into your elbow while raising the other fist. Several Black sailors jumped up and pursued him. He ran up an escalator before they caught him, struck him repeatedly, and dragged him back down the escalator.[16]

The white sailor positively identified two of his assailants, an airman and a seaman.[17] Assault charges were filed against them and their cases were referred to a captain's mast. In a decision he later regretted, Townsend chose to follow his predecessor's lead and conduct masts in the ship's TV center so they could be taped and broadcast later on the ship's closed-circuit system for the entire crew to witness.

At the Black sailors' masts a ship's investigator presented the details of the assault.[18] Both of the accused had witnesses appear in their defense, but Townsend found both guilty.

Townsend sentenced the airman to three days in the brig with a diet of bread and water and sentenced the seaman to thirty days in the ship's brig.[19] In later testimony about the escalator incident, Townsend referred to the assailants as "thugs."[20]

Townsend made a bold statement at that mast that every crew member watching on TV later remembered. He said that anyone who fights or commits an assault on his ship would be dealt with "very harshly and severely."[21] Townsend later confirmed his policy of dealing with onboard assaults. He said, "You go to the brig for 30 days . . . and you are reduced in rate."[22] The ship's crew now knew what to expect from their new commanding officer. The crew soon learned, however, that Captain Townsend's harsh punishments only applied to Black sailors. With a white assailant, a completely different standard applied.

Date: 8 June 1972
Time: 1815H
Location: Fifth deck, USS *Kitty Hawk*

The next interracial incident occurred later the same day as the escalator incident, only this time the roles were reversed. A white sailor assaulted a Black E-1 airman recruit, a crew member fresh out of basic training.

The recruit was performing extra duties in the number three machinery room, using a high-pressure water hose. His supervisor was a fireman,[23] an E-3 level white sailor.[24]

The recruit had lost control of the hose, causing it to flail about. His supervisor turned off the pressure to the hose and told him to pick it up again. The recruit reported that his supervisor said, "Either pick it up or I'm going to kick your ass," and "We don't take no static from [n-word]s down here."[25] He apparently did not respond quickly enough, however, and the supervisor struck him in the back with a clenched fist.

The white sailor was charged with assaulting the Black sailor and the case referred to a captain's mast. News of the incident circulated quickly among the relatively small complement of *Kitty Hawk's* Black crew members, which numbered 297 men, or fewer than 7 percent of the ship's total company.[26] Most waited in anticipation of how Townsend would handle the case. Commander Cloud said the feeling of the Black sailors was "Let's see what the captain will do [when an] assault was committed by a white against a black."[27]

Three days after the hose incident, the accused fireman appeared before Captain Townsend's mast.[28] However, instead of dealing with assaults "very harshly and severely" as he earlier promised, Townsend simply dismissed the charges against the white sailor.[29] In explaining the dismissal, Townsend said he didn't think the supervisor, a nonrated man,[30] should have been put in charge of an extra duty man.[31] Thus, in effect, Townsend blamed someone else for the white sailor's assault on the Black recruit.

That dismissal was especially egregious because of the supervisor's threat of bodily harm and the racial slur directed at the Black recruit. Both constituted violations of the punitive articles of the *UCMJ*.[32] The records do not reflect whether those additional charges were also filed against the supervisor, but would it have even mattered?

Black crewmen saw the mast when it was replayed and were understandably outraged. Immediately thereafter, groups of Black sailors gathered around the ship to vent their anger about the new Captain's special brand of white man's justice.

The disparity of sentencing later came to the attention of a congressional subcommittee which was conducting its own investigation of the *Kitty Hawk* incident. Townsend was pointedly asked about his disparate handling of the two masts: "Why shouldn't [the white supervisor] be punished for striking the black man?"[33]

Captain Townsend replied that the blow was struck in anger and was not a planned assault. Therefore, since it wasn't premeditated, he argued it was "not assault."[34]

That was preposterous. Premeditation is not an element of an assault under the *UCMJ*, so it is immaterial whether an assault is preplanned. In making such a statement, Townsend was apparently trying hard to justify his refusal to punish the assailant. He then said something that must have further dumbfounded the subcommittee members. He told them that by dismissing the charges, he had passed up "a great chance to win a lot of affection from the blacks. I could have thrown that man in jail and been a hero, but I couldn't have lived with myself since that time, either."[35]

The Black sailors and the subcommittee members were not alone in questioning the disparate outcomes of the two masts. A Navy lieutenant gave a sworn statement to the onboard JAG investigator. "The feeling among blacks was that the new Captain was inconsistent at best."[36] The lieutenant also talked about how some black sailors responded to that inconsistency. Following the second mast, groups of Black sailors gathered on more than one occasion to discuss their feelings of frustration and anger about Townsend's actions. They finally decided to ask him to explain his handling of the two masts.[37]

Townsend responded by meeting with approximately 150 Black sailors on the fo'c'sle.[38] During the two-hour meeting, Townsend attempted to explain his actions, and discussed problems on the ship and possible solutions. In response to the sailors' request, he agreed to establish a full-time human resources committee to address future interracial problems.[39] The sailors took the opportunity to air other grievances, including perceived discrimination in ship board assignments and advancements in rank.

That meeting, and how it came about, are important in several respects. A very large group of Black sailors responded to the two contrasting masts by holding a series of peaceable meetings, with no hint of any improper motive. Their next actions likewise revealed the spirit in which they gathered. They asked Captain Townsend to personally meet with them, a very reasonable and appropriate reaction to his unequal treatment of Black and white sailors.

Finally, and significantly, about 150 Black sailors met with Townsend out of a total Black complement of 297 men on the ship.[40] In other words, the perceived racial injustices administered by Townsend were so pervasive that fully half of the Black crewmen showed up to hear him try to explain his actions.

The grievances aired during the meeting with Captain Townsend probably included his practice of televising masts,[41] which especially angered the Black sailors. Who, after all, would want his transgressions aired publicly in such a humiliating way? Townsend himself later acknowledged the impropriety of broadcasting his masts. He said he realized the broadcasts angered the Black sailors but claimed that he only did so because his predecessor commanding officer had recommended the practice. When he first took command, Townsend said he even asked the ship's legal officer about it, "because, frankly, I thought it may be illegal."[42]

Nevertheless, he continued to broadcast the masts for months thereafter.

Date: 19 July 1972
Time: 0830H
Location: Second deck, USS *Kitty Hawk*

A few weeks later, Townsend held his third mast involving a Black sailor and a white sailor. For the second time in a row, a white sailor was the assailant. Black Airman Apprentice Perry Pettus was assaulted in the forward S-2 head on the mess deck.[43] He was on his way to sick bay to have a prescription filled and stopped to use a head a white seaman was cleaning.

The seaman told Pettus the head was secured, but Pettus thought he was kidding because they had previously worked together compartment cleaning. The seaman was not kidding, however, and threw a can of scouring powder at Pettus, striking him in the face. When Pettus tossed it back, the seaman struck him in the eye with his fist.[44]

The seaman was charged with an assault and his case referred to a captain's mast on 27 July.[45] What would Townsend do this time? The televised mast undoubtedly drew an unusually large audience. Given the backlash from his previous two masts, Townsend could easily have taken the opportunity to show his Black crew members that his future masts would be conducted without racial bias.

Unfortunately, the 27 July mast simply reinforced the Black sailors' feelings about Townsend's brand of shipboard justice. The white assailant received a monetary fine, nothing more.[46] A petty officer who attended the mast said, "I believe [he] was fined $25.00, if I recollect right."[47]

The entire ship's crew learned the result of the much-anticipated mast. The Black sailors learned about the outcome they probably expected. Not surprisingly, an interracial incident erupted immediately after.

————

Date: 28 July 1972
Time: 1930H
Location: Second deck, USS *Kitty Hawk*

The next evening two Black sailors were alleged to have gone into a berthing compartment and aggressively confronted and struck two white sailors with their fists. One of those victims was the seaman who had assaulted Pettus, and he was told by one of the Black sailors that he was being repaid for that assault. Interestingly, that Black sailor returned shortly after, asked the victim if he was all right, and told him it was all over.[48]

One of the Black sailors was charged with throwing a shoe during the incident in the berthing compartment and hitting two white sailors. His case was referred to a captain's mast.[49] Instead of meting out punishment at the mast, however, Townsend elected to take the extraordinary step of referring the case to a special court-martial proceeding. Given the alleged offense of throwing a shoe, that decision defied all logic.

The court-martial was to be held when the carrier returned to the Subic Bay Naval Base. The accused never appeared at a court-martial tribunal, however, because he was given the option of accepting an undesirable discharge in lieu of standing trial.[50] That discharge under less than honorable conditions is the most severe punishment that can be administered at other than a court-martial level, and stripped the sailor of all post-military GI benefits, as well as barring any future military service. The outcome was unheard of given the nature of the charged offense.

In his first few weeks on board, Captain Townsend dealt with four interracial incidents. His record was there for all to see. When Black sailors assaulted white sailors, the sentences ranged from three days' confinement on bread and water, to thirty days confinement, to a court-martial referral followed by an undesirable discharge. Yet when white sailors assaulted Black sailors? An outright dismissal of the charges in one case, and a twenty-five-dollar fine in the other.

Townsend tried to defend his handling of those masts by saying that Black sailors didn't understand that he took the accused's prior Service Records into account in his mast decisions.[51] However, the official record gives no support for Townsend's inconsistent mast outcomes. In addition, his dictate that all assaults would be dealt with harshly and severely is flatly contradicted by his mast record.

Those inconsistent outcomes led the congressional subcommittee to question Townsend about that "inequality." Captain Townsend simply replied, "There is equality in mast procedure."[52] He added, "They know damn good and well my record is fair."[53] In an attempt to bolster his defense of his mast records, he told the subcommittee, "In our day and time, as competitive as our business is, a guy who is purely bigoted or something like that is never given a command."[54]

———————

The *Kitty Litter*, a small publication,[55] was sometimes referred to as an "underground newspaper."[56] It was neither officially sanctioned nor officially discouraged. No one seemed to know if it was even published onboard. It was often critical of those in higher command positions, but many thought it valuable for those in mid-leadership positions who wanted to know what younger sailors were thinking and saying.[57]

An issue distributed two months before the October upheaval addressed Townsend's uneven handling of captain's masts. After detailing the outcomes of the masts and Townsend's attempts to defend his actions, the publication stated, "This is the same quality of argument as 'I like blacks okay, as long as they know their place.' Racism, it appears, is all right if the racist is in a position of power."[58]

The publication did concede that after Townsend's "incident of blatant racism," he spent several hours talking to Black sailors, and adopted one of their suggestions, the formation of a human resources council. That concession seemed to suggest that Captain Townsend might have turned the corner in dealing with race relations.

Whether he had, in fact, would be put to the test a few weeks later when the *Kitty Hawk* returned to Subic Bay. Another interracial incident occurred, and this time Townsend could not simply pass it off with dismissive or defensive statements.

3

TROUBLE IN SUBIC BAY

Date: 4 September 1972
Time: 1945H
Location: Subic Bay Naval Base

On 4 September *Kitty Hawk* disengaged from Yankee Station and set sail for Subic Bay in the Philippines. After completing her fifth line period since leaving San Diego in February, the sailors couldn't wait for the much-anticipated break. Three days later, the carrier steamed into Subic Bay and tied up at the Cubi Point Naval Air Station dock. Farther into the bay lay the Subic Bay Naval Base.[1]

It would be an understatement to say Subic Bay was a busy port. During the Vietnam War era, more than thirty Navy vessels entered the harbor each day. The Subic Naval facilities at the time spread out over 262 square miles, and it was the largest US Navy port in the western Pacific. It was a major supply and ship-repair facility and home away from home for much of the Seventh Fleet.

Just beyond the Subic Bay Naval Base's main gate and a bridge lay Olongapo City, the quintessential Navy town for sailors on liberty.[2] During the escalation of the Seventh Fleet's operations in 1972, however, Olongapo was overwhelmed with sailors because all the Seventh Fleet's ships used Subic Bay's port services. From January to October of that year more than a million sailors were on liberty in Olongapo, with the liberty party reaching twenty thousand men some nights.[3]

On entering the town, a sailor found himself in a whole new world, appearing to some as exotic but to others as seedy. From Magsaysay Drive to Rizal Avenue and beyond lay endless bars, night clubs with live music, tattoo parlors, restaurants, and brothels. Turning left at the Rizal traffic circle led to the "jungle,"[4] an area dedicated to attracting Black servicemen. Turning to the right sent you to the "strip," an area where mostly white sailors hung out.[5]

Captain Nicholas Carlucci, the CO of the carrier's Marine Detachment, believed Olongapo provided the perfect catalyst for interracial confrontations, since it was, to all appearances, a segregated town. He said the segregation fed "rumor upon rumor" that went unchecked by anyone.[6]

The town wasn't strictly segregated, however. A Black *Kitty Hawk* sailor said some white crew members liked the bars, music, girls, and nightlife better on his side of town, and they would often ask to go with him and other Black sailors to the jungle. He was perfectly okay with that, but it really upset him that many of those port buddies refused to have anything to do with him back aboard. He attributed some of that to criticism they encountered from other white sailors if they were ship buddies with him or other Black sailors.[7]

Taking the two-hour bus trip to Manila, the capital city, was an option, but not one seriously considered by most. That was especially true two weeks after *Kitty Hawk* arrived back in port. In late September 1972, Philippines President Ferdinand Marcos declared the entire country under martial law.[8]

———————

Date: 13 September 1972
Time: 2300H
Location: Olongapo City, Luzon, Philippines

During *Kitty Hawk*'s mid-September layover at Subic Bay, several Black crew members reported that a white shipmate was paying Filipino "Nationals"[9] to assault Black sailors whenever they ventured into Olongapo on liberty. Even though the white sailor was identified, no investigation occurred at the time.

The reports were confirmed on 13 September, the carrier's last night in port. Just before midnight, an incident occurred on Rizal Street in the jungle section of Olongapo. According to several Black *Kitty Hawk* sailors, a white *Kitty Hawk* sailor accompanied by four Nationals randomly assaulted them and other Black sailors.

One Black eyewitness reported that the white sailor was the instigator and was not only throwing punches, he was directing Nationals in their assaults on Black sailors.[10]

Another Black sailor said the white sailor hurled a racial slur at him and he was then struck in the face by a National, suffering a facial laceration requiring eight stitches to close.[11] Another Black sailor was assaulted and also required medical treatment. Three other Black eyewitnesses stated the Nationals were using knives and rocks during the confrontation.

Five Black victims and witnesses gave sworn statements to *Kitty Hawk*'s chief investigator. The investigator followed up by having them view a lineup on board the ship with the white sailor and four other white sailors, whom he described as having "very close likenesses" to the accused. Three of the five Black sailors picked out Radioman Seaman Apprentice Allen Sickles as the assailant.[12]

The investigators also identified the four Filipino Nationals involved, who happened to be otherwise employed as Naval Base Subic Bay security guards.[13] But before they could be questioned, two of them suddenly quit their jobs and disappeared, so they could not be interviewed. The other two admitted going to the jungle with Sickles that evening. They even called him their "American Friend"[14] and admitted to drinking with him just before to the incident,[15] yet both denied taking part in the assaults.

Sickles admitted that he and his Filipino friends were involved in a fight with the Black sailors, but denied starting the fight. The ship's investigative report concluded that Sickles and the Nationals "had trouble on their minds" when they went into the Black area of Olongapo, and that "it was the mutual feeling of the investigators that the P.I. Nationals were untruthful."[16]

Sickles was charged with an assault and appeared before Captain Townsend at a captain's mast.[17] No record was found, however, of any disciplinary action taken against Sickles, apparently for the reasons Townsend explained to the congressional subcommittee. He did so in response to a *Time* magazine article on the *Kitty Hawk* incident. Townsend said that report of the jungle incident was "circulated by blacks" and "only a few blacks made the charge" that a white sailor had hired the Nationals. He also said the ship's investigators questioned the Nationals and could find no evidence they were hired.[18] These were the same persons his own ship's investigators believed were "untruthful."

The allegations against Sickles were made in sworn statements by five sailors from Townsend's own ship. Three had positively identified Sickles and two had suffered head and facial lacerations. After hearing Townsend say he took no action because "only a few blacks made the charge," one might well ask, *How many sworn statements from how many Black sailors would it have taken for him to discipline Sickles?*

Kitty Hawk returned to Yankee Station and its sixth line period on 16 September. No onboard interracial incidents were reported during that line period which lasted until 2 October. The carrier then returned to Subic Bay.

———————————

Date: 9 October 1972
Time: 2345H
Location: Main gate, Naval Base Subic Bay

Kitty Hawk arrived back at Subic Bay on 5 October and docked at the Naval base's Alava Pier[19] rather than its usual mooring at the Cubi Point Naval Air Station. The Alava Pier was used if ship maintenance was needed. Sailors preferred it to Cubi Point because from there it was an easy walk to the night life in Olongapo, instead of having to take buses from the Cubi Point Naval Air Station.

During that October stay, several more interracial incidents occurred. They were investigated by Captain Bobby Hatch, the assistant chief of staff to the commander of the US Naval Forces Philippines.[20] That informal JAG Manual Investigation[21] produced testimony and more than thirty sworn statements.[22]

The first incident occurred just before midnight on 9 October outside the main gate of the Subic Bay Naval Base. Airman Dwight Horton, a Black *Kitty Hawk* sailor, was returning alone to the ship when two white sailors came up behind him, and one uttered a racial slur. As he turned around, one of the sailors grabbed him and threw him to the ground. He tried fighting back but had difficulty, as his right arm was in a cast, having been broken earlier. Both the sailors were assaulting him when shore patrolmen arrived. They took his assailants and two white eyewitnesses to the Naval base security office.[23]

Horton was first taken to the Naval base medical facility because of injuries to his eye, wrist, and hip, and then to the Naval base security office, where an investigator was taking statements. Horton asked to make a statement, but the investigator kept telling him to "shut up."[24] He eventually just gave up and returned to the *Kitty Hawk* on his own without anyone ever talking to him.

The two white eyewitnesses who gave statements were from another ship. They both said that Horton was the victim, not the perpetrator. One said the assailants yelled the *n*-word at Horton and then "threw him down and started hitting him."[25]

One of the assailants claimed Horton initiated the fight after his "intoxicated" friend "said loudly his distaste for people."[26] His friend admitted he was quite drunk at the time but claimed he was only "carrying on and laughing, talking about naval black shoes" as they walked up behind Horton.[27] Captain Hatch, the JAG investigator, reviewed the witness statements but took no action on the incident. He gave no reason, simply saying, "I didn't pursue the matter any further."[28]

When the *Kitty Hawk* was again at sea, Horton was summoned to the ship investigator's office. Expecting to be told of action taken against his assailants, he was instead told he was suspected of an assault against the shore patrolmen who had come upon the scene when he was being assaulted.[29] Nothing came of that allegation against Horton. Horton did tell the ship's investigator that when he returned to the ship that evening after the incident his Black shipmates asked about his injuries. When he told them what happened, they were "really unhappy about it."[30]

After the *Kitty Hawk* left port, Captain Townsend conducted his own investigation into the Horton incident. He concluded it was "black word against white word" as to who instigated the fight. He did say, however, that since Horton was alone and had his right arm in a cast, it was "not unreasonable" to believe Horton's statement that he did not initiate the attack.[31]

Despite Townsend's statement about Horton's veracity, he likewise chose not to pursue charges against the two white sailors. Identifications were not an issue, of course, given the written statements made by Horton's two assailants. And still he chose not to charge anyone because it was a "black word against white word" situation? In fact, the two disinterested white sailors who witnessed the assault had corroborated Horton's statement that he was a victim and not an assailant. Therefore, it was one Black sailor and two white eyewitnesses' word against that of the two white assailants. Townsend had again come up with a reason, however illogical and indefensible, to take no action against white sailors assaulting a Black sailor from his own ship's company.[32]

Date: 10 October 1972
Time: 2230H
Location: Sampaguita Club, Naval Base Subic Bay

The evening after the Horton incident was Tuesday, 10 October, and the *Kitty Hawk* was scheduled to set sail the next day. Ship crews took full advantage of their last hours of liberty, and the *Kitty Hawk* crew members were no exception. Some *Kitty Hawk* sailors said what occurred that evening on the Naval base was a contributing factor in the outbreak of onboard confrontations just two days later.

The Sampaguita Club on the Subic Bay Naval Base was for enlisted men,[33] and every Tuesday night was "Soul Night" which drew an unusually large contingent of Black sailors from the Naval base and Black crew members from ships in port.[34] That evening more than seven hundred patrons, Black and white, including some wives, clocked in at the club.[35]

By early evening, the security office started receiving reports of fights on and off the Naval base.[36] Some were interracial altercations, and those became the source of fast-circulating rumors. A white *Kitty Hawk* airman and his friend were in the club "getting drunk" and witnessed a "few fights."[37] The club manager reported that "most" of the fights were between white and Black sailors. Just after midnight, a fight erupted in the club that could not be controlled by the assigned Shore Patrol. Additional SPs were called, and they reported "not a riot at this time but as a fight of considerable portion going on at the club."[38] Most of those fights were between white and Black sailors and still could not be contained, so the Marine riot squad was called from the Naval base Marine barracks. They witnessed a confrontation at the back of the club between a white sailor and some Black sailors.[39]

A Marine officer decided to eject the Black sailors from the club, and his troops began pushing them toward the front entrance. No weapons were used and no blows were struck, but just then someone inside the club smashed a bottle and "All hell broke loose!"[40] Some Black sailors broke free from the marines and began picking up chairs and bottles and throwing them,[41] then ran outside. A short time later, the club was shut down for the evening.

Several white sailors were also engaged in that upheaval. Four were detained by the marines, evidently with some resistance, because two of them received head injuries. One asked, "Why is it whites you are hitting and not the blacks?"[42]

Marines then swept the Naval base "looking for large groups of blacks,"[43] even though white sailors had also been involved in the fights. Interestingly, other than the four white sailors originally detained, the only other apprehension was of a group of six Black and three white sailors who were seen leaving the club together. The investigator said the group was picked up because of the Black sailors in the group, but they were never charged "because they had whites in their company."[44] In other words, they would have been charged were it not for their white companions.

Were any Black *Kitty Hawk* sailors involved in the club incident? A group of them were seen running back to the carrier that night. A marine on security detail on the brow of the ship expected them to cause trouble, but they came aboard peacefully.[45] Another marine said he thought they had been in a brawl because of their disarranged clothes and unbuckled belts.[46] Nothing further came of it, as no one could connect that group to the club incident.[47] Captain Townsend later concluded that his ship was "relatively clean in that affair."[48]

———————————

Date: 11 October 1972
Time: 0900H
Location: At sea

Kitty Hawk sailed out of Subic Bay the morning of 11 October, and in its wake were several more confrontations between Black and white sailors. The Sampaguita Club interracial fights were the subject of many heated discussions aboard ship, even for those who only heard about the fights secondhand. Black sailors, however, were especially focused on the two unprovoked assaults on their fellow Black crew members.

The first was the assault on several Black sailors by Sickles and the four Nationals. The other was the assault by the two white sailors on Horton, who had his arm in a cast. That made four assaults on Black sailors since Captain Townsend assumed command. Two occurred on board the ship and two in Subic Bay. The only consequence was a twenty-five-dollar fine for one of the white assailants. The ship's Black sailors thus came to believe that white sailors' assaults on them would continue, especially since those assaults were not being prosecuted, regardless of circumstances or evidence. That merely reinforced their already low opinion of white mans' justice. Those feelings would not change in the coming days, and for good reason.

4

A NIGHT TO REMEMBER

Date: 11 October 1972
Time: 1200H
Location: *Kitty Hawk* at sea

By noon on Wednesday, 11 October, *Kitty Hawk* was ninety-five miles out to sea, outbound northwest of Subic Bay on her return voyage to Yankee Station. She was heading for her seventh line deployment since leaving San Diego eight months earlier. The carrier had already completed 163 days actively engaged in air strikes on North Vietnamese targets, and the crew was weary, bone-tired, and restless. The twelve- to sixteen-hour workdays had taken their toll. No end was in sight, and the crew knew it. Not even scuttlebutt hinted at an "out chop" date, that glorious day when they finally set sail back to San Diego.

The first interracial altercation of the line period occurred on the aft mess deck when sailors were eating their noon meal.[1] A white sailor carrying out his mess duties was clearing tables. He came to the table of two Black sailors and picked up an empty glass. One of them, an airman recruit, yelled obscenities at him and angrily demanded he put the glass back down. The mess man told the airman to knock off the profanity, and the airman stood up and took a swing at the mess man, which was blocked. The airman then tackled the mess man who fell against a table and struck the bulkhead behind it. The mess man later said he was not hurt, and never even considered himself in danger because of his "training in the pugilistic arts."[2]

Date: 12 October 1972
Time: 1900H
Location: Forward mess deck of *Kitty Hawk,* en route to Yankee Station

The next altercation happened the following day, an hour after sunset. A large group of sailors were eating their evening meal in the forward mess deck. A Black airman apprentice in the chow line asked for a second sandwich but the white mess cook refused, telling him to return when he finished the one he had.[3] The cook said the airman put the sandwich in his pocket and reached for a second one, but the cook stopped him. The airman entered the galley to fight the mess cook but then retreated when the cook picked up a knife.[4]

Shortly after, an officer passing through the forward mess deck saw a white sailor step out of the chow line and approach him. The sailor said some Black sailors in line were cursing him, so the officer led the sailor to the front of the line to separate him from the others.[5] The white sailor was none other than Sickles, who a month earlier had escaped punishment at a captain's mast after being accused of hiring Filipino Nationals to assault Black sailors. The Black sailors on board had apparently not forgotten what he did, nor Townsend's inexplicable failure to discipline him.

A third altercation occurred in the ship's investigative office about an hour later. A master-at-arms was trying to question a Black sailor accused of kicking his supervising petty officer while high on drugs. The sailor refused to cooperate and stormed out of the office. Several other Black sailors were listening outside the office door and the MAA asked what they wanted. One replied, "We came to see the man get a fair shake," and another said, "You won't sleep tonight."[6]

Those sailors left with him and went to the forward mess deck. A few minutes later, a white mess man who was stacking trays accidentally stepped on the accused sailor's foot. That led to an angry exchange of words, but nothing physical between them.[7]

Nearby, another verbal exchange erupted between Black and white sailors. A Black airman said he and five brothers were "giving dap," and someone came over and told them to break it up. The airman asked why, as they weren't doing anything, but they were again told they had to leave. More Black sailors arrived and started giving dap. What exactly was giving dap? Aboard *Kitty Hawk*, Black sailors called it giving dap but white sailors typically called it "giving power." That alone told a lot about the two different perspectives. Whatever the label, it was a form of greeting when two or more young Black sailors met. It consisted of a series of fist bumps and hand gestures that might last only a few seconds or up to a minute or even longer. It was not practiced among more senior Black crew members, such as petty officers.

Dap is sometimes thought to be an acronym for "dignity and pride," and among young Black sailors was a sign of unity. Many white sailors, however, felt quite differently when witnessing dapping. Some were openly irritated, while others felt uneasy or even threatened.

At the military command level, the dap was recognized as a possible source of racial friction. A Marine Corps study conducted because of increased racial incidents between Black and white marines concluded that racial tensions increased with delays in mess lines as a result of the dap. The study found that interracial confrontations occurred owing to "white antagonism to the dap and other ritual acts of black solidarity . . . although most blacks viewed such acts as a legitimate sign of unity and greeting."[8] A Black *Kitty Hawk* marine sergeant, for example, said dapping was simply a greeting, just like an "ordinary handshake" and meant nothing more than that.[9]

"Black solidarity" was another subject that sometimes evoked different emotions between white and Black sailors. One opinion was offered by a Black petty officer aboard *Kitty Hawk* who previously served as a Navy recruiter in Philadelphia. He said the Black sailors he recruited often came from economically depressed inner-city neighborhoods, many from broken homes. and they typically bonded with Black friends for a sense of unity. Therefore, he explained that when a young Black sailor came aboard *Kitty Hawk*, the first face he wanted to see was a fellow Black man, and they banded together. Black crew members "more or less pulled together," he said, giving an example. He could walk on the mess decks, not know any Black sailors sitting there, and by just giving the Black salute, "all the hands would fly up, 'Right on, brother!'" He added that young Black men have a strong loyalty to each other even before they join the military and feel they must stick together.[10]

Commander Cloud, the Black XO, talked about Black unity even more forcefully, and eloquently:

> I think we have to recognize that there is a great, great sense of unity, of camaraderie and companionship among the so called, black brothers, not only on the *Kitty Hawk* but throughout the nation. This sense of unity, of course, is very apparent even here on Kitty Hawk. The black community here has devised their own private fraternal handshake. . . . This of course, pride of unity and loyalty, exists all the time, but at the same time we can recognize the same black men every day responding to their military responsibilities and assignments in a very loyal way. So it is, in my opinion no compromise one to the other. They are Navy men . . . who just happen to be black.[11]

As the Black sailors in the forward mess were told to "break it up," they continued giving dap and the situation escalated. Black and white sailors began arguing, and one Black sailor asked, "Why is it every time a few brothers get together someone thinks there is going to be a riot?"[12] The two groups loudly exchanged insults, and a division officer, hearing the commotion, entered the dining area. He saw white and Black sailors standing around "having words" in a "cross manner," but no fighting. He estimated about eighty to one hundred men were on the mess deck at the time, which included about twenty-five Black men.[13]

A ship's investigator received a call to report to the forward mess deck, but when he arrived, he just observed loud talking. He saw some senior Black petty officers, including members of the human resources staff, trying to calm the situation. They were able to get the Black sailors to leave the mess deck and go with them to the nearby training room, which doubled as the ship's human resources office.[14]

The Black sailors immediately began airing their grievances, including the recent incidents of Black sailors assaulted by white sailors, with no resulting disciplinary action. They also talked about the assault on Horton, whose arm was in a cast, the assaults on Black sailors by Sickles and the Nationals, and the Sampaguita Club incident, where "numerous blacks were attacked that night by the Marines for no reason."[15] They also said Black sailors were mistreated by the ship's MAA force and, while in port, by Naval facilities' shore patrol detachments. They asked why, following any interracial disturbance, the shore patrol and the MAAs questioned only Black sailors.

One said on many occasions he was involved in situations where Black sailors were ordered to scatter when several of them gathered in a group. Another said, "Twenty white sailors could sit at a table but four blacks could not."[16] Others echoed those complaints, saying whenever Black sailors gathered together, no matter how innocently, the ship's MAAs would order them to disperse. By coincidence, the ship's chief investigator had witnessed just such an event right before the group entered the training room. He was talking to several Black sailors in the passageway when an MAA came over and told them to disperse, with no reason given.

The sailors also complained about being discriminated against in their onboard duty assignments and promotions. They also felt they didn't get equivalent performance marks compared to white sailors, and that in turn also limited their potential for advancement.[17]

When the training room meeting finally broke up, it was reported that several of the Black sailors were still "pretty bitter."[18]

Date: 12 October 1972
Time: 2115H
Location: Aft mess deck, *Kitty Hawk*

The next incident occurred on the aft mess deck. A white mess cook was slotting food trays when a group of Black sailors came in and started "giving the power." A Black sailor confronted him, saying, "I remember you. You gave me some [expletive] a while back. I'm gonna kick the [expletive] out of you." The mess cook told the sailor he didn't know what he was talking about, turned away, and then the Black sailor hit him in the back. He said he swung around and "smacked him with a tray," but when an MAA came to help, he said the Black sailor assaulted him again.[19] The Black sailors then left.

About an hour later, some Black sailors left the training room meeting and went down to the aft mess to eat when another confrontation occurred. Fireman Apprentice Durward Davis was among the group of Black sailors and vividly remembers the incident. He was standing in the chow line when a Black and a white sailor began arguing about something that had happened in port. That led to angry words exchanged between other Black and white sailors. The situation escalated,[20] with shouting and even "words of violence" exchanged between the two groups.[21] Several MAAs who were present tried to pacify the crew members.[22]

A mess cook witnessed the ongoing altercation and decided it was time to call in the troops. He rushed forward to the third deck Marine Detachment compartment,[23] shouted that all hell was breaking loose, and they better come fast. They did. Upwards of twenty marines grabbed their nightsticks and followed the mess cook back to the aft mess.

Upon arrival, they saw sailors trading insults, but no fighting. Nevertheless, since the marines were trained in riot control, they apparently decided to put that training to use. Fireman Apprentice Davis recalls the marines pushing right past the white sailors and confronting his group with raised nightsticks.[24] The marines formed a blocking unit and began forcing the Black sailors backward. That did not go well.

Almost immediately after that first group of marines rushed up, another group grabbed their nightsticks and swung into action. When they arrived at the aft mess, they also began confronting the Black sailors. Behind that second group of marines, bringing up their rear, was their CO, Captain Carlucci. Instead of leading his marines, he found himself tagging along behind them. While sitting in a second deck wardroom, he had heard his troops running down the passageway, so he ran out and followed them aft.

Upon arrival at the aft mess, Carlucci said a group of Black sailors were using provoking gestures and obscene, taunting language toward his marines. He had not witnessed the earlier aggressive tactics of his marines, however, so had no frame of reference to judge the situation.

He did say that he saw no real physical contact between the two groups and reported it as more or less of a "Mexican standoff."[25] The Black sailors were angry, and his troops were responding, but no blows were exchanged. He finally separated the two groups with the help of his first sergeant and a member of the ship's human resources staff.[26]

Carlucci then told his marines to stand down, and as they were doing so, another event occurred that became one of the most talked about and controversial incidents of the evening. Some Black sailors even described it as a flash point for the later confrontations and assaults.

A marine corporal who had arrived with the first group of troops was armed with his .45 service pistol. Corporal Anthony Avina might have thought his firearm was the perfect response to two groups arguing with each other. A Black sailor said that when he arrived at the aft mess, "a Marine was about to pull his pistol out and shoot a brother and a member of the human resources staff stopped him. Got in between them and stopped him from pulling his pistol."[27]

Another Black crewman said, "Yes, he did remove the pistol. He snatched it from the holster, and at that time . . . the First Class [petty officer] grabbed him."[28] While their accounts differed somewhat, the incident was verified by the Black petty officer who restrained the marine. "When the Marines arrived, they were ready to fight with clubs and all. They were also asked to leave in which they did until a fight broke out between a Marine and a black. I grabbed the Marine with a gun then I got hit with a club by a Marine. I was trying to stop the Marine from pulling the gun."[29]

Another marine, a Black lance corporal, said that "one of the brothers" thought the corporal was drawing the pistol to shoot him, and "started screaming, you are not coming to shoot me!"[30]

Corporal Avina gave his version of the event to the congressional subcommittee. He said he had his pistol with him because he had just come off guard duty and, when he arrived at the aft mess, he saw twenty-five or thirty Black sailors who "seemed to me like they were just tearing furniture apart."[31] Later, during the ongoing confrontation, when the marines were ordered to stand down, Avina said he started to leave but one of the Black sailors grabbed the shoulder strap to his pistol holster. He claimed he only reached for his pistol to keep the Black sailor from taking it, but also acknowledged that if it came to that, he was prepared to use it.[32] Captain Carlucci, his CO, backed Avina up, saying he did not draw the weapon, but merely "protected" it.[33]

In giving his testimony to the subcommittee, however, Corporal Avina must have forgotten about the sworn written statement he gave the morning after the incident, which flatly contradicted that later testimony. "I was the last one through the hatch and someone pulled me back into the crowd. I then attempted to draw my pistol, a [petty officer] stopped me and pinned me against the bulkhead and told me not to pull any pistol."[34]

Of course, the Black sailors later repeated what they actually witnessed, not Corporal Avina's later sanitized version. The real story spread like wildfire throughout the ship, and a Black marine who witnessed the event said the incident "started a whole lot of chaos right there. [The Black sailors] thought the Marines were coming at them to shoot and kill them."[35]

Other incidents contributed to the later tumult, but the pistol incident loomed large. Up to forty Black sailors had personally witnessed a marine attempting to draw his firearm on them. That was a bell that could not easily be unrung.

During his subcommittee testimony, Corporal Avina also talked about something that was very unsettling. He testified he believed he was free to discharge his pistol without a direct order from a superior. That prompted a congressman to ask, "Assume [someone's] misconduct is continuing . . . Isn't it better to have them apprehensive that the pistol will be used if they overstep?" Corporal Avina responded, "Yes, sir, it may work. I am pretty sure if you just crack down, draw the line, draw a big black line, I am sure you can put a stop to it."[36]

Afterward, Avina asked Captain Townsend, "What would happen if I would have shot one of them, or two, or whatever?" Townsend said he would have been taken to court. Avina's reaction? "It would have been on my record book. And that would have been a complete mess."[37]

Commander Cloud was called out to the aft mess deck just after the pistol incident. He was watching a movie in the officer's wardroom when someone shouted that he was urgently needed in the aft mess.[38] As he approached, he could hear shouting and glassware being broken. He witnessed the marines confronting the Black sailors with a "lot of pushing, shoving, and cursing" between the two groups.[39] He said the marines had showed up during the "already warm situation" and "attempted to isolate the [Black sailors], push them back," and tempers got out of hand.[40] Recognizing that the marines had escalated an already tense situation, his first instinct was to isolate the two groups.

He ordered the marines and all white sailors to leave the mess deck, with the exception of a couple of senior chiefs. After removal of the deck plates[41] at the bottoms of doors, he ordered the entrances secured. Isolated with the other Black sailors, he listened to them vent their anger toward the marines. He said the incident, "seemed to have inflamed them to the point where they were well beyond reason."[42]

Cloud eventually got the group of about forty sailors to settle down. Some told him they believed that, even before that evening, the marines and MAAs were out to get them. They felt singled out, especially when told to disperse whenever they gathered in small groups.

One repeated grievance was about the actions of the armed marine. A Black petty officer who was a member of the human resources staff said, "The issue about a man pulling a gun" was brought out "with a lot of shouting."[43] He said there was a "lot of talk" about a gun being pulled on them. At one point, the XO stated he would have the marine who pulled the gun off the ship the next day.[44] The petty officer also said that the discussions between the Black sailors and the XO proceeded on a "brother to brother" basis after that, and he recalls raised clenched fists being exchanged a couple of times.

The XO told the group that, for the first time ever, they had a brother in senior command.[45]

————————

Captain Townsend first learned of the ongoing disturbance at about 2130. Not knowing the extent of it, he went to the Bridge and ordered Primary Flight Control to turn up the flight deck lights.[46] He next contacted Marine Captain Carlucci and ordered him to post additional marines on the hangar and flight decks for aircraft security.[47] He then hurried down to the aft mess to check out the disturbance for himself.

Townsend arrived at the aft mess and described a situation "badly out of control." Although acknowledging his XO's good intentions, he saw Commander Cloud operating as a "black to a black," rather than as the ship's number two, which Townsend said was a mistake.[48] He listened as the XO gained the group's trust and began settling them down. As he turned to leave, however, some Black sailors asked him to stay. Now that they had Townsend's attention, they began airing a new set of grievances, but this time directed at him personally.

Their main objection was to his unequal disciplinary treatment between Black and white sailors. They asked why he hadn't taken action against Sickles who had hired the Nationals to assault Black sailors in Subic Bay. He told them the incident was under investigation.[49] In fact, the investigative report was marked closed earlier that same day.

Townsend and his XO spent almost an hour listening and responding to the grievances of the group of assembled Black sailors. Townsend appeared genuinely sympathetic and assured them they did not have to worry about the marines anymore. Together the two senior commanders succeeded in getting the Black sailors settled down.

The issue of the marines' aggression remained, however, and Townsend was again asked by the Black sailors if they had anything to fear from the marines. He again told them not to be concerned. He told them the marines worked for him, just as everyone else did, and that he would handle the situation.[50]

With the mess deck disturbance behind them, and their meeting with the Black sailors concluded, both the XO and the CO felt the evening's troubles were over. The XO said the meeting broke up around 2230 when Townsend ordered the group to disperse peacefully, which they did.[51]

One member of the ship's all-Black human resources staff witnessed the aft mess confrontation and helped quell the disturbances. When the meeting broke up, he also didn't think the Black sailors were going to cause any trouble. He felt they simply wanted to be heard and to be assured action would be taken on their complaints. He returned to his office, convinced the evening's troubles were over.[52] Sadly, he, too, was mistaken.

––––––––––

Date: 12 October 1972
Time: 2130H
Location: Aft S-8 berthing compartment aboard *Kitty Hawk*

While the aft mess meeting was ongoing, another altercation occurred in the aft S-8 berthing compartment, located on the third deck. It came about following an escalation of an otherwise innocuous event. White sailors in their berthing compartment saw several Black sailors making their way through the area and asking how they could get out the other side. During those exchanges, a Black sailor cried out "Hey, man, what you looking at?"[53] A white airman lying in his rack looked out and demanded to know "What the hell's going on here."[54] That led to more heated exchanges and, during the ensuing altercation, a white sailor was struck after a blanket was thrown over him.[55] By then, a crowd had gathered in the berthing compartment and the Black sailors left.[56] In short, one early outbreak of interracial confrontations began following an innocuous encounter with Black sailors merely asking for directions, and the situation just escalated.

Date: 12 October 1972
Time: 2200H
Location: Hangar Bay aboard *Kitty Hawk*

When Captain Carlucci received Captain Townsend's order to post his marines on the hangar and flight decks, he responded by going down to the marine berthing compartment to brief his troops. He organized them into three-man patrols in full utility uniforms, with nightsticks and whistles. He also ordered a twelve-man reaction force to the marine compartment just below the hangar bay, with quick access to the decks above and below.

Carlucci instructed his troops to patrol both upper decks to protect aircraft, firefighting equipment, and other materiel. He later testified that he also ordered them to break up groups of more than three. He said if anyone refused to cooperate, they were to be taken into custody. He authorized them to use force, if necessary, and if backup was needed, to blow their whistles.[57]

Carlucci had issued an extraordinary dispersal order by not limiting it to sailors causing disturbances. His order clearly was intended to apply even to sailors moving about the ship peaceably. It is highly unlikely that any officer on board any ship had ever issued such an order before. Groups of sailors typically worked together, ate together, and spent off-duty time together while at sea.

To make matters worse, even though Carlucci had testified his order was to break up groups of "more than three," his marines clearly heard otherwise. All who later testified about the order, including three lance corporals, said they were told to break up groups of "more than two."[58] They were not told the reason for the order, and because they were marines, they almost certainly did not question it. They dutifully formed up in their own groups of threes and double-timed to the hangar and flight decks.

An overwhelming contribution to the evening's incident was that no *Kitty Hawk* crew member had a clue that such an extraordinary order was issued. Take, for example, the large group of Black sailors who had just left their meeting with the XO and the CO. They had to go somewhere. And why wouldn't they walk together in groups, large or small, as they always had before?

One of the evening's great ironies is that the ship's crew members could easily have been told of the extremely unusual order by broadcasting it through the 1-MC, the ship's central communication center.[59] Since the crew was not told, however, the young marines on patrol had to carry out the dispersal order as best they could when they came upon any group of three or more sailors.

In addition, the marines were being asked to enforce that unusual order against sailors who were not in their chain of command and against many who were equal or superior to them in rank. The resulting confusion was amplified among Black sailors who heard about, or might have even witnessed, the earlier marine confrontation and pistol-wielding incident on the aft mess. Those sailors were undoubtedly distrustful, if not outright fearful, of the marines.

Now, imagine three Black sailors who are simply walking through the ship, minding their own business, and they are approached by three white marines who order them to "break it up." The sailors might be understandably confused, maybe angered, or perhaps even fearful of what might happen next. If the sailors asked for an explanation, all the marines could say was that they were carrying out orders.

The marines might tell the sailors they could simply walk away, but only if one of them leaves the other two and walks in the opposite direction. That would make absolutely no sense at all. And if a dozen

Black sailors were approached by a marine squad, they likewise would be "ordered" to disperse, this time in six separate directions with no more than two together at a time. That, likewise, would be incomprehensible to those on the receiving end of the order.

The reaction of many groups of Black sailors was predictable. The sailors might understandably resist, especially since they were being "ordered" by marines that, if they refused to cooperate, they would be forcibly taken into custody and hauled off to the brig.

Unfortunately, that is just what the marines did. A marine later testified, "Sir, my duty up on the hangar bay was to try and control, you know, force. . . . The reason for us going up there was a show of force and protect the ship."[60] Captain Carlucci also acknowledged that his marines used force when carrying out his dispersal order. "On the hanger deck, when they apprehended people, they naturally had to use physical force against the individual, sir, just in the process of grabbing the individual or taking him down below."[61]

The first encounter occurred when a marine squad noticed two Black sailors, one walking forward and one walking aft. One of the marines said the Black sailors stopped and "started to do their knuckle knocking thing." His squad approached them, "asked them to break it up," even though there were only two of them. In response, one of the Black sailors called them "White honky [expletives]." The marine blew his whistle for assistance, and when another marine squad came running up, the Black sailors left.[62]

In another encounter, three Black airmen had just left the aft mess meeting together and, as they were crossing the hangar bay, three marines ran up to them, one yelling they were "not to walk in a group."[63] Words were exchanged, and the marines began aggressively trying to handcuff them. A marine swung his nightstick at one of the sailors who raised his hand in self-defense. The club struck him between his thumb and forefinger, causing excruciating pain.[64]

One of his companions, Airman Apprentice Ronald Glover, said when they arrived on the hangar bay, he "saw a lot of Marines, and some brothers getting choked with sticks, getting beat in the head and before we knew it, we had got a stick in the back too." Shortly after, Commander Cloud arrived and asked Glover what happened. He said, "I didn't know but my mouth was bleeding and my back is hurting, then up came some brother crying, saying look at my brother sir, just look at him."[65] The XO took Glover to his office and then told someone to take him to sick bay.[66]

Another Black sailor and about a dozen of his friends were crossing the hangar bay when, he said, "All of a sudden the marines jumped out on us." They were told they could walk only in "pairs of twos." They didn't understand what was going on and began walking away, some with fists raised.[67] A marine sergeant "didn't like this," blew his whistle, and several more marines "came running and jumping off the planes on us," and assaulting them. He said they were trying to defend themselves. He continued:

> [But] they started beating us with clubs and choking us with them too! I got hit several times with a club. I also was getting choked. . . . We started running. I tried to run underneath an airplane, when this marine pushed me right into it. My forehead was dripping blood. Then about 4 marines grabbed me. . . . My friends tried to help me, because I was bleeding badly. They told the marines I needed a doctor. They wouldn't listen, they were throwing me around like I was a dog. My friends finally got me loose and [took] me to sick bay.[68]

Lieutenant James Martin, the ship's legal officer, saw him being taken to sick bay, bleeding from his head wound. He recalls the emotionally charged sailor crying out, "The Marines are beating up our brothers!"[69]

The record clearly indicates that none of the injured Black sailors were doing anything but simply walking through the hangar bay, following their meeting with the XO and CO in the aft mess deck, when the marines confronted them with their nightsticks.

Marine First Sergeant Binkley saw about thirty-five or forty Black sailors on the hangar bay at the time, and his marines told them to "go up and down this little painted line they have in the hangar bay and don't get around the airplanes. . . . They said the Marines don't tell us nothing."[70] Sergeant Binkley then took action clearly beyond his orders, or his authority. He directed the arrest of a Black sailor for talking back at him when he told him he would be apprehended if his group didn't disperse. "That didn't set well. I got a little more lip service, so I told a Marine to apprehend [the Black sailor], take him to legal. We got that one. Then that more or less really antagonized them because we were in fact apprehending them and taking them away. They started, all of them started, I don't know how the hell they got the word all the way around that fast, but a lot more come up from the after mess deck."[71]

Word of the marine confrontations and assaults, and Black injuries, spread rapidly, and more Black sailors began making their way to the hangar bay. Some marines reported seeing about twenty-five to thirty Black sailors walking down the hangar bay with their fists raised. While the sailors may have considered it as an act of solidarity, the marines may well have seen it as a gesture of open defiance.

The marines approached and tried to contain them, but when the Black sailors resisted, a whistle was blown and another marine squad responded. The marines were ordered to "get on line" and push the Black sailors back, but instead were getting pushed back themselves, so a virtual scrum took place between the two groups. Even more marines arrived and finally stopped the advance of the Black sailors, at which point Sergeant Binkley announced they were all under military arrest.[72] As the marines tried to apprehend several of the Black sailors, punches started flying in both directions.[73] Marines then began forcefully pinning down several Black sailors on the deck, and Sergeant Binkley then ordered them hauled off to the brig.[74]

Binkley claimed that as his marines were apprehending the Black sailors, some broke away and "returned quickly with weapons and crow bars and tie down chains and started to hit the marines."[75] That allegation was never corroborated by anyone and found no support whatsoever in all other incident and injury reports.

Another statement by Binkley, however, was never contradicted. He said, "We were apprehending them, and at the same time moving them aft in the hangar bay, trying to wedge them in against elevator 3 which was up. They had a choice to do what they were told or sit down or jump over the side."[76] The elevator being "up" meant it was level with the flight deck above. With that, the hangar bay looked out over an empty elevator shaft with only the ocean below. Thus, those Black sailors being "wedged" against the open shaft could meekly surrender or jump to their certain deaths. Apparently, Sergeant Binkley considered death a fitting option for malefactors who dared walk through the hangar bay in groups of three or more.

Besides wielding their nightsticks, the marines utilized forceful hand-cuffing of Black crew members. A Navy lieutenant said marines used arm locks and neck holds while placing handcuffs on the Black sailors. He stated, "Most blacks had stopped [resisting] and only 3 or 4 were involved in any struggle," but, he said, the marines continued to force the sailors to the deck while being handcuffed.[77] A marine even tried to force leg irons on a Black sailor as others tried to keep him from doing so.[78]

Another marine grabbed a sailor and "put the black on the deck." When he ordered another to drop a chain, the Black sailor did so but began running, so "I ran up behind him and hit him in the back with my nightstick (being careful not to hit him in the head)."[79]

About the same time, a poignant incident occurred between two Black crew members.[80] During the hangar bay incident, a very agitated young Black sailor climbed down the ladder into the MARDET berthing compartment and began screaming at the marines inside, "You caused a riot, you're responsible for this, you people caused this!"[81] A young Black marine sergeant then stepped forward to get him out of the compartment. As the sergeant began forcing him back up the ladder, he tried to reason with the hysterical sailor, and by the time they reached the top of the ladder, both were yelling at each other.

A petty officer witnessed the encounter and said, "I remember [the marine] repeating over and over again, 'How do you think I feel?' He was pulled between two loyalties, he's a young black man and he's a Marine, and I remember I really felt sorry for him. I saw tears running out of his eyes."[82]

Airman Apprentice Perry Pettus had first-hand experience with the aggressive handcuffing taking place on the hangar bay. The evening of the incident he was with two fellow Black flight deck airmen. They had taken their regular evening duty break and were eating in the aft mess when the marines arrived and aggressively confronted the Black crew members. After that incident ended, they listened as Townsend assured them they no longer had to fear the marines. Pettus and his fellow airman then left to resume their flight deck duties.

Pettus recalls to this day exactly what happened next. "As we were walking across the hanger deck, a couple of Marines came up and one said, 'You blacks, quote, you blacks, can't walk in over twos.' We're thinking, yeah right, and we kept on walking. The Marine made the comment again. Puleeze, I'm going to have a Marine tell me I can't walk with two of my friends. The next thing I know my body is up against an A-6 aircraft with a nightstick under my neck."[83]

The marines handcuffed Pettus and the other two airmen, but they clamped down the cuffs on Pettus so tightly he was in excruciating pain. The three airmen were taken below and placed in cells in the ship's brig. Pettus was still in handcuffs, but not because of security concerns; the marines weren't able to remove them. They were locked on so tightly their handcuff keys no longer worked. The pain was so intense that Pettus doesn't remember much of what happened next, but others did.[84]

Commander Cloud recalls Pettus being brought to his office by a chief petty officer. "He had with him a young black by the name of Pettus. . . . He was hysterical, and he was wearing handcuffs that were obviously very, very tight on his wrists, and were cutting into his wrists."[85]

For the next hour several attempts were made to remove the handcuffs, all without success. The ship's chief criminal investigator was the first nonmarine to try. He recalls coming down to the legal office where

Pettus had been taken and finding him "really upset to the point of tears" because of the pain. The handcuff key on his key ring wouldn't fit, so he sent someone out looking for another key. He also went looking but eventually returned to the legal office emptyhanded.[86]

One of the ship's master-at-arms arrived and noted that Pettus "had been mistakenly handcuffed by the marines on the hangar deck."[87] He, too, was unable to remove the restraints. Just then, the XO was heard on the ship's intercom ordering the Black sailors aft. Pettus obeyed the order and left the legal office, still in his handcuffs.

The comment by an MAA that the marines had "mistakenly" handcuffed Pettus was telling. That criticism came from a member of the ship's primary security force, which relied on the marines for backup security. It was fast becoming clear that, with the sole exception of their commanding officer Captain Carlucci, the marines had only critics for their aggressive actions and overreactions against the Black sailors that evening.

A petty officer who was in the legal office followed Pettus to the aft mess deck and told another petty officer, "Get these handcuffs off this man. We don't need him in that crowd showing everybody what the marines had done to him with these handcuffs on his wrists."[88] Pettus was finally relieved of his agonizing pain when the handcuffs were finally removed, more than an hour after the marine had jammed a nightstick under his chin and braced him against an aircraft.

Captain Townsend had ordered Captain Carlucci to put marine patrols on the upper decks for security, but when Carlucci one-upped the order and directed his marines to break up groups of three or more, that directly led to the night's interracial confrontations and assaults. An additional contributing factor to the resulting upheaval was how Carlucci's marines carried out his dispersal order.

Carlucci said when he ordered his marines to disperse groups, he told them it, "didn't matter what color they were, white or black."[89] However, it appears that Sergeant Binkley passed on that order with a qualifier. One of the marines said he dispersed only Black sailors on the hangar bay because he was ordered to do so by Binkley.[90] When asked whether he was ordered to break up groups of white sailors, the marine responded, "I don't recall that it was ever brought up, sir."[91]

Regardless of whether the marines were ordered to break up groups of only Black sailors, that is exactly what they did. This obviously further incensed Black sailors who saw that groups of white sailors were not being ordered to disperse. This was happening everywhere on the ship with a marine presence. That blatant discrimination understandably increased the Black sailors' resistance to dispersal orders from the marines.

Commander Cloud conducted his own investigation following the incident and concluded that the marines had in fact enforced the order only against Black sailors. He later testified that those discriminatory actions actually instigated the hangar bay confrontations and assaults:

> In the course of [the marines] executing their duties . . . they were directed by higher authority that they were to disperse groups of people, three or more. . . . However, in the execution of this order it became apparent that the Marines, instead of executing it bilaterally, you might say, blacks and whites, allowed assembled groups of whites to mill around the hangar deck, but in the course of the evening, as groups of blacks started coming to the hangar deck, three or more, they were approached by the Marines and told to disperse or disband. *And this, of course, started the altercation* [emphasis added]. From the course of my investigation, it became apparent that the blacks asked why; words were exchanged; more blacks came to the scene; more Marines came to the scene on being summoned by the Marines; and from here physical altercation took place.[92]

These were stunning statements coming from the number two ranking officer aboard the carrier, and his statements were not made lightly. He was testifying more than three months after the incident, and well after the Navy's official *Kitty Hawk* investigation was finalized.

After Captain Townsend left his aft mess deck meeting with the Black sailors, a petty officer told him that the marines on the hangar bay were "breaking up blacks in groups of more than two."[93] Townsend immediately ordered him to "tell first Sgt. Binkley to cool it and not to bother people." The petty officer hurried to the hangar bay, observed the chaos created by the dispersal order, and returned to report the situation to Townsend. He then accompanied Townsend to the hangar bay. When they arrived, the marines were attempting to run down some Black sailors and had formed a line in the aft section of the deck. Townsend saw the marines advancing on the Black sailors with their nightsticks, got between the two groups and said, "No more of this, that is the end. You blacks disperse and the marines I am going to put away right now."[94]

Just then someone grabbed a safety guardrail, taken from an aircraft work platform, and threw it toward Townsend and marine Sergeant Binkley, who was standing next to him. The rail hit Binkley on the upper leg.[95] That may have reinforced Townsend's feeling he had to "put away" the marines, especially just after witnessing the marines advancing on the Black sailors.

The hangar bay incident experienced one more dramatic event before concluding, which Captain Townsend also personally witnessed. The hangar bay confrontations drew a large group of white sailors to the mezzanine level overlooking that deck. That resulted in three separately identifiable groups present in the hangar bay area at the same time: the squads of marines, the Black sailors, and the white sailors on the mezzanine. As if the situation couldn't have gotten any worse, some of the white sailors up above began yelling and screaming obscenities at the Black sailors down below. It was reported that a white first class petty officer was leading "the whites that were on the mezzanine [who] were taunting [the Black sailors], and hurling verbal abuses, and egging the marines on in the altercation that was then taking place."[96]

That white sailor was identified by a Black petty officer who was standing next to Townsend on the hangar deck below. He said the white sailor "was instigating very strongly toward a riot by using harsh language to a group of blacks," including, "[expletive] you mother [expletive] blacks." The captain first warned the white sailor, but when he persisted, Townsend ordered him arrested.[97]

The mezzanine incident was also the clearest example of how the marine dispersal order was unilaterally enforced. No attempt was made to break up the group of white sailors as they hurled epithets down at the Black sailors. This, despite both Captain Townsend and Marine Captain Carlucci personally witnessing those actions from below on the hangar bay.

Townsend later told the XO about the incident, saying he remembered "liberal use of [n-word] and mother [expletive] . . . by the people that were on the mezzanine which, as I learned, were all white."[98]

Commander Cloud arrived on the hangar bay after the mezzanine incident. After leaving the aft mess deck meeting, he went to his cabin along with a group of Black sailors. He was listening to their grievances when a young Black sailor broke into his stateroom. The sailor was crying and near hysteria, exclaiming, "Oh, my God, oh, my God, they are at it again! They are going to kill us all!"[99] The XO said the sailor had a large gash across his head and had been bleeding quite a while. At that point, the group of Black sailors in his stateroom rushed out, heading toward the hangar bay.

Cloud immediately followed them. When he arrived, groups of marines and Black sailors were milling about. Shortly after, he saw some marines leaving the hangar bay, apparently in response to Townsend ordering them to stand down. He then saw Townsend surrounded by a large group of Black sailors. Several were shouting and cursing, and two or three of them were openly abusive toward Townsend.[100]

Captain Townsend tried to get them to calm down. And, just as he had done in the aft mess meeting, he again apologized for the marines' aggressive actions toward them:

> I had never given an order to have groups broken up if they were in more than three, and explained that to the blacks, and it was an effort at conciliation, and frankly given as such. I

said, "I am going to, at this time, have the Marines return to their quarters". . . and said: "That is an error, a mistake on the part of the Marines, there is no intent on my part to ever have you broken up in groups of three. Now go about your business, we have solved the problems for the night."[101]

As Townsend continued talking with the Black sailors on the hangar bay, Commander Cloud noticed several marines still moving about the hangar deck, despite Townsend's order for them to stand down. Seeing marines and Black sailors together on the same deck concerned him, but then someone ran up and told the XO a "big fight" had broken out in sick bay, and off he went.[102]

Townsend later gave his reason for ordering the marines to stand down for the remainder of the night. "I felt using the Marines was dangerous and put the Marines away."[103] He also told the ship's legal officer that "the blacks possibly had a belief that they had the right to congregate on the hangar bay without being dispersed."[104] Of course, they had no reason to believe otherwise, until confronted by the marines.

Townsend also acknowledged that the marines' aggressive tactics against the Black sailors on the aft mess only worsened the situation. He conceded that a mess cook should not have been able to activate that "improper response" by the Marine Detachment.[105] In an apparent effort to deflect criticism from himself for what happened, however, he also said, "The Marines were never called out by me in this incident, they were on the scene and armed, without the direct order of the CO, XO, or the Marine CO. That was one of the things that caused the problems in the after mess deck."[106]

Townsend initially activated the marines to help with aircraft security. But why did he feel he even needed to use the marines in that role? The master-at-arms division was the ship's designated security and policing force, so why didn't he just order the MAAs to step up their regular patrols without involving the marines?

We don't know the answer to that, but Townsend later conceded that after ordering the marines' mobilization, he should have ordered them to stand down. He made that statement to the petty officer who had accompanied him to the hangar bay following the aft mess deck meeting. The petty officer said, "The CO explained the Marines had been posted when he heard of the disturbance on the mess deck . . . and he failed to tell them to relax prior to the meeting breaking up."[107]

"Relax" meant having the marines stand down and return to their quarters. What changed Townsend's mind after initially ordering them out? Just after he gave the order, he met with the Black sailors on the aft mess deck and was told of the marines' aggression toward them. In "failing" to countermand his marine mobilization order, Townsend had inadvertently caused the evening's incidents to dramatically escalate.

Captain Carlucci also reluctantly admitted that the first call up of his marines that evening was a colossal mistake. He did not order them out. His first sergeant did not order them out. In fact, no one in the MARDET command structure had ordered them out. Carlucci later tried to explain how a low-ranking mess cook could have called his marines into action. He said that earlier in the evening, a chief petty officer on the mess deck had called his gunnery sergeant, a Black man, to come and quell a minor disturbance. The "gunny" responded, but when he left the marine compartment, he told them to be ready to respond, just in case. Mere minutes later, the mess cook rushed down to the marine compartment and called for help, causing the troops to run up to the aft mess and aggressively confront the Black sailors.[108]

It was three months after the incident when Commander Cloud testified that the marines unilaterally enforced the dispersal order. His statements were immediately picked up by local and national media. A banner headline in the *New York Times* exclaimed, "Kitty Hawk Officer Traces Riot to Marine Dispersal of Blacks." The *Times* quoted the XO's dramatic testimony in detail, revealing once again that many of the Navy's previous accounts of the incident were not to be believed.[109]

5

A TIME TO REMEMBER

Date: 12 October 1972
Time: 2300H
Location: Sick bay aboard *Kitty Hawk*

The sick bay confrontation erupted just after five crew members had been escorted down to the medical facility after suffering injuries in the hangar bay incident. The ethnicity of those five tells us much about what happened on the hangar bay.

The marine sergeant had reported that while his troops were forcefully apprehending Black sailors, several of them ran away but "returned quickly with weapons and crow bars and tie down chains and started to hit the marines." Given his graphic depiction of brutal assaults on marines, the number of seriously injured marines must have been substantial.

Actually not. The medical reports indicate only one marine was treated all evening, a white corporal. The marine described his injuries. "1st LT Holcomb escorted me to sick bay from the Hangar Bay for treatment of a bloody nose."[1]

So, who were the other four injured crew members? All were Black men, and all received injuries much more serious than a bloody nose, as reflected in their medical reports. A seaman recruit was pushed into an aircraft wing by a marine and suffered a forehead laceration, which

56

took seven sutures to close. He had to be held overnight for observation.[2] An airman was struck on the head and hand by marines wielding clubs, and received a "possible fracture" to his right hand.[3] An airman apprentice was, "struck with a stick" and sustained a forehead laceration that required ten sutures.[4] Another airman reported, "A couple of marines attacked me on the Hangar Bay," and he suffered a left arm contusion.[5]

One of those suffering a head wound was probably the crew member who burst into the XO's cabin that evening crying, bleeding, and exclaiming, "They are going to kill us all!"

Those four Black crew members and the marine were being treated when the sick bay incident occurred. How it started is unclear, but, incredibly, the marines showed up again in force. Townsend had just issued his explicit order on the hangar bay for the marines to stand down.

A marine lance corporal arrived the same time as two Black sailors that were carrying a fellow Black crew member who was severely injured. The marine was told by a medical corpsman to secure all entrances to sick bay, allowing in only injured crew members or medical personnel.[6] The marine complied with the "order" from a fellow enlisted crew member who was not even in his chain of command. When other marines arrived, they joined in to help seal off the entrances. No record shows that anyone ordered them there, and if they had done so, it was in direct violation of Captain Townsend's stand-down order.

More injured Black sailors began arriving from the hangar bay. Some were helped by corpsmen, and some by fellow Black sailors who were demanding treatment for their charges.[7] The marines, however, were actively resisting their efforts, and further confrontations occurred.

A senior Navy officer was outside sick bay at the time and saw several marines rush down the passageway with raised nightsticks. They ran up to a group of Black sailors, one of whom yelled, "Hey man, what are you doing with that stick?" Another group of marines came running immediately behind that first group.[8] All the marines outside sick bay were now acting in direct contradiction of Captain Townsend's explicit order to stand down.

As the confrontation escalated, four Black sailors approached the Naval officer, talking loudly. The officer said he never detected any hostility from any of them, yet a marine approached and confronted them with his nightstick held high. In response, one of the sailors, obviously scared, kept repeating, "I gotta get off this boat, can you get me off this boat?" The others then joined in with the same plea.[9]

The CO of MARDET arrived about then as he was helping to bring injured sailors to sick bay. He recalls seeing "numbers of Blacks who seemed just as frightened as everyone else."[10]

Compounding the chaos, a Black airman already in sick bay was actively resisting treatment by the corpsmen. Airman Apprentice Ronald Glover was lying on a treatment table and had a bleeding head wound from being struck with a nightstick by a marine on the hangar bay. He was delirious and finally couldn't take it any longer. He struggled to his feet and headed for the exit. A corpsman tried to stop Glover, and the marine corporal with a nose bleed jumped off the table and said he "pulled him into the treatment room with a choke hold."[11]

Just then, two more Black sailors arrived, followed by two marines. It is unclear if those sailors were injured themselves or were trying to help Glover leave the room. An argument broke out, followed by pushing and shoving. One of the corpsmen got hit,[12] and the marine corporal went after the assailant.[13]

Another marine struck Glover in the left eye with his nightstick, opening up a second wound, which Glover described:

> I got hit on the head so hard that it took eight or nine stiches to close it. I do not remember very much after that. I remember the blood covering my eyes from my forehead, and dripping down on my shirt, and I remember someone shouting, "Glover, you hurt bad! You hurt bad!" I was so messed up that I sort of went crazy almost then. . . . I remember telling the corpsman working on me that I would rather die than have needles stuck in my head. He went ahead and stuck them in anyway. I have always been afraid of needles, especially around

my eyes, or my head, and the whole situation made me want
to die anyway.[14]

Glover grabbed a nearby broom handle and started swinging wildly
at the cabinets and in the air, partially blinded by the blood in his eyes.[15]
A corpsman grabbed him from behind, and Glover struck him on the
chest and arm.[16] Glover remembers finally ending up on the floor of
sick bay, and then someone bit him.[17]

That was the marine corporal. He had grabbed a CO_2 bottle and
confronted Glover with it but ended up on the deck with two Black
sailors hitting and kicking him. Wanting to later identify Glover, the
marine said he "bit him as hard as I could on the leg. I think the right
lower calf."[18]

The sick bay incident was over in only a few minutes,[19] and the
room was finally cleared of everyone except the injured and those treating them. The head of the ship's medical department arrived soon after.
He began treating two Black sailors with head lacerations. As he was
suturing them, however, he said they had "frequent visits from black
brothers bursting into the room to check on and note the treatment
of their brothers."[20]

Date: 12 October 1972
Time: 2330H
Location: Damage Control Central aboard *Kitty Hawk*

Commander Cloud had left Captain Townsend on the hangar bay
because he had been told of the altercation in sick bay. Just outside
sick bay, the XO heard a shout of "Gangway!" and three corpsmen
came running toward him carrying medical kits. When they passed,
one yelled, "They got the captain. The captain has been hurt. They
got him!" He looked inside sick bay, saw that relative calm had been
restored, and reversed course.[21]

As he was rushing back up to the hangar bay, he passed the personnel office and heard an agitated petty officer exclaiming, "They got the captain! They killed the captain! Oh, my God!" Reacting to the tragic news, Cloud now became "very concerned about the safety and the integrity of the ship."[22] Believing Captain Townsend dead, the XO felt the exigency compelled him to take control of the situation—that is, control of the ship. He had no idea how Captain Townsend had met his fate on the hangar bay but assumed the marines and Black sailors were at it again. His first instinct was to get those two groups separated from each other as quickly as possible.

Cloud rushed down three deck levels to Damage Control Central,[23] which had a 1-MC loudspeaker for broadcasting ship-wide messages. Arriving there, he grabbed the microphone, announced himself as the XO, and issued a direct order. "This is an emergency. Do not listen to what anybody else tells you. I want you to do exactly as I tell you. I ask you, implore you, order you to stop what you are doing. . . . All black brothers proceed immediately to the aft mess deck. All Marines proceed to the Fo'c'sle immediately. This is an emergency, I beseech you, beg you, order you to do as I say."[24] He explained why he made his impassioned announcement, "I did not want these two groups to meet again."[25]

Just when one might think the onboard situation could not get any worse, it did. As if there were not enough chaos already, the back-to-back countermanding orders by the CO and XO threw yet another cruel twist in the evening's events. By now, in response to those conflicting orders, marines and Black sailors were rushing forward and aft in opposite directions, and again running into each other. Further confusion and turmoil ensued.

Cloud then heard a commotion outside Damage Control Central. He looked out and saw some Black sailors armed with makeshift weapons running down the passageway cursing and yelling. He stepped into the passageway, trying to stop them, and collided with two of them. He was knocked down but later said, "It was a collision which was just as much my responsibility as it was theirs. It was not an assault." The XO tried to reason with the group and several dropped their weapons at his request. However, one "rabble rouser" told the XO his way wouldn't work. "You told us the Marines would not hurt us, would not bother us, and they were out there again beating us up just like they had been told." He accused the XO of being no better than the others and said he was a liar.[26]

Shortly after, the XO was greatly relieved to discover that Captain Townsend had not been killed after all, nor even injured. Those rumors may have started when the rail was thrown in his direction on the hangar bay, missing him but striking the marine next to him.

Not only was Captain Townsend alive and well; he was seething. He had heard Commander Cloud's order over the intercom system while he was still talking to the group of Black sailors in the hangar bay and said the XO's order was "pretty terrifying."[27] Having ordered the marines to stand down, Townsend had no way of knowing "why the XO was taking over the ship." He did know, however, that he had to get it corrected immediately. He did not want the marines out again, and certainly not back up on the decks in the middle of a group of Black sailors. "I wanted the Marines right where I could control them."[28]

Townsend rushed down several decks to countermand the XO's order which had just countermanded his order.

Commander Cloud was still in Damage Control Central when Townsend arrived. The XO said, "The captain was obviously in good health, and, of course, as he rightfully should be, I believe, highly incensed at the announcement I had made, and told me as much."[29]

Following that one-sided encounter, Townsend immediately made an urgent announcement over the 1-MC: "This is the Captain. Disregard what the XO just said. He thought the situation was more serious than it really is. Do not go to places—blacks are not to proceed to the mess deck, Marines are not to go to the Focsle. That's the last thing we want to do, segregate into two camps. Everybody go about your normal business. Cool it, everyone. The Marines will not use weapons. There will be no weapons used unless I myself call for it on this box. . . . So cool it. I am OK and the XO is alright."[30]

Townsend's intercom announcement included a lead-in remark, "If anybody ever writes a [book] about this, this is going to be the most [expletive] up chapter."[31] Whether the countermanding orders and ensuing chaos would qualify for that dubious honor, his comment, broadcast to the entire crew, certainly captured everyone's immediate attention.

To further add to the confusion of conflicting orders, another senior officer, believing that there had been an "initial misuse" of the marines, took the extraordinary step of directly ordering their CO, Captain Carlucci, to "move only on direct order from the Commanding Officer or Executive Officer."[32] He probably did so after hearing about the marine assaults on Black sailors, but he had issued an order that could only have further confused Carlucci. Which of the senior officers' orders was Carlucci now supposed to follow? By any reasonable interpretation, the *Kitty Hawk*'s senior chain of command was now in complete disarray.

Townsend clearly recognized that the Black sailors were very fearful of the marines, or else he would not have apologized to them about the marines' aggressive actions, nor tried to reassure them that they need not fear the marines any longer. But they were not buying it. Their fear was manifested in many ways throughout the evening. When the XO was meeting with Black sailors in the fo'c'sle, a group of them in the aft mess deck wanted to join the meeting but were afraid to go there on their own. One said it "was not safe to walk through the 2d deck." They only agreed to go when a chief petty officer personally escorted them to the fo'c'sle.[33]

Shortly after, Commander Cloud heard other Black crew members saying, "Marines are killing blacks and throwing them overboard." Because of that rumor, the XO said the "blacks were convinced they had to arm for their own protection."[34] One Black crew member remembers to this day how he reacted to the rumors flying about the ship. Seaman Apprentice Durward Davis and a group of other Black sailors barricaded themselves in the forward mess compartment. Another Black sailor joined them, exclaiming that more marines were arriving by helicopters, armed with M16 rifles, to assault them and break down their barricade.[35]

Captain Townsend said on several occasions that evening he was approached by agitated and fearful Black sailors yelling, "They are killing our brothers!" Each time, he tried to calm them by saying, "Show me," but he said, "they were truly hysterical people."[36]

A Black petty officer said that numerous crew members, regardless of race, were frightened. "It was a lot of scared people on that ship that night. From scuttlebutt such as 'They are going to kill all the blacks. They are killing all the whites. The captain has been killed.'"[37]

Although all those frightful rumors later proved untrue, they had a significant impact on the actions of many sailors throughout the evening, Black and white.

Earlier, when Townsend was trying to mollify the Black sailors on the hangar bay, he told them, "Now go about your business, we have solved the problems for the night." Townsend may have believed the night's problems were over, but saying those reassuring words could not make it so. What Townsend and Carlucci and the marines had set in motion could not be undone by simply ordering the marines to stand down, especially since those marines kept showing up later and aggressively confronting Black sailors. Actions spoke much louder than words, and Black crew members continued to fear the marines because of what they had witnessed or personally suffered at the hands of the marines on the hangar bay and in sick bay.

Finally, seared in their minds was yet another example of the white man's double standard. They felt victimized by the unilateral enforcement of the dispersal order, even as the white sailors on the mezzanine were allowed to yell racial epithets at them. That likely reminded them once again of the captain's masts, where they witnessed discipline and punishment seemingly meted out only against Black sailors, and memories of assaults on fellow Black crew members in Subic Bay with no consequences whatsoever.

The spring had been tightly wound up and was about to be released.

After the hangar bay and sick bay incidents, a small group of Black sailors began roaming the carrier, venting their anger and frustration with apparent random assaults on white sailors. Shortly after, several white sailors also began roaming the ship, carrying out assaults on Black sailors.

Assaults by Black Sailors

Medical reports were issued for forty-two white crew members treated in sick bay, many of whom reported they were victims of unprovoked assaults by Black sailors. Some of those statements were verified by others, such as assaults taking place in berthing spaces when the victims were in their racks. Virtually no statements were ever taken from Black crew members, however, so we are left with very one-sided reports regarding a large number of those alleged assaults. In addition, records show that some of those sailors sustained their injuries when individuals, or groups of white and Black crew members, confronted each other throughout the night.

Three of the more seriously injured crew members were white, and their injuries were substantial. A third class petty officer suffered a depressed skull fracture.[38] He had been lying in his rack watching a movie on his portable TV. Another petty officer in a nearby rack said he heard several Black sailors come into the compartment and start beating the victim. When a ship's MAA arrived, the Black sailors left.[39] The injured petty officer underwent surgery aboard, was evacuated from the ship, and eventually flown to the Memphis Naval Air Station for follow-up medical care.[40]

A seaman apprentice had his jaw and cheekbone fractured when he said three Black sailors assaulted him as he walked through the S-6 compartment.[41] He was also evacuated from the ship and received follow-up care at the Clark Air Force Base Hospital in the Philippines.[42]

One airman, a mess cook, said he was assaulted in apparent retaliation from an earlier incident, when he refused to serve a Black sailor who had jumped the mess line. He had stopped the sailor from grabbing food, words were exchanged, and the Black man challenged him to fight. The mess cook said, "I was just teed off enough . . . that I just walked out on the mess decks and was ready to fight."[43] A Black crew member had intervened and stopped the confrontation, and the mess cook thought that was the end it.

On the night of the incident, however, the mess cook was asleep in his rack when he was awakened by Black sailors. One of them identified him as the mess cook involved in the earlier incident. They asked him if he was prejudiced, the situation escalated, and they began assaulting him. He said he was hit in the head, apparently with a fog nozzle applicator,[44] and was then "more or less just pushed and shoved on out the door and told to go to sickbay."[45]

He suffered a laceration on his eyebrow and a possible fracture to his cheekbone.[46] He was treated in sick bay and flown off the ship to the Clark Air Force Base Hospital. When it was learned he did not have a fracture, he was returned to duty when *Kitty Hawk* arrived back at Subic Bay.[47]

A white petty officer sustained lacerations on his chin and upper lip that required fourteen sutures to close. He reported that he and another sailor were walking aft to the mess hall when a group of Black sailors came from the other direction. One of them asked where he was going and then hit him in the mouth. He fell, and several Black sailors started kicking and hitting him. The next thing he remembered was being laid on a table and getting stitched up.[48]

Another white petty officer was lying in his rack when he heard other sailors getting beaten in his berthing compartment. He said he was then hit in the face and "stomped, kicked, and clubbed." He suffered facial contusions and a possible rib fracture.[49]

The ship's senior criminal investigator had been in the aft mess during the marine encounter with the Black sailors. Later that evening, he was confronted by several Black sailors including an airman who yelled he was going to put the investigator on report for striking him earlier during the aft mess incident.[50] The investigator later said he "may very well have hit" the airman earlier. The situation escalated, and the sailors backed the investigator against an outboard rail. Just then, a first class petty officer arrived and intervened. The investigator told the petty officer to take the airman and have him file a report about the accusation. As the investigator was being released, however, he said the airman leaned over and whispered in his ear, "You're dead, mother."[51]

Around midnight, after Commander Cloud was knocked down outside the Damage Control Center, he followed the Black sailors forward as they moved to the fo'c'sle. When he arrived, a large group of them were angrily telling others about their encounters with marines on the aft mess deck, in the hangar bay, and in sick bay. The XO reported that some "militant leaders" were exhorting the group to stay together and take action.[52]

Cloud said he saw many kinds of makeshift weapons among the group, including spanner wrenches, broom handles, and clubs of various sorts. He did not see any guns or knives. He estimated the group numbered about 150, and many had their shirts off.[53] As the XO made his way through the boisterous crowd, he heard someone say they should beat him and throw him overboard. As he struggled to get their attention, a petty officer finally got the group to settle down.[54]

The XO said he had to attempt to "reestablish my credibility. The credibility which, if I had any at all, had completely been lost as a result of the beatings that took place on the hangar deck at a time when we had said the Marines would not harm them."[55] He implored them to adopt the tactics of nonviolent men such as Martin Luther King Jr. and Ghandi. He said if they followed their practices "you can live today and tomorrow and the next day in pride and respect," but if they continued, they would only worsen the things they were trying to correct.[56]

Cloud described some unusual tactics he used to calm the angry crowd. He pulled off his shirt, picked up a two-foot piece of steel, and challenged them to strike him with it if they doubted his sincerity. He said that quieted the crowd. "The chant went up that 'He is a brother,' and I exchanged with them the black unity symbol, which I used for the first time in my life that evening. . . . I sincerely don't feel that there is anything militant or wrong about it. I think that it is a symbol around which black people the world over have gained and are increasingly to gain respect and honor, if it is done properly." They responded positively and he ordered them to leave and disperse. They responded by saying,

"'Right on brother,' raised the hand with the black unity symbol, and we all started to leave."[57]

Group Confrontations

Several confrontations occurred between groups of Black and white sailors throughout the evening. A white airman recruit recalls seeing several Black sailors fighting with two white sailors in front of the first class mess. He and four other white crew members grabbed some brooms and chased the Black sailors away.[58]

A division officer witnessed two confrontations between Black and white groups. At 2245 that evening in the aviation ordnance space, he saw about eight Black sailors "verbally confronting" a six-man ordnance handling crew. The officer stepped between the groups, told the Black sailors to leave, and they did.[59]

At about an hour after midnight, he received a call that another white ordnance handling crew was squaring off with Black sailors in the second deck armory. When he arrived, he saw about six Black sailors engaged in name-calling with the ordnance handlers. One of the Black sailors shouted, "That son-of-a-bitch pulled a hammer on me!" The officer identified the white airman and said he would take care of him. He then told the Black sailors to move on, which they did. The officer said he was never in fear of any physical assault from the Black sailors, and all of them responded to his direct orders.[60]

Captain Townsend personally witnessed one of the encounters between groups of Black and white crew members. Just after midnight, Townsend and a Black petty officer heard a disturbance coming from the AIME shop in the aircraft maintenance department. It had the "distinct sound of a fight," so they entered the shop and saw several white and Black sailors fighting. Townsend ordered the crew members to, "break it up," which they did,[61] and the Black sailors left with Townsend. The petty officer said a few of the crew members "had blood on them," but otherwise seemed okay, with the exception of a white airman who was on the floor and bleeding from a head wound. He had to be carried to sick bay.[62] The petty officer recalled seeing about six white and four Black crew members engaged in that altercation.[63]

Assaults by White Sailors

Seaman Apprentice Durward Davis was in the aft mess deck earlier when the marines came rushing in with their nightsticks and confronted him and other Black sailors. After calm was restored and their subsequent meeting with the CO and XO broke up, he headed forward to his berthing compartment. As he was going down a passageway, five white sailors saw him and started running toward him. One of them yelled, "There's one!" They knocked him down and began hitting and kicking him. With so many attackers, he couldn't defend himself. Suddenly, it was over, and the white sailors began running away. Luckily for Davis, a group of Black sailors saw what was happening and had come to his rescue.

One of them helped him to his feet as the others chased after his assailants. He joined them, armed himself with a hand crank he took from a bulkhead, and stayed with them for protection for the rest of the evening. Even in the company of his fellow Black sailors, however, he remained fearful throughout the night. That led to him and others barricading themselves in a mess deck compartment as protection from white sailors who were on the prowl.[64]

The first four Black sailors admitted to sick bay that evening had suffered their injuries on the hangar bay at the hands of white marines. Many other Black sailors who were injured never sought medical treatment. The handcuffed Pettus, and Davis who was assaulted in the passageway, are two cases in point.

Five medical reports were issued for injuries suffered by Black crew members in other parts of the ship following the assaults by the marines on the hangar bay. An airman was attacked by several white crew members, one of whom wielded a knife. He was sleeping in his rack just before midnight when he was told to go to the aft mess deck in response to the XO's order. As he was passing through an air squadron berthing compartment, he was confronted by several white crew members. One of them struck him on the shoulder with a metal fog nozzle applicator, and as he tried to defend himself "another guy knife[d] me in my arm." He was treated in sick bay for the laceration and trauma to his shoulder.[65]

A Black petty officer was assaulted twice that night. A marine struck him with a nightstick in the aft mess incident when he was trying to keep the marine corporal from drawing his pistol, and he was then assaulted a second time in sick bay. He wanted to go there because he heard that a Black sailor's hand was "busted open" and that "all the blacks were mad about it."[66] On his way to sick bay to check on the injured sailor, he was accosted and "kicked in the stomach by a white guy. I then was taken to sick bay. They gave me a shot."[67]

An airman apprentice suffered contusions to his right shoulder and hip[68] when he was assaulted by a white sailor at 2005 that evening. "I took one step onto the ladder which leaves from the Foc'sle and then I felt myself being pushed, I tried to keep myself from falling but wasn't able to. So by the time I had fallen to the bottom of the ladder, whoever pushed me, they were gone."[69]

Another Black airman apprentice sustained two separate injuries from assaults by white crew members. He was first hit on the head with the cover of an oxygen bottle on the forward mess deck, and later was hit on his left wrist with shattered glass on the aft mess deck. Both laceration injuries required suturing.[70]

A seaman was attacked while he was locking up a ship's store for the evening. He submitted a report of the incident and later testified in detail: "Three whites came through the passageway and jumped me; I turned around and I hit him back. He fell and I turned around to face the other two, and another hit me with a dogging wrench."[71] He sustained several broken ribs.[72]

In total, nine medical records were issued for Black crew members—four for injuries sustained on the hangar bay, and five for injuries sustained later elsewhere on the ship.[73] Most of those Black sailors' injuries were very severe, including broken bones and multiple head, facial, and body lacerations.[74]

More medical reports were issued for white sailors than Black sailors. However, many Black sailors were treated in sick bay for which no medical reports were issued. At least six hospital corpsmen worked in sick bay that evening, and one was asked how many Black sailors he alone treated. He testified, "About ten, eleven, a little bit more, maybe."[75] And that was just one corpsman out of several.

No explanation was ever given as to why medical reports were not issued for those additional Black crew members treated in sick bay for their injuries.

Throughout the evening, as Commander Cloud was making his rounds of the ship and meeting with Black and white groups of sailors, he was personally subjected to vicious racial slurs and even death threats. The details of those incidents were elicited from a somewhat reluctant XO at a later hearing in San Diego for one of my clients.[76] He was questioned about threats he received from white sailors that evening. He mentioned an incident when he was going down a ladder and two white sailors at the bottom said to him, "Here comes the black mother [expletive]. . . . I thought we had thrown his ass over the side long ago. I guess we'll have to do it."[77] The XO said the epithet "mother [expletive]" was used frequently by white sailors that he encountered while walking through the ship. One group of white sailors saw him approaching and called out, "Here comes the black mother [expletive] XO. He is no better than the rest of the blacks," and then said, "We ought to kill him."[78]

The XO also told the congressional subcommittee that he had a "collision" with a group of white sailors, during which he tried to keep from falling to the deck. His shirt was torn open and he did fall to the deck. As he was lying there, he said the white sailors stopped briefly and again hurled "verbal insults and threats" at him.[79]

Several Black sailors heard about the white sailors' threats to the XO and offered to provide him protection. Cloud said they "were bound and determined that they were going to be my bodyguard for the rest of the evening. I told them that . . . I would leave it to the integrity of the Navy men on the Kitty Hawk not to assault me that night."[80]

Later on, Cloud was alerted that a large group of white sailors had gathered in a berthing compartment and armed themselves to take action against Black crew members. The XO went to the compartment and saw a group of 100 to 150 white sailors, many of whom had weapons. He said they were "loud and boisterous" and disrespectful to him, saying he was, "nothing more than a [*n*-word], just like all the rest of them."[81] The XO told them they were to obey orders and if they had grievances, they would be addressed by legal means. He also told them if they assaulted anybody, they could be rest assured they would be taken care of by the law.[82] In the end, the XO's words had their intended effect.

The ship's chief investigator encountered a group of twenty or thirty armed and very angry white sailors who "wanted to jump in on this group of blacks," but a couple of officers stepped in, closed off the hatches, and got them to cool down.[83] Afterward, many of those white sailors held on to their weapons for several days. One of the investigators reported that, following the incident, practically every berthing compartment of white sailors "was an armed camp. You would find a chain under a man's mattress, you would find a shore patrol's nightstick, any type of weapon that you can conceive of, short of a firearm. No firearms."[84]

Fifty-one medical reports were issued that night, but fortunately most of the injuries were not serious. The ship's chief medical director reported on the treatment of those injuries and mentioned two major surgical procedures. He said, however, that they treated "mostly abrasions, contusions, black eyes, if you will, a fair number of lacerations, mostly superficial, just of the skin, and superficial subcutaneous tissues. Very little in terms of anything that would have a lasting disability. Mostly bumps, bruises and minor cuts."[85]

Almost all the injuries were treated by 0630 the next morning.[86] Except for the three flown off the ship, most were able to return to duty shortly after the incident. Only about a dozen were admitted for observation following their initial treatment, and the remainder were treated and returned to duty immediately.[87] Of those admitted for observation, all were returned to at least limited duty within thirty-six hours.[88]

Beginning after midnight, Townsend and the XO began making rounds of the ship to restore order. They moved separately, going where they heard of trouble, or where groups of Black or white sailors congregated. Without exception, they were eventually able to calm all the sailors, just as they had earlier on the mess decks. They weren't always welcome initially, but they persisted and sometimes stayed for an hour or more to listen to grievances and to visit.

Two hours after midnight the ship was relatively calm, albeit with sporadic outbreaks between some crew members. During that lull, a group of both Black and white sailors gathered in the aft mess deck for food and socializing. Commander Cloud was making his rounds and stopped off to witness a peaceful setting, including about two dozen Black sailors, and more arriving. Music was playing, food was being served, and several were playing cards. He stayed there long enough to have a sandwich before continuing his tour of the ship.[89]

About twenty minutes later, he talked to Townsend who said he heard of occasional fights. Cloud said from his perspective all was quiet, but still tense. Townsend told him, "Well, we have just got to stay on top of it until things quiet down."[90]

A short time later, Townsend expressed concern about the congregation of Black sailors on the mess deck. He thought they might be a disruptive force during the upcoming morning meal. Commander Cloud said Townsend, "likened that gathering to a victory celebration, and he felt that on his ship there certainly could not and would not be anything of a semblance to a victory celebration."[91]

Townsend then told all the crew members in the mess deck to disperse, but said if anyone wanted to visit, they could follow him and the XO to the fo'c'sle.[92] A group of about sixty Black sailors accepted the captain's invitation and followed the CO and XO to the fo'c'sle at about 0400 that morning. Captain Townsend continued to hear grievances for the next two hours, many of the same type that had been voiced earlier that night.[93] Afterward, the captain asked the group to disband, and Commander Cloud said the group of Black sailors left "without any problem, in a very sociable way." He said most returned to their berthing compartments and racks without further incident.[94]

By midmorning on Friday, the thirteenth, calm had returned to *Kitty Hawk*. One of the Black sailors recalled that, when he woke up the next morning, shipboard life had returned to normal: "Like nothing happened. We ate together, slept in the same compartments, and returned to work as always."[95]

––––––––––––

Even though relative calm had settled over *Kitty Hawk*, what followed was almost as contentious and divisive than what had gone on the night before. That was because Captain Townsend was in complete denial of what actually took place during the interracial confrontations. He steadfastly maintained that no white crew members had ever assaulted Black crew members. He did so despite the overwhelming evidence to the contrary. Some of his denials were made under oath in his sworn testimony and statements to the congressional subcommittee.

A *Time* magazine article in early December 1972 reported that unprovoked assaults were committed by both white and Black crew members: "The outline of the riot was known before the *Kitty Hawk* docked: a six-hour long melee in which sailors *attacked each other* [emphasis added] with chains and pipes."[96] Captain Townsend responded by submitting a written statement to the subcommittee denying any white crew members had committed assaults. "In fact, there was no mutual combat. Groups of black sailors, some of them armed, assaulted individual or smaller groups of white sailors. No pitched battles were fought anywhere on the ship on the night of 12–13 October 1972."[97] Apparently, the captain forgot all about the AIME shop fight between six white and four Black crew members, which he personally broke up.

Townsend also took exception to a *Time* magazine statement that "groups of both whites and blacks rampaged through the berthing quarters of the ship."[98] Townsend responded by saying, "Again, no whites were involved in any rampaging."[99] Those opinions and his attitude played a significant role in the injustices that followed for two dozen young Black *Kitty Hawk* crew members.

6

RETURN TO SUBIC BAY

Date: 13 October 1972
Time: 1030H
Place: *Kitty Hawk*, Yankee Station, Gulf of Tonkin

Perhaps it was fitting that dawn broke the next day on "unlucky" Friday, the thirteenth. Captain Townsend undoubtedly wished what happened on board would stay on board, but he knew better. Although his crew was physically isolated from the outside world, word of the incident was bound to leak. Outgoing mail was not censored, and many lower echelon sailors had access to the ship's communication center.

Midmorning on 13 October, Townsend issued the first public statement about the night's tumult. He may have had approval from higher-ups since two flag officers were aboard his ship during the incident.[1] From the outset, the Navy was clearly trying to keep the incident under wraps, as shown in a *Honolulu Advertiser* report of the incident: "The U.S. Pacific Fleet command refused on Saturday to reveal more details about a racial fight Thursday aboard the aircraft carrier *Kitty Hawk* off Vietnam. . . . The Navy issued two brief statements Friday at fleet headquarters in Pearl Harbor and has declined to amplify them despite a long list of questions posed by newsmen."[2]

The afternoon of 13 October, Townsend ordered the ship secured with a Condition II lockdown,[3] what he called "extraordinary security measures." He also doubled the master-at-arms force, and closed the second-deck passageways with Zebra fittings, meaning they had to be manually opened for passage.[4] He also kept an officer or chief petty officer in every berthing space on a scheduled watch basis, all night long.

A sailor described what Condition Zebra looked like to someone making his way through the ship. "The Captain closed off every other passageway . . . and made it kind of like a zigzag or a puzzle trying to get through the ship."[5]

Townsend's stated reason for the added security was to ensure against a "white backlash."[6] He added, "That meant restraint was applied to every soul on the ship."[7]

But Townsend didn't stop there. He also issued an order prohibiting group meetings, or even informal gatherings, unless personally approved by him. As with the marine captain's infamous dispersal order, his new order was color-blind on its face. However, Captain Townsend left no question how he intended to apply it. He wanted to prohibit any "voluntary segregation" in the assigned berthing spaces.[8] What did he mean by that?

When new crew members first came aboard, they were assigned berthing compartments near their duty stations. So long as they berthed in their designated compartment, they could exchange rack spaces with others to be near their friends. Captain Townsend's new restriction, however, prohibited any switching of racks, at least for the Black sailors. Since the new restriction was color-blind on its face, how could that be?

Black crew members constituted fewer than 7 percent of the *Kitty Hawk* personnel, about one crew member out of every fifteen.[9] Therefore, if Black sailors traded rack spaces and ended up together, that would be readily apparent, and they would be ordered to disperse. But what if a dozen white sailors rearranged their berthing to be together? How could it possibly be detected when 93 percent of the ship's company were white men? It couldn't.

The congressional subcommittee chairman asked Townsend what constituted a "gathering." Fifteen sailors? Three sailors? Captain Townsend responded, "No, sir, a group of 15 blacks who sit in a berthing space listening to music and just talking about what they are doing . . . is an abnormal group. You don't see 15 whites get together in a group that size, so you can't say why don't you break up a group of 15 whites, because *people* [emphasis added] don't congregate in groups of that size. . . . I would say any time you see a group of 10 or more . . . simply to air grievances, then that becomes an unauthorized meeting."[10]

Did the subcommittee members hear him right? If a group met "simply to air their grievances," that meeting violated his order? Townsend made it clear not even peaceable gatherings would be allowed on *Kitty Hawk* if the subject matter offended him. And who could misconstrue what he meant when he said "people" don't congregate in large groups like Black men do? Captain Townsend probably did not realize how revealing his comment was to others.

He also made it clear he didn't want Black sailors taking over his ship. "A young black who has been around blacks all his life is thrust into a major white situation, faces some problems, and I can recognize those. How much we can give to let him take over a certain section of the ship and make it like his own hometown though, I cannot accept that."[11]

Captain Townsend was so adamant about Black sailors not meeting, he even ordered his XO not to meet with Black sailors the evening after the incident.[12] Commander Cloud was the person most responsible for calming the Black sailors during the incident and, by the end of the evening, was probably the person in authority most trusted by those sailors. And now Townsend had given him a direct order not to meet with any Black sailors that evening.

Before the incident, Black sailors were frequently criticized for dapping. In fact, the first hangar bay incident occurred when only two Black sailors met, began dapping, and the marines forcefully confronted them. The day after the onboard incident, Townsend prohibited even that seemingly innocuous exchange between Black sailors. Dapping was now a chargeable offense under the *UCMJ*.[13]

Townsend told the subcommittee his reason for the dapping prohibition. "You have to break up the solidarity, that is all. One thing I will never permit on my ship again is the so-called 'dap' which is the knuckle-rapping system. . . that was the major coercive method that the blacks use. . . . This was the control form. . . . That is my opinion."[14]

Breaking up solidarity might seem odd coming from a commander of a seagoing combat force of several thousand men. Soldiers and sailors alike are indoctrinated, from basic training onward, that unit cohesion and solidarity are a critical component of a combat group's effectiveness. Townsend obviously felt differently about solidarity among Black sailors.

Townsend issued an outright prohibition of dapping based upon his "opinion." In fact, the chief of Naval operations said the Navy had no prohibition against dapping.[15] Questions of legality aside, if anyone doubted his resolve in punishing anyone who violated his new prohibition, he made it clear in his criticism of his XO who had displayed a Black power salute. "I told him [the XO] that morning if he ever did anything like that again, any more black-power salutes or anything like that, he was off the boat, I could not work with him."[16]

Townsend might have told himself, or actually believed, he harbored no racist feelings since his new prohibitions were, on their face, color-blind. After all, his prohibitions applied to everyone. But in practice, of course, they did not. Dapping, for example, was practiced exclusively by Black sailors.

At 1100 the morning of 13 October, Captain Townsend directed that an investigation of the night's incident start immediately. Captain Frank Haak, who was on board, was directed to conduct a formal JAG investigation into the incident,[17] along with Lieutenant Martin, the legal officer. The initial investigative team included them as well as the ship's criminal investigative staff of four white petty officers.[18] The investigators began their work in earnest, and within hours, were interviewing crew members and collecting statements.

Date: 14 October 1972
Time: 0800H
Place: *Kitty Hawk* at sea

Most Naval shipboard disciplinary matters were handled at sea at captain's masts, with a maximum punishment of thirty days in the brig, reduction in rank, and pay forfeiture. A ship's CO could also refer infractions to a court-martial trial with more severe punishments. Special courts-martial sentences, for example, included one year's confinement and a bad-conduct discharge (BCD). Those were also federal convictions.

Before the *Kitty Hawk* incident, Captain Townsend handled virtually all onboard assault cases at captain's masts. If Townsend felt any of the night's offenses were serious enough to warrant a court-martial, it was assumed he would do what every other commanding officer did—namely, send the case to a shore-based trial team for disposition.

But Captain Townsend took a different approach, one that was virtually unheard of. Early in the morning after the incident, he woke up his legal officer, Lieutenant Martin, and told him "that after much thought he was concerned that it might be better, from the standpoint of speedy trials and the administration of justice, to have the trials on board ship."[19]

Clearly, the mention of "trials" meant Townsend was already planning on referring the cases to courts-martial proceedings. Martin must have been surprised at the unusual request, because he told Townsend, "We [are] talking about as many as twenty courts . . . [and] we would need at least three trial teams, composed of military judge, trial and defense counsel, and a certified court reporter with equipment."[20]

The obvious question, apparently never asked, was, *Why couldn't the cases be delayed for three weeks when the ship returned to Subic Bay?* After all, the investigation had just started, and it would take some time before Martin could prepare charges against the accused. And then there was the matter of logistics. In addition to the nine members of the trial teams, most of the cases would require jury "panels" of officer and enlisted personnel.[21] In addition, the very idea of trying all those courts-martial cases on board an oceangoing vessel actively engaged in daily bombing runs seemed preposterous. But Captain Townsend was not to be deterred, and so Lieutenant Martin complied.

———————

JAG Lieutenant Dick Smith had been on active duty for only six months at the Subic Bay Naval Base Law Center when he was tagged to meet with the first of *Kitty Hawk*'s accused. He was an assigned defense counsel at the law center, which had about a dozen JAG lieutenants as well as four more senior JAG officers.

On 16 October, three days after word broke of the *Kitty Hawk* incident, Smith was informed that he and eight others from the law center would be flown out to the carrier to constitute the requested three trial teams.[22] Smith said he and the others were astonished that Captain Townsend had ordered full-out special courts-martial trials aboard a ship at sea in a combat zone. Smith said it was clearly an "improper venue," but orders were orders, so off they went.

On 17 October the JAG officers took a military flight to Da Nang Air Base in South Vietnam, and then they caught a Navy helicopter for the short hop to *Kitty Hawk* on Yankee Station. They were greeted by Lieutenant Martin, and each was then assigned to a stateroom that would serve as an office and overnight quarters. Smith was in the stateroom of an air squadron pilot who was temporarily disembarked. Except for meals and occasional meetings, he did not see the other members of the trial team over the next several days. As a defense counsel, he was busy interviewing Black sailors who had been charged after the incident.[23]

Meanwhile, the ship's investigative team had been busy, and within five days of the incident had 120 sworn statements from crew members, officers, and enlisted men.[24] By 24 October 1972, twenty-five Black sailors had been charged by Captain Townsend.[25] He charged all of them with assaults, and all but four with rioting. All except one case was later referred by him to special courts-martial for disposition.[26] No white crew members were charged.

An airman apprentice was the first of the accused to receive his "Charge Sheet."[27] Charge Sheets set forth allegations of criminal conduct under the *UCMJ*. They contain charges and specifications. Each individual charge lists an alleged violation of a Punitive Article of the *UCMJ*.[28] The specifications listed below each of the charges contain the factual details of the alleged offense.[29]

Charges are sworn to by an "accuser," which is someone with personal knowledge of the alleged offenses, either as an eyewitness or investigator.[30] Charge Sheets also list the names of prosecution witnesses and identify the place of the alleged offenses.

The Charge Sheet of an airman apprentice listed the place as "USS *Kitty Hawk* (CVA-63) at sea in the Gulf of Tonkin." Shortly after charges were preferred against him, he was personally advised of those charges.[31] The specifications in Charge I alleged assaults by striking three white crew members, two with his fists and one with a broom handle.[32] Charge II accused him of rioting and its specification alleged he "did . . . participate in a riot by unlawfully assembling with . . . others to the number of about ten (10) whose names are unknown for the purpose of assaulting passers-by . . . thereby causing public terror and alarm."[33]

As each of the accused was informed of his charges, he was directed to either Lieutenant Smith's stateroom or to those of the other two defense counsel from Subic Bay. Smith recalls his first meeting with one of the accused who had a large naturally red Afro hairstyle. Smith immediately knew that a defense of mistaken identity wouldn't probably fly.

He soon learned that the accused enlisted man wasn't quite ready to trust a white "two-striper" officer,[34] and initially clammed up. Smith decided to do something to focus his attention. He told him that initial charges can be, and often are, amended. Smith had heard scuttlebutt about mutiny charges possibly being added later, so he mentioned the maximum penalty for mutiny was a death sentence.[35] From that point on, he had the accused's undivided attention.

Not surprisingly, many of the accused were angry. Smith recalls one Black sailor in particular who stormed out of his office, later to return after he had time to cool off.[36] With those two exceptions, Smith found all the accused were initially willing to share their experiences aboard *Kitty Hawk*. They vented their feelings about how Black sailors were treated before the incident, and some told of being assaulted by white sailors during the night's confrontations.

Smith was not yet assigned to represent anyone in particular, but he advised each of the accused of their right to counsel under the *UCMJ*. He told them a JAG officer would be the first of their assigned defense counsel,[37] and they also could request another military counsel of their own choosing, provided counsel was "reasonably available."[38] He also told them they were entitled to representation by civilian counsel, but not at government expense.[39] Although requests for civilian counsel were rare, the fact that only Black sailors were charged might have suggested to the accused that the Navy could not be trusted. Smith also advised them that a request for civilian counsel would delay the disposition of their cases at least until the ship got back to Subic Bay, and more likely until the ship returned to San Diego.

For whatever reason, the idea of civilian counsel representation quickly gained traction among the accused. On 18 October, just a day after the trial teams arrived, the first of the accused made an oral request with the ship's legal officer to be represented by civilian defense counsel from either the NAACP or ACLU.[40] By 24 October, twenty of the accused had made those requests.[41]

The command forwarded the requests to the commander of Naval air forces in the Pacific, headquartered at the San Diego Naval Air Station, for further action.[42] Later, civilian counsel requests were also sent to the commander in chief of the US Pacific Fleet at Pearl Harbor.[43] Their legal offices relayed the requests to the NAACP and ACLU.

The ACLU initially turned down the request because they were looking for Constitutional issues that would justify their involvement.[44] The NAACP, however, agreed to supply legal support, which was confirmed by Nathaniel Jones, its general counsel.[45]

Three of the accused chose to forgo civilian representation. Lieutenant Smith said those three aspired to be career Navy men and felt they might get more lenient courts-martial treatment by not dragging out the legal process.[46] In addition, they would be accommodating Captain Townsend, who wanted the cases tried on board.[47]

Smith said from the outset he had a "distinct feeling" that Captain Townsend very much wanted the incident to blow over as quickly as possible. That was his logical reaction to the captain taking the highly unusual action of having trial teams flown out to the carrier. Smith felt that the last thing Townsend—or the Navy, for that matter—wanted was a long, drawn-out drama as the accused worked their way through the usual legal process at shore-based law centers.[48] If the cases were disposed of while the *Kitty Hawk* was still at sea, that would keep the adverse publicity, and the Navy's possible embarrassment, to a minimum. The captain's hopes were thwarted, or course, when virtually all the accused asked for civilian legal counsel.

Interestingly, if the captain really wanted to keep publicity to a minimum, he had complete authority to do so. Instead of referring the cases to courts-martial, he could simply have the accused appear at his captain's masts. They would not have been entitled to counsel, and he could have disposed of their cases without publicity or fanfare. Why didn't he do so?

One likely reason is because potential punishments are limited at captain's masts. If that was the reason, the captain had much harsher punishments in mind for the accused.

Smith and the other trial team members spent about a week on *Kitty Hawk*, and he and the other two defense counsel visited often with the accused. As a result, Smith learned many of the details of the night's incident, which led him to consider challenging Captain Townsend from any further involvement in the criminal cases.

In the military justice system, if disciplinary action is not taken at the captain's mast level, criminal charges are officially sanctioned by a "convening authority," who is typically the commanding officer of the military base, station, or other facility to which the accused is assigned.[49]

The convening authority quite literally "convenes" the court and may also assign the military judge, defense counsel, and trial counsel, also known as government counsel, who are prosecutors.[50] He also makes the decision what charges are sworn out, and at what level of courts-martial the case will be tried.

With all that power and authority, it is critical that the convening authority be totally neutral, unbiased, and free from any personal involvement or interest in the outcome of the trials.

Captain Townsend, the commanding officer of the ship, became the initial convening authority.[51] The *UCMJ* provides, however, that if a potential convening authority is an "accuser," the court shall be convened by another commanding officer. An accuser includes any person who has an interest "other than an official interest" in the prosecution of the accused.[52] An official interest would include the vast majority of cases brought to trial, such as a sailor charged with an unauthorized absence or an assault. In those instances, the commanding officer would have only an "official" interest because it is likely he would have little personal interest in the outcome of the case.

Did Captain Townsend have anything other than an official interest in prosecuting the accused? There could be little doubt. He was personally involved in the incident on many levels. He had issued the orders that called the marines to the hangar and flight decks. He believed the Black sailors were solely responsible for the mayhem on the ship he commanded, what many had already called a full-blown riot. In addition, Townsend had personally witnessed many of the incidents that evening, including the white petty officer's hurling of racial slurs from the mezzanine level in the hangar bay.

Finally, Townsend had a rail thrown in his direction during the incident. Some said the captain had been struck by the rail, even though Townsend later said the rail narrowly missed him. Legally speaking, the difference was immaterial, as either version would constitute an assault under the *UCMJ*.[53]

Lieutenant Smith immediately recognized that Captain Townsend fit the classic definition of an accuser, and thus subject to removal as convening authority. A couple of days later, he filed a formal motion for his removal.[54]

His motion was not well received by Captain Townsend. Nevertheless, it proceeded to a hearing in which Townsend did not even bother testifying to challenge the clearly justified motion. On 24 October a military judge who had come aboard with the trial teams granted Smith's accuser motion.[55] The cases were then transferred to the jurisdiction of the commanding officer of the Subic Bay Naval Base.[56]

Later that same day, the trial teams were helicoptered off *Kitty Hawk* to Da Nang Air Base, en route back to Subic Bay. Captain Townsend was probably happy to see them go. Things hadn't gone as he would have liked. All but three of the accused would see their trials postponed indefinitely, and that undoubtedly meant further adverse publicity for him and his ship.

That might also explain why Captain Townsend left it up to the trial teams to find their own way back to Subic Bay, instead of issuing them orders for that purpose. The nine JAG officers remained at Da Nang Air Base for two days before talking their way onto an aircraft that would take them back to Subic Bay. While there, they came under a barrage of incoming rocket fire, including one rocket that set off a nearby fuel dump.[57]

Kitty Hawk finally set sail for Subic Bay on 4 November, three sailing days away. On 7 November, when the ship docked, all but three of the accused went ashore.[58] Those three had declined civilian counsel. *Kitty Hawk* made a quick turnaround at Subic Bay, bound for the US Navy Base and Fleet Activities Facility in Sasebo, Japan.[59] Before leaving, however, a new trial team was appointed to accompany the carrier and handle the cases of the three accused, technically now "defendants,"[60] who remained on board. Lieutenant Smith was an obvious choice to serve as defense counsel, and two others from the Subic Bay law center would serve as trial counsel and military judge.

Also aboard *Kitty Hawk* would be several crew members from another ship who would serve as "court members," that is, a jury panel for the trials.[61] The reason for selecting non–*Kitty Hawk* jurors was to ensure total objectivity in deliberations. One of the defendants chose to go "judge alone"—that is, without a jury. The other two elected to have a jury panel hear their cases.

A defendant is always entitled to a jury panel, but that right is not invoked as often as might be expected. That is because of the typical composition of the panels whose members are decided by the convening authority. The number of panel members varies depending on the level of courts-martial. The *Kitty Hawk* defendants were to be tried at special courts-martial, which require a jury panel of at least four members,[62] and a guilty verdict requires the concurrence of at least three-fourths of those members.[63]

The panel can be a mix of commissioned officers, warrant officers, and enlisted men. A defendant who is an enlisted man is entitled, at his request, to have at least one-third of the members be enlisted men, so long as they are not junior to him in rank.[64] Having an enlisted juror sounds good in theory, as a young noncareer juror might be more forgiving of violations of military rules. In practice, however, if a defendant asked for an enlisted juror, he would most likely find himself facing an "Old Navy" career man, such as a chief petty officer or even a master chief. This was true throughout the Navy, and certainly at Naval Base Subic Bay. Typically, those at the higher enlisted levels didn't cut any slack with defendants.

As a result, most defendants accepted commissioned officer panels, and hoped for junior officers who always seemed more sympathetic than their senior counterparts.

After *Kitty Hawk* set sail for Japan, a training room on board was converted into a makeshift courtroom. Long tables were rearranged into a U shape, completely filling the room. The three defendants were a seaman and two airmen.[65]

On 7 November, with the ship enroute to Japan, the seaman's case was heard first. He had elected to go judge alone.[66] He was a twenty-year-old from New Orleans and had been on board just a month when the evening's incident occurred.[67] Along with a rioting charge, he was alleged to have committed assaults on white sailors in the forward mess berthing compartment.[68]

Following the submission of the government's case, Lieutenant Smith made a motion to dismiss all the charges for lack of sufficient evidence proving all elements of the offenses. The military judge dismissed the riot charge and all but one of the assault charges, then found him guilty of that remaining charge.[69] After a sentencing hearing in which the defendant was able to offer evidence and witnesses "in mitigation," he was sentenced to two months confinement, and then taken to the ship's brig.[70]

On 9 November the second trial was held before a jury panel. The defendant airman was just nineteen and had enlisted less than a year earlier in the Bronx, New York.[71] A chief petty officer testified against him, and the defendant testified that he was a victim of an assault, not an assailant. He even said he could identify his white assailant.[72] The jury panel acquitted him of all charges.

The third and final onboard trial was held the next day before the same jury panel. The defendant was a nineteen-year-old airman apprentice from Virginia[73] who was facing charges of rioting, assaults on two seamen in different locations, and a breach of the peace. Both white victims had been attacked while they were walking through compartments on the ship. The military judge dismissed the riot charge and one of the assaults, but the jury found the defendant guilty of the second assault. He received two months confinement and was escorted to the ship's brig.[74]

Meanwhile, twenty-one other defendants languished in the Subic Bay Naval Base brig.

PART II

COMING HOME

7

ADDING INSULT TO INJURY

Date: 13 October 1972
Time: 0715H
Place: *Kitty Hawk*, Yankee Station, Gulf of Tonkin

"The night before all hell was breaking loose, but the next day it was like nothing had happened,"[1] Fireman Apprentice Durward Davis, crew member and later defendant, recalls the morning after the incident as unreal. He said for the next three weeks while the ship remained on Yankee Station, it was life as usual. Black and white sailors alike reported to their duty stations, and the daily air interdictions into North Vietnam continued without letup. Shipboard life for sailors off duty likewise continued as usual, including on the mess decks and in berthing compartments.

Even after Davis and the other twenty-four defendants were formally charged, nothing changed on board for them. They were told that when the ship returned to Subic Bay, they would be billeted in a legal hold barracks to await their trials.

Legal hold did not mean confinement. It was just the Navy's way of keeping the defendants segregated in one location and accessible to their lawyers. They were promised they would still enjoy regular liberty off the Subic Bay Naval Base. From that time on, Davis and the others thought of little else. Since they had been unrestricted on board since the incident, they had no reason to distrust the command's assurance.

———————

Date: 7 November 1972
Time: 1645H
Place: Subic Bay, Philippines

The *Kitty Hawk* steamed into Subic Bay on 7 November and tied up at the Cubi Point Naval Air Station. Three of the accused were allowed to remain on board,[2] but all others were assembled on the quarterdeck and escorted to a waiting bus,[3] which took them north to the naval base. Davis was familiar with the naval base, so when the bus headed in the opposite direction from the barracks, he was confused. But not for long. The bus pulled up to the Naval Base Correctional Facility, the "brig," and pulled in.

Having been lied to about being billeted in unrestricted barracks, most of the defendants were understandably angry, even outraged. Durward Davis, however, has a distinct memory of being very scared when the bus pulled into the brig compound. He feared if confinement could be ordered under these circumstances, what might happen next?[4]

Who ordered their confinement? Technically speaking, it was the naval base commander,[5] the succeeding convening authority after Townsend's removal from that position.[6] Townsend, however, had recommended confinement of all the defendants even before *Kitty Hawk* arrived in Subic Bay.[7]

The Naval Base Correctional Facility was divided into three confinement barracks, plus a separate cell block with five cells.[8] Three of the defendants were kept in the maximum cell block, which was called a "hellhole" by some who had been inside.[9] The Subic Bay brig was never a good place to be, and certainly not during the oppressively hot and humid Philippine rainy season, which lasted six months.

New JAG officers who arrived at the Subic Bay Naval Base law center during the rainy season, and watched the rain coming down in sheets, would invariably ask, "How long is it going to rain?" The usual response, accurate but not really helpful: "Until November."[10]

As the *Kitty Hawk* defendants sweated out the coming days and nights awaiting their fate, life in confinement only worsened. Virtually none of the accused had ever before been incarcerated in their entire lives, and most did not tolerate the Subic Bay confinement well. For some, it was a nightmare.

One defendant cried uncontrollably from when he was first incarcerated, so he was sent to the Naval base hospital for observation. He was then returned to the brig, however, and his condition and depression only worsened. He was again sent to the hospital with a diagnosis of "anxiety reaction, acute," and remained hospitalized until the defendants were returned to San Diego.[11]

The brig counselor had an interesting comment about this sailor's reaction to his incarceration: "Anxiety reactions of this kind are not uncommon among individuals in confinement and such states can be induced by the individual."[12] By that, he apparently meant that the unjustified confinement in the oppressive heat was not the cause of the prisoner's mental state. It was simply self-induced.

The continued confinement led to increased tension and confrontations between the accused and guards. At the end of their confinement, the counselor said the *Kitty Hawk* sailors were "the most unruly, most disruptive, and most disrespectful" of any in his memory.[13]

These are the same sailors who did not have a single disciplinary issue on board *Kitty Hawk* in the weeks between the incident and their arrival at Subic Bay. One wonders if the counselor had even an inkling of why they acted differently after two weeks of totally unwarranted incarceration in his brig.

———————

Date: 11 November 1972
Time: 0830H
Place: Naval Base Subic Bay, Philippines

On 11 November, the naval base commander was told the NAACP had agreed to help represent the defendants. Those civilian lawyers would not be coming to the Philippines, however, which meant the trials would take place back in San Diego. That change of venue started the legal wheels turning to have yet another convening authority appointed. On 16 November, the naval air station on North Island in San Diego Bay was designated to receive the accused, and its commanding officer, Captain Robert McKenzie, became the third designated convening authority.[14]

After the defendants were told they would be flown to San Diego, they immediately wanted to know if they would finally be released from confinement on arrival. They were assured they would be billeted in a nonrestricted barracks, and free to enjoy liberty from there.[15] They had heard that promised before, but this time they really wanted to believe it. On 19 November they were escorted under guard from the brig and transported inland to Clark Air Force Base to catch a Military Airlift Command flight back to the States.[16]

When they arrived, the bus pulled up to a US Air Force Lockheed C-141 cargo plane, which was already loaded and ready to depart. They boarded and buckled into the rear-facing row of seats near the front of the huge aircraft. They were told to settle back for the seventeen-hour, three-hop flight to San Diego.[17] Their escorts were "chasers," a marine special security detail assigned to watch over them during the flight.

One of those chasers reported that the long trip from Subic Bay was "without incident and fairly quiet."[18] That should have told the authorities something. When not incarcerated, the defendants raised no disciplinary concerns whatsoever. In fact, while en route, the mood among the young men was upbeat. For some, even euphoric. And why not? They had been confined in cramped quarters for almost six weeks. First, aboard *Kitty Hawk*, and then in the Subic brig. But now they were promised unfettered liberty on arrival, in what they considered a great liberty town.[19] The plane would ultimately arrive safely the next day at Naval Air Station North Island in the San Diego harbor.[20]

Date: 20 November 1972
Time: 0800H
Place: Naval Air Station North Island

The cargo plane from Clark Air Force Base touched down at the North Island Naval Air Station runway at 0800 the morning of 20 November.[21] The twenty-one young men aboard couldn't wait to get off the plane. They were very familiar with the Naval air station, as it was their home port. Naval Air Station North Island was a city within itself. With all ships in port, its population swelled to over thirty thousand military and civilian personnel. Considered one of the best Naval stations anywhere, it had every convenience and accommodation a sailor could hope for: commissary, Navy exchange, enlisted clubs, movie theater, parks, and beautiful sand beaches. The sailors had last seen their home port island nine months earlier. It would be good to be home, check into their barracks, and then secure liberty to enjoy their newfound freedom.

As the plane taxied from the runway, however, they were told to remain in their seats. One of the marine chasers told them they were to deplane one by one, as each of their names was called out in alphabetical order.[22] There were a few groans. What was that all about? That wasn't what they expected at all.

The chasers were the first to deplane, walking toward the air terminal receiving area, what some called a quarterdeck. There followed a short delay before the sailors started coming off the plane, but they finally exited one by one as their names were called off. On the tarmac next to the receiving area, they could see marines standing by military vans, a couple of petty officers, and the new convening authority, Captain Robert McKenzie,[23] the commander of the Naval air station.

As more and more sailors deplaned, their excitement built, and they began exchanging daps. They were finally in home port after nine grueling months at sea. Then, someone started singing, and others joined in. By now, the orderly exit had turned into a celebration of sorts, at least for the sailors. Not so much for Captain McKenzie.

What happened next at the airfield, known as the "deplaning incident," was the subject of much controversy and a later hearing. The incident led to Captain McKenzie ordering the sailors into the vans, and instead of taking them to enlisted barracks, as the defendants expected, the vans exited the North Island Naval Air Station and headed for the Coronado Bay Bridge.

The defendants immediately suspected that something wasn't right, and their apprehension grew. The vans crossed the bridge and a few minutes later entered the east gate of the Thirty-Second Street Naval Station. Then they pulled up to the Naval Station Correctional Center. That really set off the sailors, and some loudly voiced their anger at being deceived, once again, about a promised liberty.

The Naval station sits adjacent to the harbor and just south of downtown San Diego. Not to be confused with Naval Air Station North Island where the defendants' plane landed, the Naval station was part of Naval Base San Diego, home to many commands and support facilities which sprawled for miles within and around the harbor.[24]

One of those facilities was the Naval Station Correctional Center. That was the official title, but to most everyone else it was simply "the brig." Since time immemorial, a brig has always meant a military lockup. Its origins are naval, named after small two-masted warships called "brigantines" used as floating prisons. Navy traditions run deep, so why give up a perfectly good word to denote one of the worst places any sailor would ever want to find himself?

The Thirty-Second Street brig was one of the Navy's major correctional facilities, with a maximum capacity of 150 prisoners, although it typically held about half that number. The marine security contingent numbered about eighty.[25] An asphalt center courtyard was flanked by several buildings and two guard towers, all enclosed by a fifteen-foot chain-link fence topped with barbed wire. Prisoners were classified as minimum, medium, or maximum, and to a prisoner, the differences in those classifications were substantial.

Maximum prisoners were classified as such because they were considered the highest escape risks, or safety risks to themselves or others. When prisoners first arrived, they were taken to the maximum facility to be screened and processed. Were they a flight risk? Would they obey orders? Did they cause any disciplinary problems? Except for those undergoing screening, the maximum building typically contained only a handful of prisoners.

The maximum facility was a two-story building—actually a cell block—containing individual cells. The doors had steel bars, and steel bars crisscrossed the top of each cell through which marine guards could observe prisoners from above. A separate section of maximum housed the cells for those in disciplinary confinement. Known as "Row 6," it was separated by a wall from the rest of the maximum cells. The Row 6 cells were each completely enclosed with a steel door and steel plates along the walls.[26]

After a prisoner passed the screening protocol in the maximum cell block, he was moved into medium or minimum housing. Those were two-story barracks with rows of bunk beds and, except for bars on the windows, were indistinguishable from any other barracks.[27]

Brig security was provided by young marines who were only slightly less unhappy than the prisoners to be there. Brig duty was often given to marines just out of boot camp, and it was the last place a young "gung-ho" marine wanted to be posted. It was those marines, many just teenagers themselves, who were called out to the courtyard to meet the *Kitty Hawk* defendants.

After the vans pulled into the brig courtyard, the chain-link gate closed behind it, and a marine sergeant ordered the twenty-one new prisoners to exit and fall in line on the tarmac. Brig security had been alerted that there might be trouble, so a dozen marine guards waited for them, nightsticks held at the ready. There could be no mistaking that they meant business.

By now, some of the defendants were openly venting their frustration and anger, but they all exited the vans and fell in line, and after a few minutes started to calm down. They were escorted across the compound to one of the outlying buildings, and then taken onto the Q deck of the maximum cell block.

The sailors immediately sensed something wasn't right when they saw the rows of small cells encased in steel bars. As the marines directed them toward the cells, some reacted by yelling at the guards, who in turn shouted back at them. The situation escalated and the marines wielded their nightsticks, trying to force the prisoners into the cells.

After a couple of minutes of further confrontations, a marine captain arrived. Upon realizing something more than brute force would be needed, he placed a call to an adjacent building that housed the brig trial center, which primarily handled UAs, unauthorized absence cases.[28] The marine officer got JAG Lieutenant Tom Phillips on the line, explained the situation, and asked if he could double-time it to the cell block to help out. Phillips responded immediately and hurried over into the brig compound. He was met by the captain who explained the situation and said someone other than a marine would be better able to handle the prisoners.[29] He knew Phillips from his work at the brig trial center, and thought he would be a good intermediary. He guessed right.

Phillips was escorted to the maximum cell block and into a spacious room where chaos ruled. A large group of angry sailors were yelling and shouting, with some pounding on the metal tables. They seemed to be venting their anger at a group of charged-up marine guards who stood facing them, nightsticks at the ready. Above them, Phillips could see other marine guards looking down from a balcony.[30]

Facing a highly volatile situation, Phillips didn't hesitate. He placed himself between the groups and raised his hands. That, plus his uniform, caught the attention of some of the prisoners, and the noise subsided somewhat. Phillips felt that if he could quiet them down enough to talk to them, he could convince them he was on their side, so to speak. As a relatively short JAG officer who probably looked as young as some of the prisoners, he definitely felt he was not threatening.[31]

After a few minutes, they quieted enough so he was able to tell them he was a defense lawyer and had been called to help them. A couple of sailors responded by saying they were innocent, and the charges against them were totally unjustified. Phillips told them the last thing an innocent person should do was to commit an offense while awaiting his trial. He urged them to consider the possibility they would be found not guilty of their original charges, only to be charged with their subsequent actions in the brig.[32]

Phillips also advised them of their legal rights, including their right to remain silent. He advised them, in no uncertain terms, not to talk to anyone except their lawyers. Several asked when they would see the civilian counsel they had requested, so he assured them he would personally contact the NAACP and ACLU on their behalf.

Phillips had been with the defendants for about fifteen minutes, and by then they had completely settled down, with some even quietly starting to enter the cells. He was not aware of it at the time, but I and another JAG officer had witnessed most of his remarkable efforts from just outside the cell block entrance.

Date: 20 November 1972
Time: 0915H
Place: Naval Station San Diego Law Center

I first learned of the *Kitty Hawk* incident on 14 October, the day after it ended. The ship had relayed the news to the Eleventh Naval District headquarters in San Diego, and the story was soon picked up by individual commands. The details were sketchy, but those of us at the Naval Station Law Center heard that the onboard interracial confrontations had lasted several hours. This obviously was something major. Also, from the beginning, the words *"Kitty Hawk"* and "race riot" had been joined together, seemingly never to be separated again.

We next learned that more than two dozen Black sailors had been charged, but no white sailors. Many of us immediately wondered how that could be. A reported race riot lasting for hours, yet only Black sailors were charged?

At the time, we assumed any legal action arising out of the incident would be handled in Subic Bay by our JAG counterparts, and then learned that some of them had, in fact, been flown out to the ship. That information did not come by way of official channels.

News between JAG officers in different commands flowed like sea water off a carrier's flight deck. The JAG officer corps was a very small contingent among an ocean of over fifty thousand US Naval officers. With only about seven hundred of us JAG officers, and frequent duty station rotations, it seemed like at least one JAG from each command knew another one at a different command.

The next thing we learned was that we would be handling the cases in San Diego. Our law center was home to JAG officers assigned to courts-martial duty for the Eleventh Naval District, and, as its name implies, brought together Navy lawyers from smaller outlying commands. That consolidation took place just three years earlier.

The law center housed a courtroom with seating for about thirty spectators, an adjacent room for deliberations by jury panels, and individual offices for the director, executive officer, military judges, legal assistance lawyers, military and civilian court reporters, and two separate wings for the trial lawyers.

We had about fifteen lawyers in the trial wing, and our group included both defense counsel, my designation, and trial counsel, also referred to as prosecutors or government counsel. We dealt with criminal offenses of a more serious nature than the unauthorized absence and other cases tried at the brig trial center. Occasionally, we appeared in general courts-martial trials, reserved for the most serious offenses, but most often served as counsel in special courts-martial hearings. Our cases ran the gamut from disobedience of orders and assaults to murder.

The law center was a short walk from the lockup where the brig drama was unfolding. The morning that the accused were taken to the brig, the executive officer[33] of the law center stopped by with Lieutenant Glenn Haase, another defense counsel.[34]

"Marv," he said, "I'd like you and Glenn to get over to the brig as soon as you can."

"Sure," I said, "what's up?"

"A marine lieutenant just called. They're having trouble with the *Kitty Hawk* sailors and wanted me to send someone over to get them settled down."

"*Kitty Hawk*? I didn't think she was due until next week."

"She isn't," he said, "but they flew the defendants in this morning and want us to get a head start on the cases."

"Are we being assigned clients already?"

"No, but we expect to make those assignments shortly."

"Why us now, then?"

"The brig officer said he hoped the sailors might listen to the lawyers who would be representing them."

"Understood."

I grabbed my cover, and Glenn and I hurried over to the brig. When we arrived, we showed our IDs to the marine corporal in the small guard shack outside the fence. He hit a switch to slide the chain-link gate open, and once across the inner courtyard, we again showed our IDs and entered a narrow hallway leading to the receiving desk.

A marine lieutenant was waiting for us, noticeably agitated.

"Thanks for coming so quickly," he said, "but we've got a problem in maximum."

"What's going on?" I asked.

"It's the *Kitty Hawk* bunch, sir. They've been raising holy hell. Our CO called the legal office here for help, and then asked me to call your Law Center."

"What's the problem?"

He explained about their promised liberty, gave some details about the deplaning incident, and told us of their anger when brought to the brig, which then escalated when they were taken to the maximum cell block.

"Why maximum?" I asked.

"It's routine, sir. New prisoners are put in max cells for a day or two to make sure they're manageable."

"Did you tell them that?"

"We didn't have a chance. They started yelling and haven't stopped, and our troops had to use their batons."

"Anyone hurt?"

"No, sir, not that I know of, but I left so I could wait for you here."

As we stepped inside the outer entrance to the cell block, we could hear shouting, along with profanity-laced outbursts. When we entered the Q deck, we saw Lieutenant Phillips standing in the middle of a very angry group of Black sailors and a very agitated group of young marines. He was trying to be heard over the din, and eventually they settled down long enough to listen to him. He seemed to be doing quite well on his own, so Lieutenant Haase and I stood just outside and watched.

The entire episode was over in minutes, but witnessing the anger of the *Kitty Hawk* sailors left an indelible impression on me. They felt they had been seriously wronged and didn't hesitate to let it be known. I also learned something else in those few minutes. Despite their clearly justified anger, the young sailors would listen to reason. That was reassuring, as I would soon be representing several of them.

8

KITTY HAWK LAWYERS

The *Kitty Hawk* defendants were not lacking for defense counsel. In addition to their initially assigned JAG counsel, several asked for civilian counsel, and a few requested alternate JAG counsel, designated individual military counsel (IMC).[1] Defendants had the option of having the civilian counsel or IMC serve as their primary counsel, or as cocounsel to their initial JAG counsel. Most of the *Kitty Hawk* defendants requested civilian counsel, and many requested IMCs. That was extremely rare. So rare, in fact, that during my time as a JAG defense counsel, I had only six cases with civilian counsel or an IMC at my side. All six were my *Kitty Hawk* cases.

The NAACP's general counsel was a Black attorney, Nathaniel Jones, who directed all litigation for his organization. He retained civilian attorneys to serve as defense counsel, when needed, and the *Kitty Hawk* cases certainly qualified as a cause worth fighting for. Jones ultimately retained five civilian attorneys, four of whom were Black. The ACLU came in later, with three of its white members stepping forward.

That brought together a group of military and civilian defense lawyers who had a lot in common. Before the trials, we JAG officers had never met the civilian attorneys, but we bonded very quickly. That was easy after learning of the appalling injustices suffered by our young clients.

Almost all of us were young, in our late twenties or early thirties. None of the defense team were in it for the money. The NAACP attorneys were paid modestly and not until a year or more after the trials. The ACLU attorneys all worked pro bono—that is, without any compensation at all. We JAG lieutenants collected our usual monthly military pay.

I met frequently with San Diego attorney Milt Silverman, who was retained by the NAACP to oversee the *Kitty Hawk* cases. I also spoke often with Nathaniel Jones, and usually met with him on his frequent trips to San Diego from New York City. The three of us worked together to coordinate the efforts of the civilian and military defense team,[2] and we were sometimes joined by one or more of the other defense lawyers.

We JAG defense counsel were fortunate to have the civilian attorneys on our defense team, as well as the NAACP's financial resources. All were needed because of the exceptional nature of the *Kitty Hawk* cases. It was the first time in anyone's memory that sailors were charged with rioting, a group offense which required defense team coordination among the cases. It was the first time a group of defendants were locked up in the brig for months before their trials. Finally, since so many defendants were tried in back-to-back trials, the cases dragged on for several months.

Date: 22 November 1972
Time: 0930H
Place: San Diego Naval Station Law Center

I received my informal case assignments on Wednesday morning, 22 November, the day before Thanksgiving. The formal assignment documents would arrive a week later. Captain Newsome, the law center director, came by my office and handed me a list of names of twenty-one Black sailors charged in the *Kitty Hawk* incident.[3] He had penciled in my name next to five of the defendants. I was later assigned to represent an additional Black crew member.

Captain Newsome also gave me the case files for my new clients. We talked about the inexplicable fact that only Black crew members were charged. As I read through the files, I noted that my clients were each charged with one or more assaults, and all but one were also charged with rioting.[4] The charged acts were alleged to have taken place on 12 and 13 October 1972 aboard the USS *Kitty Hawk*. My two youngest clients were nineteen, one having been in the Navy just six months. My oldest client was twenty-two, with over three years of Navy service.

After he left my office, Captain Newsome made his rounds of the offices in the trial wing, handing out additional assignments. He designated two additional defense counsel, and three trial counsel, to handle the twenty-one *Kitty Hawk* cases. Later, he also assigned a few more JAG defense counsel and trial counsel, as the need arose in individual cases.

Most of us stationed at the law center were Naval Reserve officers who did not intend to make the Navy a career. The majority of us assigned to the *Kitty Hawk* cases had come into the JAG Corps upon being accepted into a new program offered to first year law students. That program allowed us to complete law school in lieu of answering the US Army draft notices many of us had received.[5] After law school graduation and requisite Navy schools, we had received orders to the Eleventh Naval District in San Diego.

With one exception I was aware of, every new lawyer at the law center began as a defense counsel. The standing joke—but not actually a joke—was that the Navy wanted all on-the-job training and mistakes to take place on the defense side of the courtroom. After several months, the now more experienced lawyer could be entrusted to represent the government and prosecute.

Trial lawyers in the law center were sometimes rotated every few months between defending and prosecuting cases. During the time I was making the transition between those roles, I would occasionally move from one counsel table to the other in the courtroom within the same day. That system gave us a unique and healthy perspective into the criminal justice system. Lawyers who spend their entire careers as either prosecutors or as defense counsel might well benefit from that perspective.

With our rotating system of assignments, I just happened to be serving as defense counsel when the *Kitty Hawk* defendants arrived in San Diego. Fortunately, by then I had eighteen months of trial experience, primarily as defense counsel, and almost two hundred courts-martial cases under my belt.[6] I spent virtually every day of the work week in the courtroom with arraignments, motions hearings, and trials. I would need all that experience, and more, for what followed, seeking justice for my clients in the ensuing *Kitty Hawk* trials.

How did I find myself defending six young Black sailors charged with rioting aboard an attack aircraft carrier off the coast of North Vietnam? In retrospect, it came down to a series of seemingly disconnected events that somehow all fell together. That I happened to be serving as defense counsel when the defendants arrived was just the last in that series of events.

I came into this world in January 1945, in a farmhouse on a small farm in South Dakota. I was delivered early one wintry morning by a doctor who was handed a thirty-five-dollar check by my father for his services. World War II was in its final year, and my father and mother had their hands full on the farm, raising crops, livestock, and children. I was the fourth child born in four years and times were tough, not only for our family, but for most of the rest of the country. Our family later moved to a nearby agricultural community with a population roughly half that of *Kitty Hawk*'s crew complement.[7]

I graduated from the South Dakota School of Mines and Technology, with a bachelor of science degree in mechanical engineering. I had taken two years of mandatory US Army ROTC, and during my time on campus, America's troop levels in Vietnam escalated from a few thousand to almost half a million. I fully expected to be joining those troops when my college military draft deferment ended.

I decided to apply to law school after college graduation, and took the Law School Admissions Test. My law school applications listed my LSAT score, my college debate team experience, and graduating with honors. Northwestern University Law School in Chicago was the first to respond and offered me a three-year full-ride scholarship.[8] I was all set. Or so I thought.

Two months into my first year of law school, the Army draft blew a small envelope my way, directing me to report to Fort Benning, Georgia, for infantry basic training. That undoubtedly meant Vietnam was in my immediate future. Fortunately, I was able to get accepted into the just-announced JAG Corps program that allowed me to complete law school, in return for a four-year Navy commitment.

After my second year of law school, I headed for the Newport Naval Station in Rhode Island. I was there to attend Officer Indoctrination School (OIS), a two-month summer cram course in the "real Navy." Why OIS? Before we could become Navy lawyers, we first had to learn how to conduct ourselves as Navy officers. Our OIS group of about eighty consisted entirely of law students. We were taught US Naval history, military leadership, and even rudimentary seamanship and navigation.

I returned to Chicago that fall for my final year of law school, and, in another serendipitous moment, met my future wife, Nicki, on a blind date. I graduated in the spring of 1970, and unlike many lawyers I know, I actually enjoyed law school.[9] The next October I was off to Naval Justice School (NJS) back in Newport, Rhode Island. Before returning to Newport, however, Nicki and I got engaged, and she remained in Colorado to teach high school English.

I approached NJS more seriously than I had OIS the previous summer. I treated it with the same resolve and enthusiasm I had in law school, as did my classmates, who numbered about thirty, all white, and all male. For the preceding hundred years and more, law school graduates had been overwhelmingly male. But times were changing. The next year's NJS graduated three women JAG officers.[10]

Early on, I developed friendships with many of my Justice School classmates. We attended classes for twelve weeks and were taught military law, including the fundamentals of the military justice system and military court procedure. Military law is a unique legal system, but it shares many aspects of civilian law, such as the rules of evidence.

We studied the *UCMJ* and the *Manual for Courts-Martial, United States* (*MCM*) which would be our governing law. The *UCMJ* is a federal law originally enacted by Congress in 1950.[11]

For those thinking a serviceman's legal rights are not as robust as those enjoyed by civilians, they may be surprised. For example, the US Supreme Court ruled in 1966 that detained individuals had to be advised of their legal rights upon arrest.[12] A decade earlier, however, Article 31 of the *UCMJ* had already mandated that those warnings be given to military arrestees.

Just before Justice School graduation in December 1970, I learned my first duty station would be in the Eleventh Naval District in San Diego. En route, I stopped off in Fort Morgan, Colorado, to marry Nicki, and we spent our honeymoon driving to San Diego, arriving on New Year's Day 1971. We found a one-bedroom furnished apartment in Chula Vista, south of downtown. It was a short fifteen-minute drive to the Naval Station Law Center.

I reported to the law center on 4 January 1971 and was immediately thrust into my new assignment. Good as it was, Justice School could not give us trial court experience. It didn't have to because the Navy believed in on-the-job training. My first day in court was the beginning of a lifetime learning experience.

———————

Date: 22 November 1972
Time: 1130H
Place: Naval Station San Diego Law Center

I was reviewing my *Kitty Hawk* case files when Lieutenant Glenn Haase stepped in from across the hall and asked me to join him and other law center JAGs for lunch. Several of us, both trial counsel and defense counsel, walked over to the nearby officer's mess. That mix of prosecutors and defense lawyers was typical, but today's lunchtime conversation was different. We spent most of our lunch break talking about our new *Kitty Hawk* case assignments, including who had what cases and, therefore, whom we would face later in court.

Criminal courtroom dramas on television and in the movies often portray prosecutors and defense counsel as antagonistic, often bitter, adversaries. However, in real life, those attorneys are more likely to have a mutually respectful relationship, especially those who face each other regularly in court. Successful defense lawyers recognize that fostering good relationships with prosecutors translates into more effective representation of their clients. Plea agreements, for example, constitute the vast majority of all criminal case dispositions.

Our situation at the law center was no different. In fact, our relationships with each other were altogether congenial, for many reasons. Many of us had gone through OIS and Justice School together, and we also developed friendships with JAGs we first met in San Diego. We often ate lunch together and sometimes socialized after work. Weekends would usually find us together also, wives included, hanging out at the beach.

In our professional capacities, however, we met in a quite different setting at the law center courtroom down the hall from our offices. Some of us sat at the trial counsel table, others at the defense counsel table. In that setting, we faced off in criminal law trials, the most diametrically opposed positions in American jurisprudence.

Some may find it hard to comprehend how we could have one life outside the courtroom with our contemporaries, and another inside. How could the same lawyers who socialized the previous weekend go head-to-head in court on Monday morning, often very aggressively? Hard to believe, perhaps, but it was never a problem for us, and our friendships never caused us to back off in the courtroom. To do so would have violated not only our professional oaths of office but also our obligation to fully commit in representing either the accused, or the government.

Some of our JAG friendships were tested during the *Kitty Hawk* trials. The reason? Simply put, those trials were nothing like any we had ever experienced before or would ever experience thereafter. The challenges and pressures of those trials, which lasted for months, led to heightened tensions between trial counsel and defense counsel. But more of that later.

9

KITTY HAWK DEFENDANTS

Twenty-three Black sailors eventually faced special courts-martial charges in San Diego. Twenty-one flew into the San Diego Naval Air Station before the carrier's arrival, and two were charged later. From the outset, the defendants found themselves treated as if they were a single entity. Collective reference was typically made to them as "the *Kitty Hawk* defendants." Perhaps that was easy since almost all were charged with rioting, in itself an accusation of concerted, unified, action.

Captain McKenzie, the convening authority, also treated them as a single, unified group from when he first met them coming off the plane. He sent every single one to the brig. Was every defendant a flight risk? Even McKenzie admitted only a few conducted themselves in what he considered a disrespectful manner by singing songs and flashing Black power salutes.

The congressional subcommittee also treated the defendants collectively.

> The subcommittee is of the position that the riot on *Kitty Hawk* consisted of unprovoked assaults by a very few men, most of whom were below-average mental capacity, most of whom had been aboard for less than one year, and all of whom were black. This group, as a whole, acted as "thugs" which raises

111

doubt as to whether they should ever have been accepted into
military service in the first place.[1]

The subcommittee heard testimony from more than sixty witnesses
and issued a final report of over a thousand pages. While they were taking testimony, the daily hearings were closed to the media and public.
When they released their report in early January 1973 the public and
press still received only one side of the story. That was because they
solicited testimony almost exclusively from Navy top brass, those in
Kitty Hawk command positions, and a select few others. None offered
testimony from the standpoint of the Black sailors.

To be sure, the subcommittee "invited" the defendants to testify,
and one of our defense team even suggested some might testify, if
offered immunity from prosecution.[2] The congressmen flatly refused,
so it was an easy call for our defense team to decline the invitation.
Without immunity, all testimony and statements by our clients could
be used against them at their subsequent trials. Further, the subcommittee followed no rules of evidence, with the questioning apparently
totally random.

Although the media were barred from the hearings, they were everywhere during the trials, not only at the law center but at any other Naval
facility they could access. Therefore, a normal assumption would be that
if the defendants wanted to tell their side of the October incident, they
could talk to the press. Actually, they couldn't. Not without violating
a standing order issued by Captain Townsend the day the *Kitty Hawk*
arrived in San Diego. As reported by a news outlet, "The ship's commander, Capt M. W. Townsend Jr., said that he had ordered the crew
not to talk with newsmen because 'it's not healthy to deal in rumors.'"[3]

Among the subcommittee selectively choosing whom to question,
Captain Townsend's order prohibiting his crew from talking to the
press, and the Navy's selective investigation and prosecution, is it any
wonder the subcommittee concluded that "all" the perpetrators of the
physical assaults were Black sailors?

Who knows where the subcommittee came up with some of their other findings? The report said "most of [the defendants] were below-average mental capacity." In fact, fifteen of the twenty-three had General Classification Test scores ranging from 41 to 57, which was above the average GCT score of 40.[4] In addition, eighteen of them had a high school education or higher.[5]

The subcommittee report got one thing right, however, when it stated "most of [the defendants] had been aboard for less than one year," as if that were somehow a strike against them. The report didn't mention that, at the time of the incident, Captain Townsend had been aboard just five months, Commander Cloud two months, and the legal officer two weeks.

Most of the defendants grew up in large metropolitan areas but several came from small towns. The oldest defendant was just twenty-two years old, and eight of them were still teenagers. About all they had in common was their shared racial identity. Each was a unique individual. Each had his own distinctive family background, experiences growing up, and memories of that October night. Almost fifty years later, three of the Black sailors who were aboard that evening recounted for me what it was like for them back then.

Durward Davis had been on board *Kitty Hawk* eighteen months when the incident occurred. He was raised by his single mother in a suburb of St. Louis, Missouri. He was always small for his age but never had trouble sticking up for himself. He enlisted three days before Christmas in 1970, at age eighteen, when he stood five foot five and weighed in at 150 pounds. He never smoked, drank, or did drugs while growing up, but he started doing all of that in the Navy.

Davis scored a 50 on his GCT which, along with his other test scores, should have easily qualified him for Accession School. When he enlisted, Davis was promised "A School" in avionics, but after basic training was given maintenance training instead.

A light-skinned Black man, he had a large light-brown Afro that he kept hidden under a stocking cap when aboard the ship. He was known

Seaman Apprentice Durward Davis aboard USS
Kitty Hawk, 1972.

as "Red Two" in the Navy. His best friend was also a light-skinned
Black sailor, known as "Red One" because his Afro was naturally red.

Growing up in Missouri, Davis doesn't recall experiencing much
racism, but that changed in the Navy. Some white crew members freely
used racial slurs such as the *n*-word, "coon," and "porch monkey." Other
Black sailors, especially those from southern states, could not believe
the Navy was his first encounter with overt racism.

On board he felt like a "second-class citizen." His mother taught
him from an early age to "yes, sir" and "yes, ma'am," so giving respect to
another's rank was easy. Not so easy was being talked down to, ignored,
or how some shipmates looked at him. He felt he was mostly tolerated
by whites, but not accepted. He remembers having white shipmates

assigned to work with him because petty officers didn't think he was smart enough to work on his own.

Interestingly, on shore, some white crewmates wanted to hang out with him. In Subic Bay they liked to tag along to the "jungle" because they liked the bars, music, and girls better over there. Back on ship, however, the white sailors would often be criticized for hanging out with Black sailors, so many would revert to their usual treatment of them. Despite all this, Davis never felt the Navy itself was racist. Just some people in it.

In fact, the biggest racial takeaway he had from his Navy experience was positive. But not for reasons one might think. The Navy gave him the opportunity to visit several foreign countries where he was "treated like royalty." That included the Philippines, Hong Kong, Japan, and Kenya. He remembers being treated with more respect at overseas ports than he ever got at home, either before or after his tour of duty. He especially remembers that foreigners "didn't look at my skin first, they looked at me."[6]

He has a white friend who insists he's "color-blind," but Davis told him, "When I walk into the room you see a Black guy; you don't see me." I took that to mean white people aren't really color-blind if they see or interact with a Black man, and afterward recall having seen or interacted with a Black person, not just a person.

He vividly recalls the night of the shipboard confrontations and tumult. He was in the chow line with "Red One" when his friend saw a white sailor who had "set him up" in a Subic Bay bar and beaten him. Red One confronted the white sailor and a brief fight broke out between them. Davis later headed back to his berthing compartment.

As previously described, five white sailors assaulted him in the passageway, but he was rescued by a group of Black sailors. Later, he was on the fo'c'sle with the large group when Commander Cloud calmed them down. He remembers the XO saying white sailors had spewed racial epithets at him and threatened to throw him overboard. Davis felt if the ship's XO was threatened, any Black man on board was fair game. He was scared.

Davis left the meeting, armed himself with a brass crank, and joined other Black sailors in a self-defense pact. In a later encounter in a berthing compartment, he struck a white sailor. He was charged with assault and rioting. He recalls no one in authority would listen to his side of what happened. They likewise were not interested in investigating the assault on him by the five white sailors.[7]

———

Vernell Robinson grew up on the South Side of Chicago, relatively insulated from racism in his all-Black neighborhood. He was warned from a very early age, however, never to venture west a few blocks to Ashland Avenue and beyond. Going there put you in "their" neighborhood where anything might happen. All bad.

One day he and five other Black friends walked to the Dan Ryan Forest Preserve, but to get there they had to cross Ashland Avenue. They were enjoying themselves in the park when suddenly they saw a large group of white teenagers running toward them, carrying baseball bats. Robinson and his friends took off running back toward their neighborhood, chased for blocks by the angry mob. He also recalls a later incident when he was driving to his employment at a local post office. He passed through an all-white neighborhood and someone threw a bottle at his car, breaking the back window.

Just after turning twenty, Robinson married sixteen-year-old Jacqueline from his neighborhood. Within a couple of months, however, he received his Army draft notice. He immediately enlisted in the Navy, all five foot six and 138 pounds of him. After basic training in San Diego, he attended A School, where he learned administrative and clerical skills. He returned to San Diego and the *Kitty Hawk* as an airman assigned to the ship's crew—that is, not assigned to an onboard air squadron.

He started out as a mess cook but within a month moved on to his MOS (military occupational specialty) and was assigned to a cubicle surrounded by aircraft parts. He signed out parts to aircraft maintenance personnel who worked on the hangar deck above him. Robinson was an excellent sailor who consistently received the top 4.0 work ratings.

He liked his job and actually enjoyed living on a carrier. For the most part. He was never subject to racial slurs until the evening of the October incident, but from when he first came aboard, he was treated as a second-class citizen by some white crewmates who "thought they were gods." That was especially bothersome because some of those same sailors wanted to hang out with him ashore so they could go with him to the Black sailors' side of Olongapo.

Growing up, he was never into the "Black unity thing," but that changed on the *Kitty Hawk*. He never displayed the Black power salute while aboard, but he did learn the dap. He got quite good at it and could keep it going with another Black sailor for several minutes, even while walking backward. To him it was a unity thing, but he knew many of his white crewmates thought it was a sign of militancy.

Robinson fully embraced his ethnicity and grew a large Afro. He was asked, but never ordered, to trim it, and so it remained. He also bought a custom-made black jacket in the Philippines with African sayings that he could only wear ashore. On the ship, he wore dungarees and long-sleeved blue work shirts.

He returned to San Diego with the carrier after the October incident and continued to work on board. Everything was going well for him until 13 February 1973 when he was served with a Charge Sheet. It accused him of rioting and assaults on two white sailors during the incident months earlier. No explanation was ever given for the very late charges. The only advantage of receiving charges so late was he never had to serve any brig time.[8]

Airman Perry Pettus was an outstanding crew member from any perspective. He completed two years of college, including Army ROTC, before enlisting in the Navy. He rose quickly in the ranks and early on was picked to serve on the flight deck crew, duty which was highly

Perry Pettus aboard USS *Kitty Hawk*, 1973, receiving promotion from airman to aviation boatswain's mate third class.

prized among most. He was a member of the crash crew and operated a tow tractor "staging aircraft" on the flight deck for launches and movement from aircraft elevators. Backing up aircraft was a piece of cake for a guy who grew up operating tractors and other implements on his grandfather's farm back home.

Home was Hopkinsville, Kentucky, a small town tucked away in the far western end of the state. He has a vivid memory of his first experience with overt racism. He was about six years old and walked over to the restaurant where his mother worked. As he started to enter the front door, he was stopped and told he had to go around and enter through the back. A sign on that door said "colored." Not long after, his mother put him on the bus to visit his grandmother in the next small town. He remembers having to sit in the back of the bus "just because of the color of my skin." He also remembers the county courthouse having separate water fountains marked "white" and "colored."

Pettus took a lot of pride in his flight deck job on the *Kitty Hawk*, and experienced very little racial discrimination while on duty. Perhaps that was because the flight deck was the place on the ship with the highest risk of personal injury, and everyone had to look out for each other. In its best moments, he said it was "like a symphony," with all hands working together. But then came the moment that stays with him to this day.

He watched as his division officer stepped over the safety line onto the flight deck just as an F-4 jet landed and caught the steel arresting cable. The suddenly tightened cable took off the legs of the officer, just above the ankles. Pettus remembers seeing a boot come flying across the deck with part of a leg still in it.

Pettus also recalls the evening of 12 October, and the long line periods of unrelenting duty which preceded it. He especially remembers the last liberty in Subic with fights breaking out between Black and white sailors. He was outside the Sampaguita Club when the fighting broke out. When everyone came pouring outside, he and others ran back to the ship as fast as they could.

He was on duty the night of the October incident when he and his two buddies were manhandled and handcuffed by the marines as they walked across the hangar deck on their way back to work. He recalls the excruciating pain of the handcuffs and hurrying to the fo'c'sle following Commander Cloud's order. While there, he remembers the XO dramatically baring his chest and inviting anyone to strike him. Pettus says the XO "soothed a lot of souls" at that meeting with his calming voice. To this day, he considers the XO a hero of the evening.

Pettus was never implicated in any of the incidents during the night, but he did move about the ship with fellow Black shipmates following their fo'c'sle meeting with the XO. His most vivid memory is seeing a young white sailor getting beaten "just because of the color of his skin." He was so sickened by that, he immediately returned to his berthing compartment where he remained the rest of the evening.[9]

Date: 22 November 1972
Time: 0830H
Location: Naval Station Law Center

The law center director had dropped off the *Kitty Hawk* case files the day before Thanksgiving. I spent that morning and afternoon at the brig talking to my five new clients. Since the legal process had just started, it didn't take me long to review my clients' case files. The only documents in the files were copies of their Service Records and Charge Sheets.

A Service Record contains a sailor's civilian background information, his scores on his Armed Forces Qualification and General Classification Tests, his duty performance marks, and his prior disciplinary record, if any. My five clients ran the gamut in rank from seaman recruit (pay grade E-1), to seaman apprentice (E-2), airman apprentice (E-2), seaman (E-3), and aviation machinist's mate third class (E-4).[10]

Defendants facing courts-martial are almost never kept in pretrial confinement. It was so rare, in fact, that I seldom found it necessary to go to the brig to meet with my clients. Now, with all of them in the brig, I walked over to the facility after lunch. The marine desk sergeant told me one of my clients was in the medium barracks, but the other four were still in the maximum cell block.

I was escorted by a marine guard to see those four clients. I was curious why they were still there, because prisoners were normally processed out of maximum after just a day or two.

When I arrived, it seemed like a replay of two days earlier when I witnessed the standoff between the *Kitty Hawk* sailors and marine guards, with prisoners yelling and the guards yelling back. The only difference from before was that most prisoners were in their cells, while others were being escorted about.

I told the duty sergeant I wanted to see my seaman apprentice client first. The sergeant told me he was in the cell directly across from his desk. When I asked where I could interview him in private, the sergeant just shrugged. Unlike other brig facilities, maximum had no meeting rooms for lawyers and their clients.

Since my client's cell was within earshot of the sergeant, I told him it would not do. He checked his roster, took my client out of his cell, and escorted us down Row 6 to an empty cell at the far end of the corridor. We entered the tiny space enclosed by a steel door and steel-plated walls and furnished with only a toilet and a bunk tied against the wall.[11]

The sergeant lowered the bunk, and I sat down on it next to my client. He was clearly agitated and would not make eye contact. As with all new clients, I wanted to make him as comfortable as I could, but in the cramped cell I knew it would be difficult. In addition, as we used to say back home, he "didn't know me from a load of hay." For all I knew, he might be seeing just another white officer in authority.

When I told him I had been assigned to represent him, he didn't say a word[12] and just stared at the floor. It took a few minutes, but I finally got him talking. He let me know he did not want a law-yer picked by the Navy. He wanted to pick his own lawyer, a JAG lieutenant[13] whom he met on board *Kitty Hawk*. He also wanted an NAACP lawyer.

I told him he was entitled to both but explained the process of get-ting an individual military counsel, and since his requested IMC was stationed at Subic Bay, I told him it might take some time before he arrived. As for NAACP counsel, I said I had no idea when they might be available.

He repeated he did not want me to represent him. He would wait. I told him that was fine and stood up to leave the cell. As I did so, he must have realized his situation.

"Wait. Wait," he said, following me out. "Can you get me out of here?"

"Not unless I'm representing you. In the meantime, I'll see about getting the other lawyers for you."

"What happens to you if I get someone else?" he asked.

Once we returned to the cell, I explained how the system worked. He could either dismiss me, or ask me to stay on, either as lead counsel, or as cocounsel. That seemed to satisfy him, and he told me about the October incident. He insisted he had not assaulted anyone and poured out his grievances. He talked about his treatment aboard *Kitty Hawk*, at the Subic Bay brig, and at the Naval station brig. The more he talked, the angrier he became.

When we finished, I walked him out to the corridor and the marine sergeant brought in my next client, a seaman recruit. He likewise said he wanted a Subic Bay JAG officer[14] as well as an NAACP lawyer to represent him but wanted me to help him in the meantime. While talking about his experience since the incident, he also became quite agitated and angry. I could see I had a couple of very distressed clients, and after listening to them, I could see why.

My next two clients were also in the cell block, and one of them, Airman Apprentice Glover had quite the story to tell. He was the sailor who had been assaulted by the marines on the hangar deck, struck on the head in sick bay by another marine and bitten on the leg. Several times as he explained those assaults, he started crying. I was left with the distinct impression of a very depressed young man.

When I finished with the clients in the maximum cell block, I returned to the main building. I told the desk sergeant I wanted to see my client Seaman Cleveland Mallory who was in the medium barracks. He directed me down the hall to a private meeting room to wait. The interview room was sparse, with just a steel gray table and four steel gray chairs. I took off my cover and laid it on a chair, opened my briefcase, and removed Mallory's Service Record.

His record included his name, rank, social security number, birthdate, and monthly pay. The details showed he had enlisted in Pittsburgh on 15 November 1971, just a year earlier. He had excellent work performance marks and had been promoted from pay grade E-1, to E-2, and then E-3, in less than a year. That was impressive. He also had a GCT score of 57, the highest of all twenty-three defendants. I did notice one disciplinary mark on his record, a captain's mast punishment for an unauthorized absence five months earlier. What struck me as extremely odd, however, was that his stated absence was for only an hour and a half.[15]

I stood when the marine guard escorted Mallory into the interview room. Mallory immediately braced at attention and then hesitated, perhaps wondering if he should salute since we were not aboard ship and I was not wearing my cover.

He stood taller than me, and with his square shoulders and military bearing was a sharp looking young sailor. He wore his shipboard utility uniform, a blue long-sleeved shirt and dark blue dungarees. He had round facial features, sported a short Afro, and wore large plastic-rimmed glasses. I asked him to sit down and introduced myself by name, not rank, and told him I was his appointed lawyer.

"How are you doing?" I asked.

"OK, sir," he said, with no hint of emotion.

"How are they treating you in here?"

He hesitated, then said, "I guess OK, sir."

"Listen," I said, "I know you must have a lot of questions, so let's start with those. And you can skip the yes sirs and no sirs."

"Yes, sir."

I smiled at him and I think I saw a hint of a smile in return. "Can I call you Cleveland?"

"Yes, sir, I mean yes."

"Good. Any questions?"

"When can I get out of here?"

"I don't know, but let's talk about it."

He told me about all the broken promises of liberty before ending up in the Subic Bay brig and again at the San Diego Naval Station brig. That, coupled with the extreme rarity of pretrial confinement, immediately focused my attention. I told him my first priority, and that of the other defense counsel, would be to try to get all of them out of the brig.

After that, I asked him some more questions, but not about the charges against him. At least not yet. At the outset of most interviews with new clients, I avoided mention of their alleged offenses. I found it easier for them to talk about themselves first, get comfortable, and then hopefully begin to trust me.

He said he was from Pittsburgh and was raised by his single mother. He had a younger brother and sister who were twins. I told him my wife was also a twin. When I asked about his father, he simply replied, "We didn't really see him."

He said he got good grades in high school and played sports. He got his Army draft notice right after his eighteenth birthday in October 1971, but then he enlisted in the Navy. He had basic training at the Great Lakes Naval Station training center, north of Chicago, and *Kitty Hawk* was his first duty assignment. He reported on board in San Diego just two days before it set sail for WestPac.

His first seven months were spent as a mess cook, then compartment cleaning. A few weeks before the October incident, he was promoted to seaman and was given a new duty assignment.

"What was that?" I asked.

"I started working in the Ge-Dunk store on the O-3 level."

"What's that?"

"We sell cookies, sodas, and that sort of stuff. That's where I was attacked."

"What? You were attacked?"

"Yes, sir. That night after I shut the store I heard about the fighting and then went to a meeting a bunch of us brothers had with the XO. I then remembered I forgot to take out the petty cash box. I got it and was closing the store when three white guys jumped me."

"What happened?"

"One guy hit me, and I hit him back, but another guy hit me with a dogging wrench. He broke three or four of my ribs."[16]

Mallory now had my undivided attention. None of the news reports had ever mentioned Black sailors as victims, and in one afternoon I learned that two of my five clients had been assaulted, one by white marines and the other by three white sailors. Every single account of the *Kitty Hawk* incident had reported that Black sailors were the only assailants.

We then talked about the charges against him. He was charged with striking a white sailor in the face with his fist, and participating in a riot with two named sailors and about twenty "unknown persons" while assaulting others. Mallory told me he was innocent. Not because he acted in self-defense, or had an alibi for when the alleged assaults occurred. He simply said he had no idea why he was charged. It wouldn't be the first time a client professed innocence when it was not true, but something about Mallory was different. I saw before me a quiet, self-assured, and sincere young man of nineteen, and I wanted to believe him.

———————

It was midafternoon when I returned to the law center, and by then I had a fairly clear picture of what my clients had gone through. Not just during the onboard incident, but in the weeks before and after. All I could think of was how little those sailors had to be thankful for, and the miserable Thanksgiving ahead of them the next day.

Six weeks earlier they were sailing the high seas off the coast of North Vietnam, honorably serving their country in the best way they knew how. They were undoubtedly looking forward to whatever futures young men dream about, a future in which they would always be recognized as proud Navy veterans.

Today, however, they were all sitting in the brig and facing courts-martial trials. Those trials could brand them forever with federal court convictions and shatter any possible plans they had for a Navy career, or perhaps any other honorable future they imagined.

Several hours earlier, I thought I'd be representing a group of Black sailors who had been assaulting innocent white sailors. Now, I had a completely different kind of representation ahead of me. I had learned of possible trumped-up charges, assaults by white marines and white sailors with no follow-up investigations, and clients in pretrial confinement for no legally justifiable reason.

Finally, I was left with a nagging question: why were five of my clients charged with rioting? Based on their descriptions of the confrontations that evening, it seemed like nothing more than random incidents of assaults by both Black and white crew members. There was no indication whatsoever of any preplanned, unified, or organized actions by anyone. Even if the allegations against my clients were true, that might justify the assault charges, but nothing more.

Since publicity about the *Kitty Hawk* incident was already widespread, I could only guess as to the origin of the riot charges. That decision was initially made by Captain Townsend. But was there more to it? News of the incident became public days before the charges were sworn out—that is, filed. Was Townsend influenced by someone higher up in the Navy chain of command? Did someone want to send a message that harsh discipline would be meted out against anyone, especially Black sailors, whose actions ordinarily would draw only an assault charge? I didn't know.

What I did know was that was the first time I had seen, or even heard of, a riot charge in the Navy. I later learned no other JAG officer I knew had ever heard of one either. In fact, further review led me to believe the *Kitty Hawk* riot charges were unprecedented in the history of the modern Navy. The more I learned about the incident, the more I was convinced the riot charges were unjustified.

I visited my clients regularly. One of those visits, on 1 December, bears mentioning. On that day four of my five clients were still in the maximum cell block. I was talking to one of them in an empty cell when two other defendants came running down the Row 6 corridor and into our tiny cell. Close behind were several marine guards blowing their whistles.[17]

What followed was a standoff, with everyone talking at once. One of the guards told me that one of the sailors, an airman apprentice, had been let out of his cell to get a haircut, but took off running instead. I asked about the other sailor, a seaman recruit who was one of my clients. The guard said that sailor refused to return to his cell after being let out temporarily. I asked my client why he refused, and he said the cells had no place to sit down except on the floor. Since I had been sitting on a bunk when they rushed in, I asked him about that, and he said brig rules prohibited lowering the bunks from the walls during daylight hours.[18]

I had no reason to disbelieve him because none of the guards disputed what he had just said. When angry exchanges started up again between the guards and the defendants, I decided to try to take charge of the situation. I told the guards to step back and asked the three sailors to follow me. I walked with them back to their cells with the guards following. On the way, I told my two clients and the other defendant that we were working very hard to get them out of the brig. They finally calmed down and entered their individual cells without any further trouble.[19]

As I was leaving, however, I heard more yelling between the sailors and the guards. At the time, my clients had been in the maximum cell block thirteen days, and I could see their situation only getting worse. More than ever, I vowed to do whatever could be done to get them released.

10

PRETRIAL CONFINEMENT

"The Navy just completely overreacted. There was no reason to lock them up."[1]

That was my statement to a *New York Times* reporter on 1 April 1973. Prior to that, the defendants had spent an unconscionable amount of time in pretrial confinement. Those still in the brig toward the end of February, for example, had already been incarcerated 114 days, or almost four months.[2] Even a few days of incarceration would have been totally unwarranted and legally unsupportable.

Those held in the maximum cell block suffered the most. Nineteen of the *Kitty Hawk* defendants were still in maximum in mid-December 1972,[3] and a dozen were still there almost a month after their arrival in San Diego.[4] On Christmas day eight were still in maximum.[5] Many remained in maximum until their trials, including one of my clients, still there three months after arriving at the brig.[6]

Holding that many men in pretrial confinement, and especially in maximum, for that length of time was unprecedented, and unforgivable.

After the trials, having had a chance to reflect on all that had happened, I concluded that the injustice of only Black sailors being initially charged was matched by the injustice of their pretrial confinement. The key term is "pretrial." They were not confined following a conviction for an offense. How could that be? Why were the *Kitty Hawk* sailors confined at all when, under our American system of justice, the accused are presumed innocent until proved guilty?

Pretrial incarceration is extremely rare in the Navy. The majority of those incarcerated in the brig are serving postconviction sentences of confinement. At any given time, a much, much, smaller group are in pretrial confinement, which is typically limited to those considered extreme flight risks. That group includes those charged with extremely serious offenses, such as murder, and those facing charges of unauthorized absence which constitute most of those in pretrial confinement. In all those cases, if the accused are released prior to their trials, they might be expected to run.

The *Kitty Hawk* accused, however, were placed in pretrial confinement with charges of rioting and assaults. Before their cases, I had, of course, never heard of anyone charged with rioting, and had never known of pretrial confinement for someone charged with an assault.

Date: 22 November 1972
Time: 0930H
Location: Office of Captain McKenzie, Naval Air Station North Island

Shortly after my first meeting with my clients, four of us JAG defense counsel gathered at the law center to address the brig issue. We quickly agreed our first priority should be the release of our clients. Our subsequent efforts to try and correct that injustice took up an inordinate amount of our time.

I called the convening authority's office at the North Island Naval Air Station, and within minutes we were on our way to meet with Captain McKenzie. On arrival, we were escorted into a small conference room where McKenzie and his JAG staff judge advocate waited. We told McKenzie his pretrial incarceration order was totally unprecedented in assault cases. I told him that the defendants had been returned to their regular shipboard duties immediately after the October incident, had remained unrestricted for three weeks thereafter, and no further disturbances occurred. Why, then, should they be incarcerated now? Not only at Subic Bay but again in San Diego? When I mentioned that our clients were promised liberty when they reached San Diego, he quickly acknowledged he was aware of that promise.

The obvious follow-up question, therefore, was what had changed that caused him to order them to the brig? Captain McKenzie told us that he had an "open mind" about confinement before the plane landed and only decided to order them to the brig because of their "disrespect" toward him during their deplaning. That was an astonishing admission, as disrespect to a senior officer could not possibly justify pretrial confinement. Later in the meeting, however, perhaps realizing what he had just said, he tried to backtrack on his prior statement.[7]

We left the meeting without achieving the release of the men. Four days later, one of our JAG defense counsel again made the trip over to the North Island Naval Air Station, this time accompanied by three NAACP defense lawyers. They again urged Captain McKenzie to release the defendants. Again, he refused. We didn't back off attempting to convince McKenzie to reverse his draconian pretrial confinement order, but all our pleas fell on deaf ears.

During this period, the defendants' confinement was a frequent topic throughout the law center. Even career JAG officers could not believe what was happening. Captain Newsome, the law center director, was especially outspoken on the issue. He had never heard of pretrial confinement for anyone charged with an assault. In addition, Newsome said Captain McKenzie was totally inconsistent in ordering pretrial confinement when he had referred the cases to medium level special courts-martial trials. If the charges were serious enough to justify pretrial confinement, he said, they would have been serious enough to be sent to general courts-martial trials.[8]

We finally gave up trying to convince Captain McKenzie, so we filed a motion with the military judge assigned to our cases, Captain Bobby Day Bryant, seeking our clients' release from confinement.

During the later hearing on the motion, McKenzie testified and readily conceded the defendants were told before arrival they would be free to go on liberty when their plane landed.[9] He was then asked about what came to be known as the "deplaning incident." He said as the defendants came off the plane, they acted in an "unmilitary-like manner."[10] One of our defense counsel asked him to explain what he meant.[11] "We directed that they come off alphabetically one at a time and go through our screening procedure we had set up at the time. After the first two, they started coming off before they were told to come off, and they gathered around in a somewhat unmilitary manner."[12]

He then testified to what he called their "unmilitary" behavior:

> A: At this time the group did group together, not all of them, maybe a third of them or a half grouped together and started singing some songs, and they were using the DAP handshake. I think it's called the DAP handshake. I considered the singing of the songs to be unmilitary . . . and I considered the DAP handshake to be an unmilitary-like thing. . . .
>
> Q: What were they singing, Captain, if you can recall?
>
> A: I am not familiar with the song. I understood the words: "Tain't nobody going to turn us around," and "Turn around, turn us around." . . . They did at one point, I think in their singing, say, "Tain't no captain going to turn us around."[13]

He was asked if he remembered telling us defense counsel he considered the accused's actions "disrespectful and disobedient" to him. "I remember using the term 'unmilitary,' very clearly. I don't, I honestly don't remember using the term 'disrespectful.'"[14] Captain McKenzie's "failure to remember" without outright denying what he was alleged to have said, was a pattern he repeated several times in subsequent testimony on other issues.

In a surprising response, he denied the defendants' behavior led to his ordering them into confinement. He even went so far as to say he made the decision before the plane landed. That sworn testimony was surprising because it was contrary to what he had told seven of us on the defense team in the two earlier meetings in his office. I personally recalled him clearly stating during our 22 November meeting that he made the incarceration decision only after the defendants had treated him with disrespect. Another JAG officer testified at the motion hearing about what Captain McKenzie said at the first meeting.

> Q: Would you please explain to the court the subject of the meeting and what Captain McKenzie related to you?
>
> A: Yes sir. Our basic purpose for going over there . . . was to get the men released from confinement. . . . We asked Captain McKenzie why these men were confined and he stated that he had had an open mind in regard to confining them until the incident at the deplaning at North Island. And he stated at that time, because of the men's actions, I believe he stated they clenched their fists and they were singing songs, that at the time they had to order each of them personally, and he was upset about it, he had decided to confine them. . . .
>
> Q: Could you describe his behavior such that we might get an idea of his state of mind during the conversation?
>
> A: Okay. As I said earlier, he originally, in response to a question I believe by Lieutenant Truhe, said that his state of mind when they had come into the airport was such that he made no decision to confine them.[15]

At the hearing, Captain McKenzie was asked if he remembered making those statements during our meeting. As before, when asked about his "disrespectful" statement, he didn't deny it but simply asserted, "I don't remember making such a statement."[16]

Milt Silverman, one of the civilian defense lawyers present at the second meeting with McKenzie, had previously signed an affidavit relating McKenzie's statements. "The Captain stated . . . that their attitude was surly. He stated that they showed disrespect to him and the chasers. . . . It was indicated to the group of lawyers assembled in the office that it was only after this incident on the quarter deck, and the behavior of the prisoners in arriving, that the Captain decided to confine the men."[17] That affidavit was admitted into evidence.

Again, Captain McKenzie made that statement to seven of our defense team during two separate meetings, but later claimed he "did not remember" saying it.

So what was McKenzie's ostensible reason for confining the accused, if not because of their deplaning behavior? By the time of the motion hearing, he had a ready answer. He testified he confined them because of the charges against them, and because he believed they were flight risks.[18] That was convenient because his words parroted language in the *Manual for Courts-Martial*'s listing justifications for pretrial confinement.[19]

Why did it matter when or why Captain McKenzie made his incarceration decision? In point of fact, it mattered a great deal. If he made his decision to confine them before the plane landed, it could have been for at least an arguably valid legal reason. If, however, he decided to incarcerate them because they were "disrespectful" or were acting in an "unmilitary-like manner," that is clearly not a justifiable legal reason. In addition, even if he had made his decision based on the nature of the charges or because of a flight risk, military law had strict guidelines restricting his options under those criteria.

Military law provides several forms of pretrial restraint. By far, the most severe form is confinement, and it may be used only in extreme circumstances. One reason for those strictures is because there is no bail in the military like that found in civilian criminal courts. Quite simply, brig prisoners cannot post bail in order to gain release from pretrial confinement.

In addition, any form of restraint may be imposed only if probable cause exists for that level of restraint.[20] That dictate in the *Manual for Courts-Martial* is bolstered by the *Department of the Navy Corrections Manual*, which provides: "Confinement not imposed as punishment should be strictly limited to cases fully justifiable and wherein no alternative action is practicable or appropriate."[21]

Those alternative actions include several less restrictive options than the brig to ensure the presence of the accused at trial. For example, the defendants could have been restricted to the Naval air station facility, or even been billeted in a legal hold barracks designated for that specific purpose.[22] With the added security of a military base, the latter option should have satisfied Captain McKenzie.

In addition, military law dictates that all restraint decisions must be made on a "case-by-case basis." McKenzie clearly disregarded that stricture when he ordered all the defendants into pretrial confinement. No determination was given to the unique circumstances of each of the accused. By McKenzie's own admission, "maybe a third or half of them" engaged in what he called unmilitary-like behavior. And even if he sent them to the brig because of their flight risk or the seriousness of their offenses, certainly some differences existed among them using those criteria.

Just a week after McKenzie's testimony, I was able to question his operations duty officer who handled the arrangements for the defendants' flight from Subic Bay to the Naval air station. That officer actually witnessed the deplaning, albeit from a distance. He testified he noticed a "reluctance" by some defendants to obey McKenzie's orders as they deplaned. I followed up on that comment.

> Q: Commander, to the best of your recollection, were all
>   the blacks that were debarking from that plane—Were
>   they all taking part in this reluctance?

A: No. No, I would say probably five out of whatever jumped off.[23]

Military law expressly prohibits pretrial confinement as punishment, regardless of the offense charged. For those of us on the defense team, it certainly looked like all our clients were confined as punishment for what McKenzie thought was disrespectful behavior by a third to half of them, or, according to his operations duty officer, only five of them.

Release from pretrial confinement may be ordered by the person imposing the confinement, or by a military judge detailed to the court-martial of the accused.[24] That is why we brought our motion to get our clients out of the brig before the military judge initially assigned to our cases.

After Judge Bryant heard all the evidence, including Captain McKenzie's purported justification for the confinement, he recommended their release. He clearly had seen that the pretrial confinement was legally unsupportable. However, for some unknown and inexplicable reason Judge Bryant merely "recommended" that they be released.[25] This, despite his having explicit legal authority to order it done. In merely making a recommendation, Judge Bryant knew full well that his recommendation would land right back on Captain McKenzie's desk, the very man he just heard testifying and defiantly resisting their release. As everyone expected, McKenzie simply ignored the military judge's recommendation.

Our motion was heard in late January 1973, and by then our defense team had experienced enough setbacks that we realized we were bucking high-level opposition and unknown forces that were resisting all our attempts to effectively defend our clients. It was a very disheartening realization on our part, but our disappointment paled in comparison to what our clients were experiencing. Most of them were still sitting in the brig, getting more depressed and angry with each passing day and each passing week.

Brig life is difficult under any circumstances, but life for the *Kitty Hawk* sailors was especially oppressive and, in some cases, downright inhumane. Marine guards are not naturally predisposed to treat prisoners kindly, but some of them made a point of being especially cruel to the accused. One of the defendants said during their incarceration they were "treated like prisoners of war."[26]

Strong verbal exchanges became commonplace between some guards and defendants. One of the defendants later told me about an incident with a guard whom he considered friendly, one that would stop by his cell to visit. He told the guard about his girlfriend waiting for him back in St. Louis, giving her name and where she lived. Not long after, the guard said he was going on temporary assignment to Missouri and planned to look up the girlfriend. He said much more than that. The defendant tried, without success, to strike the guard through the bars of the cell.[27]

Some of the defendants were eventually moved to the medium and minimum confinement barracks within the brig compound. But, as stated, an inordinate number of them remained in the maximum cell block for months. It would be difficult to overstate the pressures endured by sailors in maximum. Because it typically served as only a transient place during initial screening, most young men could tolerate it for a day or two. But not multiple days or weeks. Certainly not months. The defendants didn't belong in the brig in the first place, so maximum confinement was especially intolerable.

Their occasional protests and outbursts led to tighter restrictions, which led to more outbursts, and even more restrictions. That vicious circle kept many of them confined indefinitely in maximum.

Some even spent time in Row 6. Prisoners called it solitary confinement, where life was even more unbearable. A marine guard described "disciplinary confinement" as a place where prisoners were "quite reluctant" to go. They were confined day and night, denied physical exercise, and not even allowed into the adjacent mess area for meals.[28]

One of my *Kitty Hawk* clients spent almost two months in Row 6 disciplinary confinement and was finally able to talk about it at his trial. By the time he faced his special court-martial, his charges included an add-on of assaulting a marine guard while in disciplinary confinement. As mentioned, it was a vicious circle. His trial testimony, which was transcribed in narrative form, is graphic and disturbing:

> Prior to today, I have been in the brig 100 days; I have been in Row 6 more than half of that. Row 6 is solitary . . . I was on Row 6 and [another *Kitty Hawk* defendant] was on Row 3 and my cell was unlocked, apparently 'cause the turnkey [guard] didn't check it. . . . [The other defendant] hollered over to me, said they was ready to bring him on Row 6 . . . so he screamed to me, "Here they come." So then I heard a lot of noise and banging, like that; I heard [him] screaming, you know, for me. I came out of my cell and stood in front of the entrance of Row 6 and hollered out, "Let him go." Tears filled my eyes and I felt like black bondage. I feared he needed help, so that's when I went forward to strike [the guard]. My relationship with [the other defendant] is as close friends. . . . All the guards are white. By "black bondage" I mean slavery; that's the impression I had. . . . I got "indefinite Row 6."[29]

Because of my client's extreme difficulty in enduring his prolonged confinement in the maximum cell block, he was seen by a Navy psychiatrist.

> At times he becomes very angry and starts beating against the wall. He relates sometimes having dreams in which he dreams that he is free and then he wakes up and sees all the wire and cells around him. . . . The patient feels that he has become much more militant since being in confinement and that he has become much more aware of his own blackness. He feels very strongly that he cannot serve any more confinement.[30]

My client survived his time in maximum and Row 6. Another *Kitty Hawk* defendant, also one of my clients, almost did not. A San Diego newspaper broke the story.

> Cmdr. Chester Edwards, executive officer of the San Diego Naval Station where the brig is located, confirmed a defense attorney's report that one of the sailors tried to hang himself in his cell with his belt last Friday. After being cut down "almost immediately" the sailor was taken to Naval Hospital for psychiatric treatment and returned.[31]

That other client of mine had attempted suicide on 30 November 1972, just ten days after his initial confinement in San Diego.[32] His psychiatric report indicated he was told if he "did well" in maximum confinement, he would be released within three days. Despite that assurance, he was still in maximum ten days later when he was spotted "rigging a noose."[33] His psychiatrist stated, "It is strongly recommended that the patient be released from the brig as soon as possible."[34] Instead, according to that local newspaper account, my client was immediately returned to the brig and, following an altercation with a guard, "was sent back to solitary confinement."[35]

That made a total of three *Kitty Hawk* defendants who received psychiatric treatment and/or hospitalization during their periods of incarceration, one in Subic Bay and two in San Diego. In every instance, their psychiatrists had recommended their release from the brig after treatment, which was, after all, necessitated by their incarceration. In all three cases, they were returned to the brig, two back into solitary confinement.

———————

After Captain McKenzie denied all our requests for brig release, the NAACP lawyers took up the battle to try to get our clients out. They spared nothing in their efforts. The NAACP lawyers immediately sought relief with the next-highest authority above Captain McKenzie, which was the Commodore of Fleet Air for the Western Pacific.[36] Their 30 November 1972 legal brief sought release of the nineteen defendants still remaining in the brig, citing Article 138 of the *UCMJ*, Complaints of Wrongs.[37] That provision allows for redress by any service member who is denied relief when he makes a complaint against his commanding officer. His complaint is then referred to even higher-ranking officers.

The NAACP's brief was factually and legally sound. Most would say legally compelling. But not for the commodore, who summarily rejected the request. The prisoners would remain in the brig.

Even as those legal efforts were ongoing, Nathaniel Jones, counsel to the NAACP, was actively pursuing relief at the highest military and political levels.[38] He had that access because he was a nationally recognized and revered champion of civil rights in America. He had argued many civil rights cases before the US Supreme Court and had previously served on President Johnson's Kerner Commission studying civil unrest in American cities. In addition, six months before the *Kitty Hawk* incident, he agreed to cochair a special Department of Defense Task Force on the Administration of Military Justice.[39] In that role he had gotten to personally know Secretary of the Navy (SECNAV) John Warner, Secretary of Defense Melvin Laird, Chief of Naval Operations Admiral Elmo Zumwalt Jr., and Judge Advocate General of the Navy Admiral Merlin Staring. Admiral Staring also served on the DOD task force with Nathaniel Jones.[40]

In fact, Jones's first contact with the Navy's top brass on the *Kitty Hawk* affair came at their invitation. On 6 November 1972 even before the carrier reached Subic Bay, he was contacted at his NAACP office in New York City by Admiral Staring. He asked Jones to come to Washington, DC, to visit with him and SECNAV Warner about the *Kitty Hawk* incident.[41] Jones flew to Washington, DC, the next day, and visited with Warner and Admirals Staring and Zumwalt.

I learned of that meeting later when I met with Nathaniel Jones in San Diego at the law office of NAACP-retained attorney Milt Silverman. Jones reported to us that he had a prolonged meeting with the Navy top brass in SECNAV Warner's office. He said Warner wanted to talk about the "racial problems" on the *Kitty Hawk*. Jones told them of his concern about only Black sailors being charged and said that no one in the NAACP believed the Navy's claim of "unilateral" confrontations, that is, a totally one-sided riot. He also pressed them as to what actions they were taking with regard to discrimination in the military. Jones said he received no satisfactory answers, and no response at all about why only Black sailors were charged.[42]

Jones also told Silverman and me that in a later meeting with Admiral Staring, he asked him to order the release of the *Kitty Hawk* defendants from the San Diego Naval Station brig. Staring was the most senior JAG officer in the Navy and could have easily done so. Staring refused. Jones came away feeling that Staring and even Secretary Warner were not calling the shots, as they may have been following orders directly from the White House.[43]

Even as Jones continued his efforts, the NAACP lawyers continued their appeals within the military judicial system. They argued for relief from the unjustified pretrial confinement and also requested a writ of habeas corpus ordering the defendants out of the brig. They were denied at every level, and several weeks later ultimately ended up before the United States Court of Military Appeals in Washington, DC.[44]

In a split decision, the USCMA denied the appeal. Incredibly, the two-member majority held that the court did not have jurisdiction over the cases. In a well-reasoned opinion, the third judge dissented, stating the court did, in fact, have jurisdiction, and should immediately issue a writ releasing the accused, "In view of the confinement already served."[45] On that date, 3 January 1973, the defendants had already spent more than seven weeks in pretrial confinement.

The NAACP lawyers relentlessly pressed on with appeals, also directed to President Nixon, and all without success. In late January 1973 their efforts were ultimately stymied at the highest legal level, when Associate Justice William Douglas of the US Supreme Court denied the NAACP's petition for review.[46]

And so, our clients remained confined. The majority were released only after their trials. Six of them spent more than three months in pretrial confinement, and another six were incarcerated just short of four months.[47] That travesty of justice was one of the most egregious of all injustices perpetrated against the *Kitty Hawk* defendants.

PART III

DEFENDING THE ACCUSED

11

COMMAND THREAT

Date: 27 November 1972
Time: 0930H
Place: San Diego Naval Station Law Center

That Monday started out like most every other day at the office. How could I know that before it was over, the Secretary of the Navy would be hearing about JAG Lieutenant Truhe. And not in a good way.

"Want to feel the spray of salt air, Marv?" It was Lieutenant Haase[1] from across the hall.

"Sure," I said, smiling. "How do I do that?"

"By getting on an actual ship at sea."

"Really, which one?"

"The *Kitty Hawk*. She's on her way back, but she's still a day out."[2]

He had just received a call from Milt Silverman, the San Diego attorney who wanted to fly out to the carrier. I returned the call to Silverman who had been told he needed military help to fly to the ship. He wanted to check out the scene of the incident, especially when he learned a *Kitty Hawk* prosecutor, JAG Lieutenant Jim Bradley, was flying out that morning. I told him I would see what I could do and called the air terminal at the Naval air station.[3]

When I told the North Island Naval Air Station flight control officer that I was a law center JAG officer, he was very accommodating.

145

He told me the carrier was about one hundred miles off the coast of Los Angeles, and a COD (carrier onboard delivery) flight was about to leave for the ship. He patched me into the pilot of the COD aircraft, which ferried mail, cargo, and personnel to ships at sea on an irregular schedule.[4] The Grumman C-1 twin props could be recovered on deck with arresting cables and do takeoffs with a catapult assist.

I identified myself to the pilot and asked if a civilian lawyer and I could catch a ride. He said we were welcome but that he was leaving in half an hour.[5] I called Silverman and told him to meet me at the Naval air station. When I called the pilot back to confirm, he said his flight was the last of the day, so anyone going out would have to spend the night on the carrier. Since I had a hearing the following morning, I told him I would not be able to accompany Silverman.

I picked up Silverman at the Naval air station entrance and drove the short distance to the air terminal. When we arrived at the plane, I saw two JAG officers that I knew personally waiting to board. One was the prosecutor, Lieutenant Bradley, and the other the staff judge advocate— that is, legal counsel—for Captain McKenzie, the convening authority.

Another civilian was also waiting to board. I did not learn who he was until much later, but his presence added a whole new twist to the drama that was about to unfold. It began when the plane was en route to the carrier, and the pilot was asked to alert the ship that an unauthorized civilian attorney was on the flight.[6]

The plane landed on *Kitty Hawk's* flight deck at about noon,[7] and Silverman was met personally by the XO, Commander Cloud. He greeted Silverman warmly, and then escorted him to the ship's bridge and introduced him to Captain Townsend. Townsend was not happy to see Silverman and told him so in no uncertain terms. He even accused Silverman of misrepresenting himself to get aboard the carrier. Silverman was taken aback and tried to explain how he got on the aircraft. He even asked Townsend to check with the plane's pilot, but Townsend wasn't buying his explanation, so Silverman left the bridge.[8]

The ship's legal officer, Lieutenant Martin, gave Silverman and the two Navy JAGs a tour of the carrier to point out where some of the

October evening's assaults had occurred. Silverman was then shown a berthing compartment in officer quarters where he would spend the night.

That evening, Silverman was again escorted to the ship's bridge, this time to witness simulated night operations by the air squadrons, with the entire ship cloaked in semidarkness. He wasn't looking forward to seeing Captain Townsend again, but, to his surprise, Townsend's demeanor had completely changed from earlier. In fact, Townsend couldn't have been more ingratiating.

Did Townsend have a change of heart about Silverman's presence? Not at all. In fact, he tried to call back the plane that delivered Silverman, but it was too late.[9] He later said, "I didn't want him aboard, but I was in a damn tough spot about not keeping him. We would have lost an awful lot more if we didn't treat him graciously."[10] He was probably referring to the likely adverse publicity if word got out about his treatment of a *Kitty Hawk* defense lawyer.

That afternoon at about 1400, the director of the law center came to my office. Captain Newsome said another Navy captain was on the phone in his office wanting to speak to me. It was the staff judge advocate for the commander of fleet air for the western Pacific.[11]

That senior JAG officer told me Silverman's flight that morning contravened a regulation that required special authorization for civilians to board aircraft carriers. I told him I was unaware of the regulation and explained how I had arranged Silverman's flight.[12] He seemed satisfied with my explanation, and I left the director's office thinking that was the end of it.

About two hours later, three civilian attorneys from Los Angeles came to my office.[13] The ACLU had asked them to help defend some of the accused, including one of my clients, and they asked if I could take them to the North Island Naval Air Station to meet with Captain McKenzie.[14] They wanted to ask him to release the *Kitty Hawk* defendants from the brig. Though several of us had been rebuffed earlier when we made that same request to McKenzie, I felt it was worth another try. With the attorneys sitting in my office, I called McKenzie's office. His secretary answered and switched me over to him.

Captain McKenzie was livid.

He angrily demanded to know if I was the one who had gotten Silverman on the plane to *Kitty Hawk* that morning. I confirmed that I was, but those were the last words I was able to speak for several minutes. He began loudly berating me, nonstop, as I just sat there, dumbfounded. His one-sided castigation was so loud that I moved the receiver away from my ear, and just stared out the window as the bewildered attorneys in my office looked on.

He told me my conduct was inexcusable and accused me of intentionally violating Navy regulations.[15] His state of agitation was such that I thought Silverman must have said or done something unforgiveable while aboard the carrier. McKenzie then declared he would have me removed as defense counsel from the *Kitty Hawk* cases. That focused my attention, as he certainly had that power as convening authority. He then told me he would contact the most senior judge advocate in the Eleventh Naval District, Captain Benrubi, and have him carry out my removal.[16]

When McKenzie finally ended his tirade, he demanded to know why I had called. Not once had he given me a chance to explain my side of the incident, nor, obviously, did he care to hear it.[17] By now, I was angry myself, but I tried not to show it. I told him about the civilian attorneys who wanted to talk to him about the defendants' confinement. He declared he had a Naval air station to run and couldn't spend all his time talking to lawyers. He finally settled down long enough to say he would see us, but only if we arrived within the hour.

I told the civilian attorneys to go see McKenzie without me, explaining that I felt my presence would only hurt their efforts. After they left, I was still angry about McKenzie's castigation, and especially his accusations that I had intentionally violated Navy regulations. I took it as a personal attack on my integrity.

I then called Captain Newsome, the law center director, and told him what had just happened. He assured me I had done nothing wrong, said he personally had never heard of the flight regulation, and doubted any shore-based officer would have either. He also said McKenzie's threat to remove me as counsel was so inappropriate and unprofessional, that he doubted the threat would ever be carried out.[18]

Still not satisfied, I called the senior JAG officer that McKenzie had said he would ask to carry out his removal order. Captain Benrubi, the senior judge advocate for the Eleventh Naval District,[19] took charge. He drove immediately to North Island, talked to McKenzie, and then called me back. He said he told McKenzie it was all a misunderstanding and that I knew nothing of the regulation. Like Captain Newsome, Benrubi also assured me that I would remain as defense counsel and that the matter was now behind us.[20]

Or was it? Little did I know that news of a civilian defense lawyer hopping a flight to the *Kitty Hawk* in connection with the cases was burning up communication lines across the fleet. By late that afternoon, it had even reached the private residence of Admiral Clarey on the Hawaiian island of Kauai. Clarey was the commander in chief for the US Pacific Fleet, and he was told that Silverman was aboard the carrier. His chief of staff suggested that they have Silverman off-boarded to one of the carrier's escort destroyers, but Admiral Clarey did not think that was a good idea. Instead, he placed a call to the Secretary of the Navy John Warner in Washington, DC, even though it was after midnight there.[21]

Why all the uproar over a civilian aboard the *Kitty Hawk*? It turned out that Silverman's being there was not simply a violation of some obscure regulation. It was in violation of a standing order from none other than the SECNAV himself, which Warner had issued about a month after the *Kitty Hawk* incident. "In order to afford the defendants every possible protection of due process . . . . [I have] determined that no outside person will go aboard the U.S.S. *Kitty Hawk* on her return voyage to the United States."[22]

Warner had issued his order after the Navy received several requests from civilians to accompany the carrier on its homeward transit, some from congressmen and other high-ranking officials. Well-known civilian defense attorney Melvin Belli had even tried, unsuccessfully, to get aboard.[23]

SECNAV Warner recounted the incident when he later testified before the congressional subcommittee. "Late on the evening of 27 November . . .

Admiral Clarey telephoned me at my residence advising that a civilian defense attorney had been taken aboard the U.S.S. *Kitty Hawk* on that date contrary to our instructions, [however, my] instructions . . . were not in turn passed on to the Commandant Eleventh Naval District, whose staff legal personnel subsequently made arrangements for the civilian defense attorney to board the COD flight to U.S.S. *Kitty Hawk*."[24]

Admiral Clarey also duly reported to the subcommittee. "Lieutenant Truhe called the North Island Air Terminal and . . . based only on the word of Lt. Truhe, the Air Terminal personnel cleared [Silverman] to board the COD."[25]

One of the great ironies of the entire episode is that Captain McKenzie had blistered me for violating an obscure regulation at the same time a SECNAV fleetwide order was in effect prohibiting civilians from boarding *Kitty Hawk*. In fact, that order, which had been messaged personally to Captain Townsend on 21 November 1972, explicitly stated, "No one other than personnel with an official responsibility to be aboard will be permitted to ride *Kitty Hawk* for any part of your transit home."[26]

Since that order applied specifically to the *Kitty Hawk*, and was messaged to Townsend personally, surely he must have seen it? Not according to Townsend's sworn testimony before the subcommittee when asked about the SECNAV order. After he said he was not aware of the order, his legal officer, Lieutenant Martin, who was sitting next to him, said the ship had in fact received the message order. That clear contradiction of Townsend's testimony led a subcommittee member to say, "You don't have to be embarrassed, Captain, we know what the situation is." Townsend, caught in his denial, replied, "OK, you got me over a barrel. . . . You are smiling, that means I lose."[27]

At the time it happened, I was unaware of the storm waves Silverman and I had stirred up. Townsend's anger over the incident even extended to the flight crew that deposited his unwanted visitor. He suspended the pilot from flying for "about a month and a half or two, until he understands the magnitude of the problem."[28]

The incident triggered a formal Navy investigation,[29] which resulted in an official report being issued by the Commander, Naval Air Force,

U.S. Pacific Fleet. The congressional subcommittee also spent an inordinate amount of time on the subject and uncovered a large amount of message traffic that had flown around Navy commands all the way to the western Pacific.

All of this commotion was generated because an unauthorized civilian had gone aboard the carrier? It wasn't as if anything untoward had happened during Silverman's time on the carrier, and no one ever suggested it had.[30] So why was the secretary of the Navy awakened from his slumber after midnight that evening? Was it simply because his message order had been violated? I didn't think so.

The reason I felt there had to be more to it was because another unauthorized civilian had flown to the carrier that morning in the same COD plane, but for some reason, no one took any special notice of him. It was the man in civilian clothes I had seen waiting to board the aircraft when I dropped off Silverman. Why wasn't anyone upset about his getting on board? That question was never answered. We did learn his identity, however, from Captain McKenzie, who later testified the civilian was an airline ticket agent that flew out to the ship to sell tickets to sailors returning from the cruise.[31]

In that testimony, McKenzie admitted the ticket agent likewise did not have confirmed orders to board the plane. The agent had arranged a spot on the COD plane by simply making a phone call, as I had. Later, the Navy also officially conceded the ticket agent was not authorized to board the carrier.[32] So why the firestorm over Silverman, but only passing mention of the airline agent? Could it have been because Silverman was a *Kitty Hawk* defense lawyer?

Of course it was.

For example, SECNAV Warner identified Silverman as a "civilian defense attorney" no fewer than three times in his short message to the subcommittee, with no mention of the other civilian. I believe the entire episode would have gone virtually unnoticed, but for the interloper being a defense attorney for Black sailors accused of causing a shipboard riot on the very ship he had boarded.

One thing was certain: two high-ranking Navy captains were incensed that Silverman had unexpectedly shown up on *Kitty Hawk*'s flight deck. Captain Townsend had accused Silverman of deceit in getting aboard his ship, and Captain McKenzie, the convening authority, had threatened to throw me off the *Kitty Hawk* cases.

Shortly after the incident, some of our defense team gathered to discuss the ramifications of McKenzie's threat to remove me as defense counsel. We felt he was no longer an impartial convening authority, if he had ever been one. We had our misgivings from the outset when he placed our clients in pretrial confinement against all logic and prior precedent, and thereafter refused to release them despite compelling legal arguments.

I told the civilian attorneys that military law obligates convening authorities to be scrupulously impartial, with no personal interest in the outcome of trials they convene. I told them the original convening authority, Captain Townsend, had in fact been removed because of his personal interest and involvement in the onboard October incident.[33]

In our case, McKenzie's threat to remove me as defense counsel was about as personal as it could get. If he had carried out his threat, that constituted a clear interference with my clients' legal rights to counsel. But what if he never carried out the threat, as now appeared to be the case after Captain Benrubi interceded on my behalf? Legally speaking, it didn't matter. McKenzie still wasn't off the hook.

Military regulations speak directly to McKenzie's threat, regardless of its aftermath. "No convening authority or commander may censure, reprimand, or admonish a court-martial or other military tribunal or any member, military judge, or counsel thereof, with respect to the findings or sentence adjudged by the court-martial or tribunal, or with respect to any other exercise of the functions of the court-martial or tribunal or such persons in the conduct of the proceedings."[34]

Captain McKenzie had clearly overstepped the line by reprimanding me in the exercise of my functions as defense counsel, so I decided to file a motion with the military court to have him removed as convening authority. Our defense team concurred.

My client Seaman Mallory was the second of the defendants to stand trial, so the motion against McKenzie was filed in that case. The *UCMJ* does not have a specific provision addressing removal of a convening authority, so we invoked another *UCMJ* Article providing redress against alleged wrongs committed by commanding officers.[35]

A hearing on our motion was held on 15 December 1972 at the Naval Station Law Center, two months after the October incident. Our military judge was again Judge Bobby Day Bryant. Since I was going to testify in support of our motion, my cocounsel handled most of the questioning.[36] I testified about my one-sided "conversation" with Captain McKenzie, his anger, his accusation that I intentionally violated the regulation, and his threat to remove me from the *Kitty Hawk* cases.[37]

I was asked how the incident affected my ability to represent my clients, and responded, "I think that without question I can pursue this—these cases with the same vigor that I had hoped to do so before. But there is in my mind a very real problem with regard to my continuing in these cases with Captain McKenzie continuing as the Convening Authority."[38]

I explained that as defense counsel I often interacted with convening authorities in preparation for trial, including witness requests and negotiations of pretrial agreements. I testified that my role was compromised because of what had transpired between McKenzie and myself. I gave as an example my decision not to accompany the civilian counsel to his office after the phone call because I felt my presence would hinder our brig release efforts.[39]

Government counsel asked me on cross-examination what my reaction was to the McKenzie telephone call.

> Q: Your immediate reaction, I take it, Lieutenant Truhe, was that, in fact, you might be taken off the cases. Is that correct?

> A: Well, my first reaction, I guess, was that. But when I started thinking about it on my way home, I really

couldn't see any way that I would be removed. I have more faith than that in the military justice system and in my superiors at the Law Center. . . . I was not really that concerned about being physically removed from the cases. What was upsetting me the most was the fact that Captain McKenzie was challenging my integrity.

Q: You did feel that your integrity had been called into question?

A: Definitely. . . and he let it be known that he felt that . . . I had done something dishonest intentionally.

Q: Have you continued to act in an active way in the defense of your client[s]?

A: Yes . . .

Q: And there is no mental intimidation there about your role as counsel?

A: When you mean—if you mean literally intimidation, fearful, timid; no. I am not fearful and I am not timid. . . .

Q: Have you ever been chewed out before? . . .

A: I guess I cannot remember any instances of being chewed out. I—let's put it this way; I have never before in my life had my integrity challenged like I did in this instance.[40]

Judge Bryant then questioned me about my conversation with Captain Benrubi after he had interceded with Captain McKenzie on my behalf.

Q: Did [Benrubi] use the word "misunderstanding"?

A: Well, the conversation started off on—a light note. When I picked up the phone he said: "You are going to be court-martialed for this." At the time I didn't think it was particularly funny, but then he said, "No, it's all right. Everything is fine. Don't worry about it." . . .

Q: What did you understand him to mean when he said everything was okay?

A: I assumed by that that he had mollified Captain McKenzie . . . although . . . the very next day . . . I was told by the Air Terminal Officer that Captain McKenzie was highly upset about the whole thing; that he had personally been chewed out about it, and that also the pilot had been called on the carpet concerning the situation.[41]

The government counsel next called Captain McKenzie as a witness, and he was asked his reaction when he found out I was the officer who got the civilian aboard the aircraft.

A: I felt that he had exhibited some poor officer-like characteristics. . . .

Q: Would you tell us whether you conveyed that to Mr. Truhe?

A: I stated that . . . his actions in this matter had been improper. . . . I did, I would say, rebuke Mr. Truhe. . . . Further, I did state to Mr. Truhe, during our conversation, that I intended to bring his actions in this matter to the attention of his immediate superior in command, Captain Benrubi. . . .

Q: Captain, would you tell us what your attitude was with
       respect to any concept of Mr. Truhe being overly eager
       as a defense counsel, going too far as a defense counsel?

A: Mr. Truhe's actions as a defense counsel never entered
       my mind really at this point. Those were not germane
       to the thing that I had felt he had done wrong at this
       time.[42]

With that last answer, the government's defense to our motion became
clear. They were contending that the "rebuke" Captain McKenzie leveled at me was totally unrelated to my being a defense counsel. He
contended he was simply trying to set a junior officer straight for "poor
officer-like" conduct. That defense was intended as a direct challenge to
my testimony of his threat to remove me in my role as defense counsel.
Thus, the threat was specific to me as a defense counsel, and not simply,
as he claimed, as a rebuke to a junior officer.

Captain McKenzie then spoke about his visit from Captain Benrubi.

A: [Benrubi] informed me that Mr. Truhe was indeed sorry
       for the precipitous manner in which he had acted. . . .
       He told me further that Mr. Truhe was a fine young
       man and a good officer and good lawyer. . . . I had met
       Mr. Truhe a few days prior to that time and he did
       indeed seem like a fine young man to me.[43]

Q: Captain, Mr. Truhe testified under oath here today that
       you made various remarks to him concerning remov-
       ing him from the cases. Now, do you remember those
       remarks?

A: . . . I cannot remember making any such remarks.

Q: Do you deny that any such remarks may have been
       made?

A: No. No, I can't deny that they could possibly have been made. I just don't remember making such remarks.[44]

Our defense team later learned that JAG Lieutenant Thomas Grogan,[45] a member of McKenzie's staff, overheard his end of the telephone conversation, so we questioned him at a subsequent hearing.

Q.   During that conversation did you hear Captain McKenzie make a statement with reference to Lieutenant Truhe's participation in the *Kitty Hawk* cases?

A: Yes.

Q: And what was that statement?

A: The Captain made some reference about speaking to Lieutenant Truhe's superior, Captain Benrubi, about the possibility of removal of Lieutenant Truhe from participation in the *Kitty Hawk* cases.[46]

McKenzie later responded to that staff officer's testimony, which directly contradicted McKenzie's earlier testimony.

A: Mr. Grogan stated that he believed I might have said something to Mr. Truhe that might have led him to believe that I was going to take him off the cases. . . . I know it was never in my mind to take Mr. Truhe off, nor have I ever made any effort to get him removed from the cases. To the contrary, I think he is one of the finest young defense counsel we have got on these cases, and I would hope that he would continue.[47]

As I sat there in the courtroom, listening to McKenzie's self-serving statements, I realized how hard he was trying to remain as convening authority. After all that had transpired between us, including my legal efforts to have him removed from the cases, I did not believe for a minute he wanted me to continue as defense counsel.

Captain Benrubi testified at that same hearing that I never asked him to apologize to McKenzie,[48] despite McKenzie's statements to the contrary. I personally never saw a reason to apologize, having no knowledge of a flight regulation that apparently neither the air control officer nor the pilot knew about. After Captain Townsend suspended that pilot's flying status, I felt genuinely sorry for him. My "rebuke" and threat of removal paled in comparison.

During Captain McKenzie's testimony, he admitted he had never asked me whether I even knew about the obscure regulation, even up to the time of his trial testimony.[49]

Ironically, the same day McKenzie was giving that testimony, Chief of Naval Operations Admiral Zumwalt was testifying before the congressional subcommittee about my lack of knowledge of the SECNAV order prohibiting civilians from boarding *Kitty Hawk.*

Mr. Hogan: [Captain Benrubi] evidently was not aware of the order. As I understand it, it was his judge advocate who made the arrangements for the individual to go out there [to the *Kitty Hawk*].

Admiral Zumwalt: Certainly the COM 11 lawyer [Lieutenant Truhe] was not [aware of the order].[50]

I found it interesting to learn that the chief of Naval operations was quite willing to give me the benefit of the doubt regarding my lack of knowledge of the order, even if Captain McKenzie was not. And that brings up a very interesting twist to the end of Silverman's flight to the carrier.

Captain McKenzie was asked whether he knew about the SECNAV order. He testified, "If there was such a message, I have not seen it." He was then asked, "To this day, you know of no message by which the Secretary of Navy indicates that no civilian should fly to the *Kitty Hawk*?" His response? "That's correct. I do not know of any such message."[51]

That SECNAV order, of course, was the same one that Captain Townsend had also claimed he had not seen. Apparently, not just lowly junior officers can be derelict in knowing about Navy orders or regulations.

A sort of poetic justice eventually prevailed in the matter of Silverman's flight to the *Kitty Hawk* that November morning. Admiral Zumwalt testified, "Let me just assure you that the responsible persons as far as the military is concerned are the commanding officers in each case."[52] Those commanding officers were, of course, Captain McKenzie, CO of the North Island Naval Air Station, and Captain Townsend, CO of *Kitty Hawk*.

———

At the conclusion of all the testimony on our motion hearing, my cocounsel argued that Captain McKenzie fit the classic *UCMJ* definition of an "accuser" and, as such, was disqualified from continuing as convening authority. He said that McKenzie's failure to actually carry out his removal threat was legally inconsequential. To contend otherwise would suggest a convening authority can threaten defense counsel with no consequences, so long as the threat isn't carried out.[53]

Judge Bryant recessed the court briefly, then simply announced. "The motion to dismiss is denied."[54] No reasons given, no reference to any legal or factual basis for his ruling, just "denied." That denial meant we would have to continue to deal with McKenzie as convening authority for the remainder of the trials. From that point on, we fought a constant uphill battle against McKenzie, and others in authority, in the defense of our clients.

Our failure to remove McKenzie from his convening authority role gave me a resolve that remained throughout the months to come. His actions toward me were a constant reminder of the adversarial role I felt McKenzie was taking toward our entire defense team. That role was in direct violation of his obligation to deal with us defense counsel, and our clients, fairly and impartially.

I had testified that I was "pretty upset" about McKenzie's challenging my integrity. In fact, I was extremely angry, and remained so long after because of subsequent adversarial actions he and others in authority took against us and our clients.

My challenge to remove Captain McKenzie as convening authority stirred up a hornet's nest that genuinely surprised me, with the hearings garnering far more media attention than I thought they deserved. But what did I know? From my perspective, all I had done was try to ensure that our clients received fair trials, free of bias and undue command influence.

To some, however, I was an overzealous junior officer who went too far by publicly challenging a very senior officer. And I did so by alleging McKenzie had done something highly improper by threatening to remove me as defense counsel.

It didn't help when Captain Benrubi told me "You are going to be court-martialed for this." He meant it as a joke, of course, but it almost came true. Two other attorneys confirmed that later. One was an NAACP defense lawyer, the other, one of the *Kitty Hawk* prosecutors.[55] They said that just after I filed the motion against McKenzie, "someone in authority" at the Naval air station contacted Captain Benrubi and demanded I be court-martialed and charged with the *UCMJ*'s "Conduct Unbecoming an Officer and a Gentleman."[56]

Conduct unbecoming is "action or behavior in an official capacity which, in dishonoring or disgracing the person as an officer, seriously compromises the officer's character as a gentleman, or . . . seriously compromises the person's standing as an officer. There are certain moral attributes common to the ideal officer and the perfect gentleman, a lack of which is indicated by acts of dishonesty, unfair dealing, indecency, indecorum, lawlessness, injustice, or cruelty."[57]

What became of the demand that I be court-martialed? Cooler heads prevailed, and I remained as defense counsel for the duration of the trials. I doubt the Navy really wanted publicity about the court-martialing of a JAG defense counsel, certainly not one previously threatened with removal from the *Kitty Hawk* cases.

I never did learn the name of the "authority" at the North Island Naval Air Station who asked that I be court-martialed, but I had a fairly good idea whom it might be.

12

JUSTICE ON TRIAL

Date: 3 January 1973
Time: 0645H
Place: San Diego Naval Station Law Center

I pulled out of our apartment complex in Chula Vista and headed north on I-5. Five minutes later, I could see the skyscrapers of downtown San Diego. I took the next exit and drove west toward San Diego Harbor and the Thirty-Second Street Naval Station. What I saw told me it was not going to be just another day at the office.

As I approached the Naval station's front gate, I saw a large group milling about holding banners trumpeting antiwar slogans and declaring, "Free the Kitty Hawk 21!"[1] I slowly drove through the group, flashed my military ID at the marine corporal at the gate, and within a minute pulled up to the law center.

Two Shore Patrol trucks were parked outside next to three local TV news trucks.[2] Several reporters approached me as I exited my car, but I told them they'd have to wait until after the trial. As I walked into the law center, I realized the next day would be two years to the day since I first walked through those doors to report for active duty.

I said good morning to Betty, our civilian receptionist, and walked down the hall to my office in the defense wing. I hung up my Service

JAG Lieutenant Marvin D. Truhe, Eleventh
Naval District, San Diego, 1972.

Dress Blue uniform coat and white cover and sat down at my steel gray
metal desk next to my steel gray bookshelf. I stared at the pile of files
on my desk that I had been poring over just five hours earlier when I
went home for the night.

Today was the day.

At 0900 I would step into the nearby courtroom to defend the first
of my *Kitty Hawk* clients to go on trial. For the past six weeks, I had
been cramming for the biggest exam of my life. If I failed that exam, I
would be personally and forever after responsible for the military court-
martial conviction of Seaman Cleveland Mallory, an innocent Black
teenager from Pittsburgh, Pennsylvania.

Shortly after, I was ready to see Mallory. Ordinarily, I would simply
call the marine sergeant from down the hall and ask him to bring my
client over from the brig. But seeing the TV news trucks outside, I
didn't want the evening news showing Mallory in handcuffs, escorted
by armed marines. I drove over to the brig and spent a few minutes

Seaman Cleveland Mallory, USS *Kitty Hawk*, 1972.

convincing the marine duty sergeant I was authorized to escort prisoners. His hesitancy? I wasn't wearing a "chaser's badge."[3]

Mallory came out looking sharp in his Service Dress Blue enlisted
uniform: dark blue pants, open V neck pullover jumper with square
sailor collar, white tee shirt, and distinctive white round stiff cloth cover.[4]
He looked solemn, as usual.

I had only seen Mallory smile a few times since we first met six
weeks earlier. Those times were in my office when I called his mother,
Ruth, on my desk phone and handed the receiver to him. I usually
stepped out of the office to let them visit. More than once when I
returned, Mallory would be quietly wiping away tears. I often spoke to
her, keeping her current on her son's case. On one occasion, she said
others were praying for Cleveland back home and that she told him to
"look to God" for strength.[5]

As we drove the short distance to the law center, I asked Mallory not to talk to the reporters. When he got out of the car, a reporter asked whether his mother was coming to the trial. "No comment," he said, and I had to smile. I hadn't suggested he give that response.[6]

In my office, we picked up where we left off the afternoon before, again reviewing what Mallory might expect at his trial. I always had that conversation with my clients, and always walked them down the hall to check out the inside of the courtroom. I wanted to keep their apprehension level as low as possible when they returned to the courtroom for real.

I again reminded Mallory that whatever happened in the courtroom, and whatever was said about him, including possible outright lies, he should not betray his emotions at any time. I intended to do the same, as best I could.

I still hadn't decided if he should take the stand to testify on his own behalf because that decision was entirely dependent on where we stood after the government rested its case. How solid was it? How effective were their witnesses? In a perfect scenario, he wouldn't have to testify at all.

With all the uncertainty, however, I knew one thing without a doubt. Mallory trusted me. That trust was important. When defending any criminal case, issues frequently arise that require the client's consent. Does he plead not guilty? Do we ask for a jury panel? Will he testify? Mallory and I had shared enough by this time that I knew he would follow my advice. Now, I had to justify that trust and do everything in my power to secure justice for him. Justice being an acquittal.

Just before 0800 my cocounsel, JAG Lieutenant Ernie Lindberg, arrived. I had asked—or technically, Mallory had asked—Lindberg to fly in from Subic Bay to assist me in the trial. He was stationed at the Subic Bay Law Center and was one of the JAG officers flown out to *Kitty Hawk* after the October incident.[7] After a week on board, Lindberg knew details about what happened that night that my clients couldn't provide. His formal title during the upcoming trial was IMC, individual military counsel.

Shortly before 0900, Lindberg and I walked with Mallory down the hall to the courtroom. When we entered through the side door, I noticed that all the spectator seats beyond the railing were filled with news people, other civilians, and several men in uniform. Behind them, through the open double entrance doors, another dozen or more stood in the hallway trying to see inside.

We took our seats at the defense counsel table on the right side of the room, and on our left sat the trial counsel and assistant trial counsel.[8] The rest of the courtroom looked the same as always. Sometimes we had male chief petty officers as court reporters, but this time one of our two regular civilian female reporters sat facing us just below the military judge's raised bench.

A couple of minutes later, the back door to the courtroom opened and we all rose as Captain Bobby Day Bryant walked in and took his place in the large cushioned chair on the judge's bench. Military judges don't wear robes. He wore his Service Dress Blues, the same as mine, except his had four gold stripes on his sleeves denoting a Navy captain. He motioned for us to be seated and called to order the Article 39(a) session,[9] the *UCMJ* section governing court-martial proceedings.

I had previously advised Mallory to go "judge alone" and so we had no jury panel for the trial. Judge Bryant would not only preside over the court proceedings, he would serve as fact finder to determine Mallory's guilt or innocence.

Judge Bryant first took care of the preliminaries. He swore in the court reporter, had counsel identify themselves, and then asked the defendant a litany of questions: Are you satisfied with your counsel? Do you waive the reading of the charges? Are you aware that with a not guilty plea, the prosecution must prove your guilt beyond a reasonable doubt? How do you plead? Do you wish to waive your right to a trial by members—that is, by a jury?

The military judge was designated MJ in the later trial transcript, TC was trial counsel, ATC was assistant trial counsel, I was DC as defense counsel, and Lieutenant Ernie Lindberg was IMC as individual military counsel.

The assistant trial counsel would handle most of the witnesses. He was a very able adversary and didn't miss much. In the hours to come, however, I had a little surprise for him. At least I hoped it would be a surprise.

He gave a short opening statement. He said the government would call seven witnesses, including the victim who was assaulted the night of 12 October 1972 at about 2330. He said some witnesses would testify to experiencing fear, and even terror, during the night's upheaval.[10]

I chose to waive my opening statement, not wanting to reveal our defense strategy.

The government's first witness was Aviation Ordnanceman Third Class Walter Unland, who was part of the ship's company. He testified that around 2300 he was working in the aft bomb transfer compartment on the second deck, just below the hangar bay. He and other airmen were bringing bombs up in elevators from the magazine compartment several decks below. From there, they would be lifted up two levels to the flight deck and loaded on the jets.

Unland said the five-hundred-pound bombs were high-explosive Mark 82s, already tail fused. In that state, there was some risk of detonation. As he was working, he heard a commotion and witnessed a group of Black sailors moving down the passageway, some carrying makeshift weapons. He testified they were shouting and arguing, and even claimed he saw several white crew members coming by "with blood dripping all over them."[11]

The witness said he next saw a white sailor running by, chased by "about 25 or 30" Black sailors. They cornered that sailor against some equipment, and one of the Black sailors, armed with a club, confronted the sailor, who had his fists raised in defense. Unland said he "proceeded over" to the group of sailors and told them to "knock it off," as they were in a very dangerous area to be fighting. He then asked the Black sailors to "please vacate the area and leave," and most of them did. Just then, he said a tall Black sailor came up to him and yelled, "Hey, we got one here. We are going to get this whitey," and then "used a phrase with Kill in it."[12]

At this time, I interrupted the witness and told the military judge that attorney Benjamin James had just entered the courtroom after being delayed in coming. James was a Black NAACP retained defense counsel, who would serve as another cocounsel. He was sworn in and joined us at our table.

Unland continued his testimony, saying the Black sailor struck him and he started swinging back. As they fought, Unland was able to get his assailant down and underneath him but started receiving kicks and blows on his back from other Black sailors. He then heard a voice yell "Hey!" and everything stopped. He got up and went into a nearby elevator. He estimated that about thirty Black sailors were gathered around him, carrying broom handles and dogging wrenches.[13]

According to Unland, the entire incident lasted only a minute or two. He said his back was bleeding from a scratch or scrape, but he did not go to the dispensary.[14] When asked how he felt during the incident, he said he was "scared to death."[15]

During my cross-examination of Unland, I knew I had to respond to his claim that just before he was assaulted, he saw several white sailors coming by "with blood dripping all over them." I had interviewed over a dozen witnesses to the incident, and no one else had mentioned anything like it. Likewise, his testimony of telling the group to "please vacate the area and leave" was inconsistent with a scene of chaos and tumult.

I did understand that painting a bleak scenario fit into the government's narrative of ship-wide bedlam that would help to support its riot charges. By this time, however, I knew the facts did not support a riot claim. In order to portray the true situation aboard, and counter the riot charges, our defense team took every opportunity to lay to rest all hyperbolic testimony of uncontrolled mayhem. In my cross-examination of Unland, for example, I got him to admit that at the same time and place he claimed to see white sailors running by awash in blood, members of the bomber crew came into the compartment, sat down, and took their regular evening break as if nothing were happening.[16]

Unland testified he could identify three of his attackers but admitted he did not see Mallory among his Black assailants. That led to an interesting exchange between the witness and the ATC.

ATC: Now, you said that you did not see the accused there. Can you say the accused was not there, or did you not recognize him with these other individuals?

DC: I object, your honor, that calls for speculation on the part of the witness.

MJ: I will sustain the objection as phrased.[17]

When a judge sustains an objection "as phrased," he is often sending a signal for counsel to try again. The prosecutor immediately picked up on the signal, but then repeated essentially the same question.

Q: Unland, I'd like you to look at the accused in court today. From this experience can you say he was not there at 2330?

DC: Same objection, Your Honor.

MJ: Objection overruled.

Unland: No, I cannot.[18]

A minute later, on recross, I decided to demonstrate the absurdity of what the judge had just allowed, what I came to call a nonidentification identification.

DC: Petty Officer Unland, you have testified that you have taken a close look at Cleveland Mallory and you could not say that he was not there? Is that correct?

A: That's correct.

Q: Would you take a close look at Mr. Benjamin James, the [Black] defense counsel sitting at the table?

A: Yes.

Q: Could you say he was not there?

A: No, I cannot.

Q: He could possibly have been there, too?

A: He could have been.

DC: I have no further questions.[19]

The ATC next called an airman who witnessed the assault.[20] He said he did see a tall Black sailor confronting the victim, Unland, but from that point on, he might have witnessed an entirely different incident altogether. His and Unland's testimonies demonstrated how two eyewitnesses to the same event can offer substantially different accounts.

During my cross-examination, the eyewitness admitted he didn't see the Black sailor actually land a punch on Unland but did see "Unland's arm going out for a defensive punch."[21] Unland had testified there were "25 or 30" sailors surrounding him, but the airman said, "I'd say about ten."[22] Unland had testified the Black sailors were wielding metal dogging wrenches, but the witness said they were holding "metal canisters for napkins in the mess decks and . . . broken broomsticks or mops or whatever."[23]

The witness also testified he saw Unland being kicked.[24] During my cross-examination, however, he admitted that two weeks earlier in another hearing he remembered Unland being hit "just by fists that I could see."[25] He also said he never saw Mallory during the incident.

Another eyewitness testified he saw only "five or six guys" around Unland during the assault.[26] Thus, different witnesses swore they saw twenty-five or thirty, ten, and finally five or six sailors around Unland.

At that point in the trial, the government had called six eyewitnesses, and none had seen Mallory at the scene of the assault. That included two eyewitnesses who said they knew Mallory personally, having mess-cooked with him.[27]

During a lunch recess, our defense team gathered in my office with Mallory. We were all feeling very good. We believed the government's entire case would rise or fall on its final listed witness, Airman Michael Laurie.

Laurie was a white airman, and not a member of the ship's crew. He was assigned to one of the air squadrons temporarily deployed on the carrier. He testified he also witnessed the assault on Unland, and saw Mallory land three blows on the victim.[28]

The ATC asked how he was able to identify Mallory, and he said Mallory was a friend of his. He testified he had first met him in the Pussy Cat Bar in Hong Kong the evening of 6 July while the *Kitty Hawk* was there in port.[29]

Laurie had told me the same story when I interviewed him before the trial. When I told Mallory afterward what Laurie had said, however, he adamantly denied a Hong Kong meeting ever happened. Accordingly, I returned to the ship and had Laurie repeat his story into a cassette recorder, which I laid on the table between us. Laurie was now committed to telling how he met Mallory, and he knew it. If he changed his story at the trial, I would testify and introduce the tape recording to contradict him. Because of that possibility, my cocounsel IMC Lindberg conducted Laurie's cross-examination.

> Q: Now, you have identified having met Mallory at a bar in Hong Kong. Do you remember the name of that bar?
>
> A: Pussy Cat.
>
> Q: And you're sure it was the Pussy Cat bar?

A: Yes.

Q: It couldn't have been the Playboy Club or Susie Wong's, but it was the Pussy Cat bar?

A: Yes. . . .

Q: And you were there for a period of approximately four hours during which time you had continuous casual conversations with Cleveland Mallory, or even sporadic conversations—that's true?

A: Yes.[30]

Laurie admitted he got into "trouble" with the British Shore Patrol for being disorderly that night at the Pussy Cat Bar. He also conceded a friend of his had been arrested by the Hong Kong Police that night. When asked if the arrest was because his friend was fighting with a Black sailor in the bar, Laurie said, "I didn't know why he was taken away."[31]

Laurie also made another significant admission.

Q: You have also testified in the Article 32 session that was held in this room about a week ago that one of the words in your vocabulary is [n-word], is that true?

A: Yes, it is.

Q: And that's a word that you used on the date of October 12? It was in your vocabulary on that date?

A: Yes, it was.[32]

The last person to question Laurie was the judge. He asked a question that really drew my attention.

Q: I am going to ask you a question now that I want you to think about very seriously before you answer. Do you think it possible that any of your testimony could possibly be due to a faulty memory or anything that you might have unconsciously forgotten or remembered during this period of time?

A: No.[33]

In a military courtroom it is rare for a judge to ever directly question a witness, especially as here when the judge was also the fact finder. When a judge does, my attention is immediately riveted because he might telegraph his feelings about the case. The judge's question to Laurie, however, left me wondering what he was thinking. When he asked whether Laurie's memory might be "unconsciously" affected, was he expressing skepticism about his testimony and giving him a chance to, in effect, recant? Or did he really believe Laurie, and just want to determine the certainty of his testimony?

At this point, Laurie was excused, and the government rested its case. Shortly after, the judge called a fifteen-minute recess.[34]

I had alerted Mallory to Laurie's expected testimony, but he was still devastated by what Laurie had just said. When we returned to my office, Mallory immediately burst into tears. He said he was innocent and asked why Laurie was lying.[35]

I had no answer to give him.

We opened our defense with the testimony of a recently retired former chief petty officer who was a *Kitty Hawk* crewman on 12 October and knew Mallory personally. He witnessed the assault on Unland, had even broken it up but testified he did not see Mallory.[36] That made seven eyewitnesses to the assault that did not see Mallory, three of whom knew him personally. In direct contrast to other eyewitnesses, the petty officer said none of the Black sailors were armed.[37]

For our next defense witness, I called Lieutenant Junior Grade Leslie Beassie, who was Mallory's division officer. Beassie testified that the *Kitty Hawk* had departed Subic Bay in late June and was in Hong Kong from 30 June to 7 July 1972. He said that Mallory was on authorized leave in the days leading up to the ship's departure, and his leave orders required him to report back to the ship in Hong Kong no later than 0600 the morning of 7 July. I then asked him:

Q: Did Cleveland Mallory make that trip to Hong Kong?

A: No, he didn't.

Q: Where was Mallory at?

A: Cleveland Mallory was on leave in Subic Bay, Philippines . . .

Q: And he was on leave in the Philippines at the time the ship was in Hong Kong?

A: Yes, sir.

Q: He never got to Hong Kong?

A: No, sir.[38]

Beassie next testified that, having missed his flight to Hong Kong, Mallory immediately turned himself in to the Subic Bay Naval security police at 0730 the morning of 7 July. He said Mallory was later charged with an unauthorized absence of just ninety minutes. I introduced documents evidencing Mallory's leave status, and his UA mast record showing the time he turned himself in to the security police.[39] Beassie concluded his direct testimony by again confirming that Mallory had never been to Hong Kong.[40]

If ever I had a gotcha moment in court, this was it. The division officer's testimony had cut the heart out of Laurie's testimony and credibility, and destroyed the government's entire case in one fell swoop. Laurie had testified unequivocally that he first met Mallory in Hong Kong on 6 July, and based on that meeting had later identified him as Unland's assailant. However, since Mallory had never been to the Pussy Cat Bar, let alone to Hong Kong, Laurie had clearly lied in his sworn testimony.

With no further questions from either counsel, Mallory's division officer Beassie got up to leave. The judge, however, stopped him. He asked him a series of questions about the logistics of air travel between Subic Bay, Philippines, and Hong Kong.[41] Those questions took me by surprise. That subject had never come up during the trial, and, ordinarily, questions from the bench are limited to clarification of prior testimony.

In fact, I had never before had a judge raise an entirely new issue in a trial in that manner. It left me confused, but we simply moved on. The trial counsel then asked for a continuance until the following day,[42] and I understood why he did. As far as I could see, the government's case was in shambles.

When our defense team and Mallory gathered back in my office, we were very optimistic about the likelihood of an outright acquittal. After the others left, I visited with Mallory. He was looking and feeling good, the best I had seen him. I continued encouraging him to keep up his spirits, while reminding him the trial was not yet over.

As I gathered up my files before heading home, the law center director stopped by my office. He said something I'll always remember. He told me the surprise testimony that Mallory had never been to Hong Kong was a "Perry Mason moment."[43] Knowing that the fictional TV defense lawyer never lost a single case, I hoped he was right.

———

Date: 4 January 1973
Time: 1300H
Place: San Diego Naval Station Law Center

The next afternoon, the trial resumed with the government calling a witness in rebuttal, a witness we had never heard of. The prosecution is obligated to notify the defense of all witnesses they intend to call, but an exception exists when witnesses are called in rebuttal to defense evidence or testimony. We, of course, wondered who this mystery witness was. Would he testify he also saw Mallory assault Unland?

Fireman Apprentice Francis Tucker was called as the government's rebuttal witness.[44] We learned later how the government had come up with Tucker as a witness. Lieutenant Martin, the ship's legal officer, was told by the prosecutors of Beassie flatly contradicting Laurie's testimony. Martin returned to the law center with Laurie and asked him who else was in the Pussy Cat Bar that evening that could back up his testimony about Mallory. Laurie named Tucker, among several others. Martin said of those named, however, only Tucker claimed to have seen Mallory that evening.[45]

When Tucker took the stand, he testified he knew Mallory well, having mess-cooked with him the previous year. He said he saw Mallory in the Pussy Cat Bar the evening of 6 July, just as Laurie had said. He said Mallory came in with about twenty other Black sailors and that Mallory "just kind of looked" at him. He testified he had no doubt it was Mallory.[46]

The trial counsel then turned the witness over to me for cross-examination.[47] Unlike the other prosecution witnesses, I knew nothing about him. Well, almost nothing. I knew he was blatantly lying under oath. But why? And who was he? Someone who knew Mallory, who just happened to be in the bar that night, and who just happened to remember seeing Mallory? I immediately thought he must be a friend of Laurie's, and that Laurie probably asked him to bolster his Pussy Cat Bar fabrication.

Even if that explained why he was in court, how would Tucker explain his incredible memory? The bar incident was six months before his trial testimony, and yet he claimed to have seen Mallory in a group of twenty sailors. I didn't believe for a minute that he did, but I had to find a way to elicit that from him.

I opened my cross-examination of Tucker by asking him how many times he had gone to the Pussy Cat Bar during the Hong Kong stopover. He said five times, and claimed he saw Mallory the last night. I then asked him who he was with or saw his first night in the bar. He said he was probably with friends, but couldn't remember which ones. I then walked him through nights two, three, and four. Again, he said couldn't remember anyone he was with or saw on those other nights.[48] Having set him up, I then had asked him, "Who were you with the fifth night?"[49]

Tucker quickly ticked off a list of seven people he claimed to be with that night. Oh, he also saw Mallory.

DC: First four nights you don't remember seeing anybody?

A: No, sir.

Q: Even the friends that you were with?

A: That's right, sir.

Q: But the last night you were there, you saw Webber, Bliss, Murphy, Clonch, Burritt, Beehler, Krochek, and Mallory?

A: Yes, sir.[50]

Tucker's remarkable memory kicked in just when it was needed—on the fifth night after four nights of not functioning at all.

I then asked Tucker about a conversation he had with my cocounsel, Lieutenant Lindberg, in the hallway that morning before the court reconvened. I asked him if it was true that he told Lindberg he wasn't sure he had actually seen Mallory in the bar. He readily admitted he said that to Lindberg earlier that morning.[51]

I also asked Tucker if he recalled talking to me in the hallway about thirty minutes after his conversation with Lindberg. He said he did remember, and I asked:

> DC: And then what did you tell me?
>
> A: Then I told you about—I thought about it.
>
> Q: For how long did you think about it?
>
> A: Half-hour.
>
> Q: You thought about it for half an hour and then what did you decide?
>
> A: I decided he was there.
>
> Q: Uh-huh. When you first talked to Lieutenant Lindberg, you weren't sure whether or not you had seen him . . . and half an hour later, you're sure you saw him?
>
> A: Yes, sir.
>
> Q: Absolutely sure you saw him?
>
> A: Positive.
>
> Q: Absolutely? No question?
>
> A: No question . . . When he just asked me a question that happened seven months ago you have to think about it.[52]

I felt that the witness's identification of Mallory had been totally discredited. At a minimum, his dubious identification could not possibly establish Mallory's guilt beyond a reasonable doubt.

In most instances during cross-examination, if you establish the point you are trying to make, it is time to sit down. And, under ordinary circumstances, I would have. However, if I was right that Tucker showed up to testify only because he was Laurie's friend, I wanted to pursue that. I, of course, had noticed that when Tucker listed the seven friends he was with in the bar that evening, he failed to mention Laurie. There had to be a reason, and so I asked.

> DC: On the evening of 6 July was there a fight in the bar that night?

> A: Yes, sir.

> Q: What kind of fight was it?

> A: It was a racial fight.

> Q: Between blacks and whites?

> A: Yes, sir. . .

> Q: Did Laurie take part in the fight? . . .

> A: Yes, sir.

> Q: And this is a fight between blacks and whites?

> A: Yes, sir. . . .

> Q: Were you sitting at the same table with Laurie that night?

A: Yes, sir.

Q: For how long?

A: Well, I was in the bar all night long, so . . .[53]

My suspicion was confirmed. He was at the bar with Laurie but purposely didn't mention that earlier when he listed those with him. He next admitted he was a friend of Laurie's and had even left the bar with him that evening. Tucker said as they exited the bar, Laurie was arrested by the Naval shore patrol, presumably for fighting with Black sailors in the club.

Since he had admitted to sitting with Laurie that night, I asked him the obvious question.

DC: Did you ever see Mallory with Laurie that night?

A: No, sir, not together, talking, I didn't.

Q: You never saw them talking?

A: No.

Q: Not at any time?

A: No.[54]

My instinct to keep questioning Tucker had paid off. He had admitted he was with Laurie at the club, and now flatly contradicted Laurie's testimony that he and Mallory spent several hours together that evening. We had caught Laurie in a deliberate lie. Not just one, but yet another. I now had to ask myself whether to stop or keep plowing ahead. So far, so good, so why not?

I then asked Tucker if he had talked to Mallory that night in the club. He said he had not but that Mallory gave him a "sort of unfriendly-like type look."[55] Given that response, I asked him about his personal feelings about Mallory.

> A: I ain't got nothing again' him, but I just don't particu-
> larly like him.

> Q: You don't like Mallory?

> A: No.[56]

Revealing bias is, of course, one of the classic ways to discredit testimony. Tucker was giving us more than I could have ever hoped for,
so I continued:

> Q: What if we had evidence that Mallory was, in fact, in
> the Philippine Islands the next morning at 7:30?

> A: That wouldn't affect nothing. . .

> Q: What if we had evidence that he was in a hotel in the
> Philippines, the Eden Hotel on the night of the 6th?

> A: He was still in Hong Kong on the night of the 6th.

> Q: What was your answer when I asked you that same
> question about half an hour ago?

> A: The same answer.

> Q: Do you remember saying if a guy wanted an alibi he
> could get one?

> A: Yes, sir.

Q: So if there was evidence that he was in the Philippine Islands at the same time, your feeling would be that it would be some sort of an alibi?

A: If the man wanted one, he could get one. That's not hard to do. . . .

Q: Why do you think Mallory would want an alibi?

A: Maybe he was going to do something illegal.

Q: Like something four months later, going to attack somebody?

A: No, like something that night or that week.[57]

Tucker had told me his "alibi story" in the hallway just before he came into the courtroom to testify. It was his immediate response when I told him Mallory was in Subic Bay that night. That quick response told me someone had tipped him off about the logistics issue raised by the judge the day before. But who had primed him to be ready with his alibi response? I believed that the judge's intervention in the trial the day before, when he raised the logistics issue with Lieutenant Junior Grade Beassie, had given rise to Tucker's alibi story.

When Tucker finished answering questions from counsel, the judge had some questions for him about his remarkable memory of an event six months earlier.

Q: What triggered your recollection of Mallory being there in Hong Kong on the night of July the 6th?

A: Well, just thinking about it. And, I mean, like, when the first time he asked me, you know, "Where was you July the 7th of '72?" you know, you know, I just answered, you know, because I didn't know the importance of the question. So I just said, you know—So I just thought about it.[58] . . .

Q: Do you know that some evidence has been intro-
      duced that Cleveland Mallory was on leave during
      this period of time and was to go on leave in the
      Philippines?

A: Yes, sir.

Q: And that he, in fact, did turn himself in at the Kitty
      Hawk beach detachment at Cubi Point at 0730 on 7
      July 1972?

A: Yes, sir.

Q: In view of this you still maintain without a doubt that
      you saw Mallory that night, on 6 July?

A: Yes, sir.[59]

I liked what I had just heard. Judge Bryant's questions appeared to
telegraph loudly and clearly his disbelief of Tucker's testimony and,
by extension, Laurie's testimony. An optimistic take on his last question would be that he had offered Tucker an out from facing perjury
charges, and Tucker had declined. Things were looking good for
Mallory.

But not for long. The judge also asked Tucker questions that were
totally unsettling to me.

Q: You said that a fellow could leave Hong Kong and go
      down to Subic or Cubi?

A: Yes, sir.

Q: And stay there while the ship was on the line?

A: Yes, sir.

Q: How do you know he could do that?

A: All you have to do is fly from Hong Kong to the Phil-
      ippine Islands.

Q: Do you know of other people doing it?

A: No, sir.[60]

Despite the illogic of it, the judge seemed to be trying to establish in
his own mind the thorny logistics of how Mallory could have been in
two places at once.

I would have thought the whole Subic-to-Hong-Kong-and-back scenario was not worth visiting again, but with the judge having asked Beassie,
and now Tucker, about it, I felt I had to pursue it. I decided to use Tucker
to respond, in effect, to the judge's logistics questions.

Q: How late were you in the bar that evening?

A: They closed it down, I think, sometime between—
      between 9 and 11. . . .

Q: And you remember seeing Mallory there until it was
      closed down?

A: Yes, sir.[61]

His testimony put Mallory in the Hong Kong bar as late as 2300 that
evening, and Mallory was due to report back to the carrier in Hong
Kong at 0600 the next morning. Our indisputable evidence had already
shown that Mallory turned himself in at Subic Bay at 0730 the next

morning, so the idea of Mallory having been in Hong Kong late the night before was absurd.

We next called two previous government witnesses who knew Mallory personally. Both testified they were in the Pussy Cat Bar the evening of 6 July but did not see Mallory.[62] With that, we rested our case, and the government had no rebuttal witnesses.

In my closing argument, I reminded the judge that seven eyewitnesses to the assault, including the victim, had not seen Mallory, including three who knew him personally.[63] That contradiction of Laurie's claimed identification was important, but obviously we couldn't prove the negative. That is why our primary defense, simply stated, was that Laurie had lied.

I then outlined the seemingly unbelievable scenario the judge would have to accept in order to find Mallory guilty. I took the judge back to the evening of 6 July when Mallory was allegedly with Laurie in the Pussy Cat Bar in Hong Kong.

> Now, this is the evening, Your Honor, before [Mallory] is supposed to report to the Kitty Hawk. He is supposed to report back to the Kitty Hawk at 0600 the next morning. The evening before that, around midnight, he decides instead of going a few blocks and getting aboard the Kitty Hawk, that he is going to take a little circuitous route. He's going to fly to the Philippines . . . midnight or thereabouts, he takes the ferry, goes to the airport. Now this, I understand at midnight, all the way back to Subic takes four or five hours flying . . . and the plane landed in Subic just in time to turn himself in an hour and a half late UA for the Kitty Hawk that he had just left seven or eight hours before. . . .

> If Cleveland Mallory would have wanted to go UA at that time, he would have gone UA. He had absolutely no reason at that point to turn himself in back in the Philippines. So if we would have the Government believe that Cleveland Mallory was in that bar in Hong Kong, that is exactly what would have

had to have happened. . . .And I maintain, Your Honor, that that is entirely ludicrous. The testimony of Lieutenant Beassie yesterday was that he never made the trip; that he took leave; and that he, in fact, reported back to Cubi Point at 0730 the next morning, which we have documentary evidence of. I maintain, Your Honor, that Cleveland Mallory was never in the Pussy Cat Bar in Hong Kong.[64]

Since that was the close of all argument, the normal procedure would be for the judge to call a recess so he could review and consider all the evidence before reaching a verdict. Under the circumstances, however, with only two government witnesses implicating Mallory, and both being completely discredited, I assumed the judge would immediately announce a "not guilty" verdict. The very next exchange is precisely how the trial ended.

ATC: We have nothing further. Thank you.

MJ: Very well. Does defense have anything further?

DC: Nothing further, Your Honor.

MJ: Very well. Will the accused please rise. Cleveland Mallory, it is my duty as Military Judge to inform you that this court finds you: Of both Charges and the Specifications thereunder: Guilty. You may be seated.[65]

Mallory, my two cocounsel, and I sat there in stunned silence. What had just happened? Was I that oblivious to what had transpired in the courtroom the past two days? Had I missed something? What I did know was that I felt devastated for Mallory.

The judge then called a recess.

I don't remember what was said among our defense team at that point, but I have a distinct memory of going out the back door of the law center with Mallory and sitting down on the steps. My wife, Nicki, who had been watching the trial, came out a few minutes later and sat down with us. We all sat there speechless for what seemed forever, as Mallory struggled to hold back his tears.[66]

Just before we returned to the courtroom, a *Washington Post* reporter asked for my reaction to the verdict. I told him I was shocked. I then asked him his reaction. He said he was "flabbergasted," and "there wasn't a single person in the courtroom who was not surprised at the verdict, except for the judge."[67]

Soon after, the trial counsel told me he too was totally surprised by the verdict, especially when the judge had Mallory stand so quickly after the close of evidence.[68]

Nicki later told me she had been sitting next to a *Newsweek* magazine reporter in the courtroom when the verdict was announced. He turned to her and said Judge Bryant could not have heard anything during the trial, adding, "He must have been a Neiman Marcus dummy up there."[69]

The sentencing of a defendant in a military court typically takes place shortly after a finding of guilt, sometimes almost immediately after. This differs markedly from civilian criminal courts where sentencing hearings are generally held weeks or months after a guilty verdict.

Military sentencing procedure is set out in the *Manual for Courts-Martial.* The prosecutor puts on evidence in "aggravation" that would tend to increase the severity of the sentence. In an assault case, that might include the seriousness of the victim's injuries and the defendant's disciplinary record, including civilian criminal convictions.[70] The defense then puts on evidence in "extenuation and mitigation" of the offense, which is intended to lessen the punishment. That might include the defendant's past good conduct.[71]

The trial counsel told the judge that Mallory had been in pretrial confinement for sixty-nine days. The TC then presented information from Mallory's Service Record, which included Mallory's prior captain's mast for being in Subic Bay when he was supposed to be aboard the ship in Hong Kong.[72] I doubt the irony of that evidence was lost on anyone in the courtroom, unless, of course, it was the presiding military judge, Captain Bryant.

During the extenuation and mitigation phase of the hearing, Mallory testified about being assaulted that evening by three white sailors. He was the sailor, previously mentioned, who was attacked outside his store. The evening of the incident, he locked up the store at 2300, and then he returned an hour later when the unrest began, so he could retrieve the petty cash as a precaution. Mallory testified that three white sailors jumped him and one hit him in the side with a dogging wrench.[73]

Mallory knew he was seriously injured—in fact, he had "three or four busted ribs."[74] He headed down to sick bay and, en route, came across a seriously injured, semiconscious white petty officer. With extreme effort, he pulled the sailor to his feet and began half-carrying him down several deck levels to sick bay. When they arrived, he told the corpsman in charge to take care of him, and then reported his own injury.[75]

We presented several other witnesses, beginning with the ship's master-at-arms. He testified he knew Mallory personally and saw him shortly after he was assaulted.

Questions by Lieutenant Lindberg:

Q: You said you saw Mallory on that occasion?

A: Yes, sir. As I proceeded back aft I saw Adair [the injured white sailor] was—Mallory had him. He was struggling with him, trying to take him to sick bay. . . .

Q: How was Mallory struggling with Adair? . . .

A: Just carrying him, you know, down on the second deck. And I said, "Can I help you?" And he says, "Sure, Smitty" . . . and I said, "Okay, follow me." So

I told the people to get out of the way and jump
aside, to move aside as we proceeded to sick bay. And
we took him into sick bay because he was in very
bad shape.

Q: Was he conscious?

A: You could say he was conscious, but incoherent. He
      was all cut up and bleeding.[76]

We called another petty officer who testified that Mallory was "quiet,
soft-spoken . . . he believed in the Chain of Command because, I mean,
he really was sincere."[77]

A third petty officer testified that Mallory worked for a time as
a compartment cleaner and was the best he had ever seen. He had
assigned Mallory to the candy store and testified, "I think [Mallory is]
an outstanding man, good potential. He'd make an outstanding petty
officer in the Navy."[78]

The most serious nonconfinement sentence Mallory could receive
was a bad-conduct discharge. A BCD carries harsh consequences for
a service member, rendering him ineligible for GI Bill educational
benefits as well as Veterans Affairs' benefits such as medical care and
housing programs. A BCD also precludes future service in any military branch.

BCDs are a rarity in special courts-martial proceedings and are
reserved for the most egregious offenses. BCDs were typically imposed
for offenses such as violent assaults resulting in grievous injury, hardcore
drug cases, or UAs of several months or more. Since Mallory's "victim"
had not even sought medical help, none of us thought a BCD was likely.
Nevertheless, we wanted Mallory to tell the judge the impact a BCD
would have on his future Navy plans.

Questions by Lieutenant Lindberg:

Q: Do you like the Navy?

A: Yes, I enjoy it . . . .

Q: If given the opportunity, would you desire to stay on in the Navy and to serve honorably?

A: Yes, I do. . .

Q: Prior to this time had you ever considered making the Navy a career?

A: When I first came in, I thought about it. My mother told me before I came in that if I do stay here, make it a career, that the United States Government would take care of me for the rest of my life. So I had an idea that I would try to stay in for a career.[79]

Following arguments by both sides, the judge took a nine-minute recess "for deliberation" and then announced his sentence.

MJ: Cleveland Mallory, it is my duty as Military Judge to inform you that this court sentences you: To be discharged from the service with a bad conduct discharge; and to be reduced to pay grade E-1. In arriving at this sentence, I have considered, in addition to other matters before this court, your pretrial confinement of nearly two months. This court is adjourned.[80]

Our entire defense case in mitigation was focused on avoiding a BCD so that Mallory could remain in the Navy. But yet again, we fell short. Despite all our efforts, Judge Bryant gave Mallory a federal criminal conviction and took away his dreams of a Navy career.

I spent the next twenty minutes with Mallory in my office. He mostly just sat looking out the window, choking back his tears. Neither of us said much, not unlike when we sat on the back steps of the law center following the guilty verdict. Because his sentence did not include incarceration, Mallory was now free of the brig, so we talked about getting together later.

I called his mother in Pittsburgh and handed him the receiver.

13

UNDERCOVER

A fter I left Mallory in my office talking to his mother, I went back to the courtroom where my cocounsel Ernie Lindberg and Ben James were waiting. They were as devastated and emotionally drained as I was about the tragic injustice we had just witnessed. I suggested we leave the scene of the outrage and gather at a favorite after-work hangout for the law center lawyers, but this time the mood was going to be decidedly different. Before we left, I placed a call to attorney Milt Silverman and asked him to join us. He had also been in the courtroom witnessing the travesty of justice.

Date: 4 January 1973
Time: 1830H
Location: Boathouse Restaurant, Harbor Island

After a short drive, we entered Harbor Island and pulled in at the restaurant where Milt was waiting. I asked for a back table so we could have some privacy. At first, we simply vented our anger and frustration, with Ben James vowing to spend the rest of his life, if necessary, vindicating Mallory.[1]

We began by revisiting our trial strategy to see what had gone wrong. Try as we might, we kept coming back to the cold, hard fact that our innocent client had been convicted on perjured testimony. We well knew that defending an innocent client imposes an incredible burden because only a complete acquittal is acceptable. And we had failed miserably.

As for trial strategy, I brought up two of my decisions that could be second-guessed. The first was my pretrial decision to go judge alone, which I had recommended to Mallory. I didn't have to defend that decision to the other counsel, but I wanted to talk about it anyway. I had previously told them I had defended fifty or more cases with Judge Bryant sitting without a jury, and never had reason to doubt his impartiality or fairness.

Perhaps in an effort to make me feel better, someone mentioned a *New York Times* story from the day before. The article reported on the *Kitty Hawk* trial immediately preceding ours, also with Judge Bryant. At the outset of that trial, in order to decide whether to waive a jury, the defense counsel asked Bryant concerning "his attitudes about black people." He responded, "As far as I know, I am not a racist and I harbor no grudge or prejudices towards blacks."[2] That article also mentioned Bryant was from a small town in Georgia.

But was Judge Bryant bias-free? Ben James commented that one of the more insidious forms of racism can come from those who sincerely believe they are free of any racial bias. That statement, coming from a relatively young Black man, really resonated with me. It still does today.[3]

I next wanted to talk about my decision that Mallory not testify in his own defense. Again, I didn't have to justify that decision to the others because at the end of the government's case we all thought we were looking at a flat-out acquittal. In those circumstances, defense attorneys generally keep their accused clients off the stand for that reason, and two very good additional ones. First, in our system of justice, defendants have a presumption of innocence. Second, the government must prove the accused's guilt beyond a reasonable doubt. So, with those two fundamental precepts of criminal law in our favor, why fix it if it isn't broken?

I knew in advance I might not have Mallory testify because I thought the evidence would play out just as it had. We had an ironclad alibi for Mallory's whereabouts when Laurie claimed he was in Hong Kong. That also was a factor in my decision to go judge alone. If a military judge, a law-trained fact finder, could disregard the cardinal rules of presumption of innocence and the government's burden of proof, those cornerstones of American criminal law were meaningless.

Someone then mentioned something we were probably all thinking. Would the verdict have been any different if Mallory had taken the stand and professed his innocence? None of us thought so because Judge Bryant had simply disregarded our clear exculpatory evidence of Mallory never having been in Hong Kong. Our belief that Mallory's testimony would not have altered the outcome was a sad reflection of our feelings about the verdict, and the military judge.

We spent almost an hour looking backwards. Now it was time to look forward. I told the others I would immediately begin to prepare an appeal of Mallory's conviction. Under ordinary circumstances, an appeal in our case would succeed solely because of the evidence in the trial record. It would be hard to imagine a stronger case for justice gone wrong. At least that was the logical conclusion for us to make right up until the judge's verdict threw all logic out the window.

We realized how naive we had been. The verdict caught all of us off guard simply because none of us thought it even remotely possible. Based on the buzz in the courtroom afterward, we weren't the only ones shocked by the verdict.

We discussed the new reality facing us. Nothing could be taken for granted anymore. We could no longer assume that an appeal based solely on the evidentiary record would succeed. And none of us were willing to stake Cleveland Mallory's future on that supposition. The more we discussed the situation, the more we felt we needed some dramatic additional support for our appeal. That support had to be so compelling, so overwhelming, that it couldn't be ignored in the appellate review process.

An hour later we had a plan, sort of. We would ask the NAACP to hire an undercover agent to tail Laurie, hoping against hope he would somehow acknowledge his perjury. That, in turn, would lead to a reversal of Mallory's conviction on appeal. Looking back, our plan seems wildly farfetched, but it was the best we could come up with at the time. Ben James called Nathaniel Jones in New York City, and we were encouraged when he said the NAACP would spare no expenses in supporting our efforts.[4]

After we left the restaurant, Milt Silverman made some calls and came up with the name of a private investigator, whom I met first thing the next morning. That investigator proposed a three-member team to tail Laurie virtually around the clock, wearing body mics. He quoted a fee of ten dollars per hour for each member, plus fifteen cents a mile.[5] His plan seemed far too complicated, and unlikely to succeed, so I thanked him and we continued our search.

Later that day, Silverman came up with the name of a second investigator that we met. His plan also included a hidden mic, but with a twist. He first suggested he'd have a woman seduce Laurie and get him to admit to his perjury. When we understandably balked, he suggested abducting Laurie and taking him across the border into Mexico, presumably to coerce an admission.[6] What? Where did these guys come from anyway?

I felt it critical that any admissions from Laurie could not be tainted by unseemly, let alone illegal, means. If we were fortunate enough to get useful information, powerful enough to help overturn Mallory's conviction, that information would eventually become part of the public record. We certainly did not want to use methods that would put our defense team in the same league as Laurie himself. Even putting aside the propriety of using the suggested tactics, we could not rely on evidence that was sure to be challenged because of how it was obtained.

We kept looking.

Two days later, on 7 January, Ben James came up with a third prospect, recommended by his San Francisco contacts. Lipset Service, an investigative agency, told James about an excellent undercover agent in San Diego they had used in drug cases. After further discussion, the NAACP signed a retainer contract with Lipset Service, and they in turn hired the man for the *Kitty Hawk* undercover work.[7] In addition, the NAACP provided Milt Silverman with funds to use in carrying out the plan, including financing the agent's activities.[8]

And that is how, shortly thereafter, Billy L. Hicks came to my apartment in Linda Vista, a northeastern suburb of San Diego.[9]

I was impressed with Billy Hicks. A thirty-four-year-old white man, he looked younger. He stood six feet tall, had long black hair, and sported a mustache.[10] Not quite a hippie look, but you certainly wouldn't mistake him for a former US Marine officer or FBI agent. In fact, he was both. He was also a part-time law student at California Western School of Law in San Diego.[11] Hicks and I spent that evening talking about the plan for him to go undercover, meet Laurie, and try to befriend him.[12]

Even before he left our apartment, I knew Hicks would be an invaluable member of our team. As a former FBI agent, coupled with his ongoing undercover work, he knew what kind of information to elicit from Laurie, and how to go about getting it. Additionally, since he was a third-year law student, I felt he would understand exactly what I needed in order to use that information in a legally effective way.

My next assignment was to have Hicks see Laurie in person, but surreptitiously. I felt the best place was the law center where Laurie often showed up since he was a key prosecution witness in several of the trials. In fact, Laurie seemed to spend an inordinate amount of time there. On more than one occasion, while I watched him visiting with reporters, I had the distinct impression he considered himself a celebrity.

I even once witnessed one of our civilian defense lawyers approach him and ask sarcastically, "How are things in Hong Kong?" Laurie apparently did not pick up on the sarcasm because he lit up and asked, "Oh, did you read about me in the *L.A. Times*?"[13] I began to think that Laurie's arrogant attitude might actually help Hicks's undercover work.

Laurie was scheduled to testify at the law center in a couple of days, so Hicks was already there when Laurie arrived. Hicks stayed in the background, mingling with the reporters and spectators, and got a good

look at Laurie. Afterward, Hicks said two reporters told him they were
convinced Laurie had lied during Mallory's trial, which really angered
them.[14] I doubt Hicks needed any further motivation to proceed, but
that certainly didn't hurt.

We next had to find out where Laurie was living. I had checked
with the North Island Naval Air Station barracks where most *Kitty
Hawk* witnesses were billeted. I was told Laurie was living off base,
but they didn't know where. They said the *Kitty Hawk* legal office had
that information, but I didn't want to draw attention to my interest in
Laurie specifically, especially where he was living. Accordingly, I called
the ship's legal office and asked for the addresses of seven government
witnesses, with Laurie's name included on my list.

A couple of hours later a typewritten note was delivered to me at
the law center with seven listed names and addresses.[15] Laurie was living on Coronado Island,[16] where the Naval air station was located, in
a small two-story apartment complex. He had recently married, which
probably explained his moving off base. I gave Laurie's address to Hicks
and a decision was made for him to rent an apartment in the same
building.[17] When I next spoke with Hicks, he had already found an
available apartment across a small patio from Laurie's.

Everything seemed to be going along swimmingly, but I think all of
us on the defense team felt our undercover effort was an almost impos-
sible long shot. It always seemed to work in detective novels, television,
and movies, but in real life?

Once retained, however, Hicks wasted no time. He moved into
the apartment, posing as an unemployed truck driver and construction
worker from Houston, Texas. It took him only two days to meet Laurie,
and before long they occasionally dropped by each other's apartments
to have a beer and just talk.[18]

Since the *Kitty Hawk* trials were daily news, it was easy for Hicks to
steer conversations in that direction. In the process, Hicks led Laurie to
believe he was racially prejudiced. That, in turn, caused Laurie to open
up to Hicks. During those conversations, Hicks had a small recording
device concealed in his shirt pocket.[19]

———————

While Billy Hicks worked his end of Mallory's case, I was preparing a formal appeal of Mallory's conviction. I utilized the strongest argument I had. Well, actually, it was my only argument. I would ask the reviewing authority to reverse the conviction because the military judge's ruling was not supported by the evidentiary record of the trial. In other words, a reversal "on the facts."

A reversal on the facts is the most difficult of all appellate strategies. In effect, I would be asking the reviewing authority to second-guess the judge's verdict. The same would be true if a jury had rendered the verdict.

Reversals on the facts are extremely rare, and with good reason. If you are sitting in the courtroom as the fact finder, you see the witnesses up close and personal. Do they sound credible? Do they pause before answering, or fail to make eye contact? Those nuances do not show up in a transcript of court proceedings, and thus are unseen by the reviewing authority. A given witness may have come across as much more, or less, credible in person than his spoken words on the transcript suggest.

On the other hand, reversals on procedural or other legal grounds are much more commonplace. For example, a judge's refusal to admit a defense document into evidence, or to refuse certain testimony.

My appellate brief was directed to Commander Fleet Air Western Pacific Captain Charles Merryman. He was the reviewing authority, with headquarters at the North Island Naval Air Station, and would sign off on the decision granting or denying my appeal. As a practical matter, however, I knew that senior officers typically relied heavily on their staff judge advocates before making legal decisions.

I completed Mallory's appellate brief the last week in January 1973 and hand-delivered it to COMFAIR headquarters. On arrival, I was shown into the office of a fellow JAG officer, Lieutenant Commander Michael Rapp. He was a staff judge advocate who reported to Captain Merryman and was a career Navy lawyer whom I knew both professionally and personally. He and his wife sometimes joined our weekend gatherings of JAG lawyers and spouses. When I handed him my appellate brief, we didn't talk about the case, but he assured me he would review my pleadings as soon as possible. It meant a lot knowing Mike Rapp had been tasked with evaluating the appeal, and I left his office feeling cautiously optimistic.

14

WITHHOLDING EVIDENCE

How do we feel when someone doesn't play by the rules? We can get pretty upset if we find someone cheated in a sporting event, or even in a friendly game of cards. But what if someone's cheating results in unfair trials and possible miscarriages of justice? I had a chance to witness that firsthand.

In late January 1973 our defense team filed a motion alleging that Captain McKenzie, or someone acting on his behalf, withheld evidence critical to the defense of our clients beginning in November 1972 and continuing ever since.[1] Our "discovery motion" sought disclosure, as well as production, of all such evidence in the government's possession.

The Fifth Amendment to the US Constitution provides, "No person shall be deprived of life, liberty, or property without due process of law." Sadly, our "presumed innocent" clients were already deprived of their liberty, locked up in the brig while awaiting their trials, but the courts have also long held that the government's withholding of "exculpatory" evidence favorable to the accused likewise violates their basic due process rights. In a landmark decision, the US Supreme Court held, "Society wins not only when the guilty are convicted, but when criminal trials are fair."[2]

The mandate of the Supreme Court on withheld evidence applies equally to the military justice system, and is also decreed in the *Manual for Courts-Martial*. The *MCM* requires prompt disclosure to defense counsel of "any sworn or signed statement relating to an offense charged in the case" as well as other evidence in the government's possession.[3] That disclosure obligation takes effect "as soon as practicable" following service of charges on the accused.[4]

The ramifications are severe for withholding evidence from the defense. If the mandate is violated, the government may be precluded from using the evidence at trial, or even prevented from presenting witness testimony. "The purpose of this rule is to ensure the prompt, efficient, and fair administration of military justice by encouraging early and broad disclosure of information by the parties. Discovery in the military justice system is intended to *eliminate pretrial gamesmanship* [emphasis added]."[5]

The *MCM* further obligates the government to provide the defense with evidence which "reasonably tends to . . . negate the guilt of the accused of an offense charged."[6]

Military law does not require defense counsel to submit a written discovery request to the government because its strict disclosure obligations apply regardless of any such defense request. Nevertheless, our defense team made numerous and ongoing requests for disclosure including in letters in November[7] and December 1972,[8] and several additional letters after that.

One of the December letters was submitted on behalf of all our clients and was addressed to Captain McKenzie who had possession, or at least control, of all the discoverable evidence we were seeking. That letter specifically asked "that all statements and photographs in the hands of the government which are reasonably related to the *Kitty Hawk* cases be provided to the defense."[9]

The government disclosure obligation is a continuing one. Therefore, even if the government initially complies with the request, it must continue to turn over any additional evidence it possesses, even during an ongoing court-martial trial. In the words of the *MCM*, that includes evidence "previously requested or required to be produced."[10] In short, the government disclosure obligation is mandatory, continuing, and not subject to question.

Airman Laurie testified at Mallory's January 1973 trial that he had known him since July 1972, having met him in the Pussy Cat Bar in Hong Kong. He even said Mallory was his friend. That was very compelling testimony against any challenge we could make at trial to his identification of Mallory as one of Airman Unland's assailants.

We later learned, however, that Laurie had much earlier given a sworn testimony that flatly contradicted his trial testimony. Just eight days after the incident, on 21 October 1972, Laurie testified at an onboard hearing into that same assault.

Q: And would you please describe what happened?

A: Well, we were sitting in the shop, working . . . and we noticed a disturbance in the passageway, and we looked out there, and a friend of mine, Unland, works in G Division, was out there and some blacks were beating on him. . . .

Q: Now were you able to identify any of those individuals?

A: Yes sir. . . .

Q: Which ones were you able to identify by name?[11]

Laurie named two Black sailors, neither of them Mallory. Back then, he could not identify Mallory, yet two months later at Mallory's trial, he positively identified him as an assailant, his personal friend, no less.

Despite the standing obligation to produce all evidence favorable to the defense, Captain McKenzie, or someone acting on his behalf, made a conscious decision to withhold Laurie's prior inconsistent sworn testimony from our defense team. We first learned of its existence three weeks after Mallory had been convicted.

How we became aware of that prior inconsistent statement is a story in itself. The Navy completed its onboard investigation of the incident while the carrier was still at sea. Its investigative report contained hundreds of pages of sworn statements and oral testimony by witnesses to the night's events. When the *Kitty Hawk* stopped in Pearl Harbor on its way home, Lieutenant Martin, the ship's legal officer, immediately dispatched a copy of the completed report to the new convening authority, Captain McKenzie, in San Diego.

McKenzie's office received the report on 22 November 1972,[12] but our defense team knew nothing of its existence. In addition to much else, it contained the sworn statements and testimony that gave rise to all the charges against our clients. That report was vital to the defense of our clients.

In mid-December, one of our JAG defense lawyers learned about the existence of the report when someone mentioned it in passing.[13] We fired off a letter to Captain McKenzie demanding its production. McKenzie simply ignored our letter at first, and when we persisted, he began a long delaying action. He first claimed the report contained classified information about the ship and its operations. In effect, he contended the information was so secret it couldn't be entrusted to other Naval officers, including us JAG defense lawyers.

What possible classified information did the report contain that we or even our own clients didn't already know? That nuclear warheads were on board? That the ship was conducting bombing raids into North Vietnam? All that information, and more, was already well known, including to the public. And, even if classified information was contained in the report, the rules of military evidence explicitly provided that those portions could simply be excised before the report was delivered to us.[14]

Captain McKenzie's next stalling tactic was that the documents were being declassified, so an NAACP lawyer asked who was conducting that declassification. McKenzie steadfastly refused to reveal his identity. A month later, McKenzie finally produced a name, but only after our defense team filed a federal lawsuit to compel its disclosure.[15]

McKenzie's next artifice was a claim that someone had to determine what information in the report was "relevant" to our defense.[16] That was a preposterous assertion. The government was going to determine what we on the defense team considered relevant? Military law does not allow the government to pick and choose what evidence to turn over to the defense. Its mandate compels the production of "any sworn or signed statement relating to an offense charged in the case,"[17] and it certainly does not permit a subjective determination of relevance.

There are good reasons for that mandate. At the early stages of any case, even defense counsel may not know what documents will later prove relevant to the defense of their clients. Seemingly unimportant documents may later turn out to be key evidence. An otherwise innocuous statement, for example, may provide an alibi by placing an accused at a different location at the time of the offense. The statement may also reveal the identity of other eyewitnesses to an assault who were not listed as government witnesses.

Week after week, the government's delaying tactics continued to stall the production of the report, in blatant violation of military law.[18] On 23 January 1973, we finally had the hearing on our discovery motion against the government. That motion was heard at the outset of the trial of Airman Apprentice Ronald Glover, one of my clients.[19]

That morning, the trial counsel dropped a small stack of documents on my desk that I later learned were part of the investigative report we had been requesting. Among the papers was a sworn statement signed months earlier by my client Glover, while he was still aboard the carrier.[20] In that statement, Glover gave details of his activities the evening of the October incident right up to the time of the assault he was alleged to have committed. The government was compelled by military law to have given me that document, as well as the other documents, two months earlier.

I was furious.

Later that morning when I testified in support of our discovery motion, I told the presiding military judge, Captain Bryant, of the government's latest deliberate violation of military law. I told him of receiving the documents that morning.

> And in that stack was a two-page, single spaced typewritten statement by my client, Glover, that we had no idea existed. Now it is beyond my comprehension . . . that particular statement could exist and not be provided for us . . . it is inconceivable to me that my own client's statement, which in part could be construed as a confession, was not provided to me even right up to and including the day we had scheduled for trial.[21]

On cross-examination, the government counsel tried to deflect the government's blatant disclosure violation by blaming me for not asking for a statement I did not know existed.

> Q: Now, with respect to the statement of Glover, did it ever occur to you to ask your own client if he made a statement?
>
> A: When these cases first came over here . . . I made inquiry around as to whether or not any confessions had been made because, of course, in an assault, a confession is a pretty lethal thing, and I was told at that time that the only confession had been made by [another defendant]. . . [Also], I have at no time in my practice of law here and 150 or 200 cases, ever had a statement that was made, especially a two-page typewritten statement of my own client withheld from me. So it was inconceivable to me that my client could have made a statement that was not given to me by the Government because . . . that would be the very first piece of evidence that would come across my desk.[22]

The documents given to me that morning included statements of those who had been listed on the Charge Sheets as government witnesses in the upcoming trials. Because of that, my first instinct was to assume that the *Kitty Hawk* prosecution team had access to the report from the outset. However, I also testified that when the trial counsel gave me the documents, he told me he was unaware of my client's statement as recently as two days before the hearing.[23] In the two weeks leading up to the hearing, he had also told me of his unsuccessful efforts to get other requested documents. That suggested someone other than the prosecution team was withholding the evidence.[24]

I also testified about three eyewitness statements that I knew existed, but which had never been produced. I only learned of their existence when I interviewed witnesses who revealed they had given prior statements. It may have been just a coincidence—though probably not—but I noted that all three statements were made by Black crew members. One of the withheld statements was made by a Black chief petty officer who had been the victim of a threat by a white sailor. His detailed statement was withheld from us until just before another trial. Another withheld statement by another Black chief petty officer was never provided to us because, "the Government did not know where it was."[25]

After I testified about those and numerous other withheld statements, the government counsel asked me some very pointed questions.

> Q: I ask if your conclusion from [your testimony] is that the command has consciously and purposefully kept statements from you in order to convict the blacks who have been charged?
>
> A: Well, not just simply with regards to these particular statements; with regards to quite a bit of other evidence that has been requested in this case . . . let me say that I have become highly suspicious at the com-

plete absence of statements of blacks and the complete absence of black witnesses inasmuch as most of these incidents involve blacks and whites; and in at least some cases I know of some statements of black witnesses that were never provided to us. . . . And so, in answer to your question, I would have to say that at some level there appears to be a preponderance of evidence which would indicate somebody is keeping some evidence from us. . . .[26]

Q: But I am asking you if your conclusion . . . is that the command consciously and intentionally has kept evidence from you? . . .

A: When you refer to the command are you referring to anybody that might be responsible for getting evidence to us?

Q: I am referring . . . Let me ask you the question one by one. Do you feel that the CO has done this?

A: I don't think the Commanding Officer has consciously kept evidence from us.

Q: Do you feel that the XO has done this?

A: No, I do not.

Q: Do you feel that the legal officer has done this?

A: Yes, I feel he has.

Q: Do you feel the legal investigative office has done this? . . .

A: I think that they do have information that was not supplied to us. I do not know who is responsible. . . . I do know the blacks' statements that were not provided to us, that we made the requests through normal channels, and that the information did not come to us.

Q: Okay . . . based on your testimony here is that the legal officer has intentionally kept information from you . . .

A: It is kind of hard to pinpoint this . . . we are asking for information, and then trying to pinpoint it at the level which it didn't come.[27]

I felt I had made myself clear that I couldn't identify who it was that withheld evidence from our defense team. I, of course, knew Captain McKenzie was resisting our attempts to obtain requested documents, but I couldn't know who else was withholding evidence from us. I thought it could have been anyone at any level of command, or even several individuals. Nevertheless, the government counsel pursued his same line of questioning.

Q: And I want to ask, Mr. Truhe, whether you feel that in each case a statement has not been provided to you that was the intentional conduct of the Government to prevent you from having a statement?

A: Yes, and if I can explain myself: The closest I can pinpoint most of this absence of . . . statements and evidence . . . is the Legal Office itself. . . for instance . . . photographs have not been provided to me and we made specific requests for all photographs used for identification purposes as far as two months ago. . . .

Q: Fine. But, I want to direct your attention on what it is that is your conclusion?

A: My conclusion is that at the legal office level that there is evidence that exists that has not been provided the defense, even though we have directly asked for that particular type of evidence.[28]

Later in that same hearing, I cross-examined *Kitty Hawk*'s legal officer about the two-page statement by my client Glover that had been withheld from me.

Q: Lieutenant Martin, you indicated that Glover made a statement to you in your office personally?

A: He wrote out a statement in my office, yes.

Q: And that was later typed up?

A: Yes, it was. . .

Q: Did you consider that statement by Glover to be relevant to the Glover trial?

A: I certainly did not.

Q: You did not?

A: I considered it, that it was not relevant.

Q: And did you not think it important that defense counsel should see the statement by its client?[29]

At this point the government counsel objected to the witness answering my question, and Judge Bryant stopped me from continuing. I was taken aback. I saw no plausible legal reason why I couldn't continue my line of questioning. I asked the judge, "Your Honor, are you saying that I cannot ask any further questions with regard to the Glover statement and the reason it did not come to me?"[30]

Judge Bryant affirmed that no further questioning would be allowed on that subject of withheld evidence. This was especially infuriating since he was then hearing our motion alleging the improper withholding of evidence. Perhaps I should not have been surprised, given his conviction of Cleveland Mallory two weeks earlier in a decision that stunned so many of us in the courtroom.

————————

Defense counsel, in both civilian and military criminal courts, have a limited obligation to provide discovery information or material to the government. They must, for example, provide a list of witnesses they intend to call at trial, and provide documents they intend to introduce as evidence. Beyond that, they have virtually no obligation to provide anything to the government in advance of trial. As a result, defense counsel's trial tactics usually can be kept from the government until the actual trial.

Under ordinary circumstances, we JAG defense counsel could directly contact any Navy personnel we wanted to interview. If, as a result of those interviews, we decided to call someone as a witness, only then would we be obligated to identify that person. Likewise, if we wanted to view the scene of an offense, we could contact the ship or shore facility directly for access without notifying the prosecutors.

However, that freedom of access to both witnesses and alleged crime scenes was shut down for the duration of the *Kitty Hawk* trials. Virtually all government-listed witnesses were billeted in a specially designated barracks at the Naval air station. In mid-December 1972, all of us JAG defense counsel received a typed memo from the head trial counsel informing us to direct all our requests for witnesses to the "Kitty Hawk Legal Officer," using two designated phone numbers only.[31]

Those new restrictions were unprecedented. Much to our exasperation, that new policy meant the government would know in advance what witnesses we felt important to our cases, and those we were likely to call as witnesses. I couldn't imagine why the ship's legal officer should be involved in our interview requests. Lieutenant Martin, after all, was the one who helped lead the investigation and who prepared the initial charges against our clients. We certainly did not appreciate that level of familiarity with our trial strategy.

Shortly after, defense counsel Lieutenant Glenn Haase discovered an even more troubling aspect of the new witness contact system. He learned that each time when he finished interviewing a witness in his law center office, the witness was immediately ushered down the hall to the offices of one of the prosecutors. The witnesses weren't our clients, so our conversations with them were not privileged. As a result, those witnesses could freely discuss any conversations they had just had with members of our defense team.

Lieutenant Haase was incensed. But what could he do? Simple. Each time he finished an interview, he gave the witness a direct order to return from where he came, without, under any circumstances, talking to anyone else about the case. The situation mostly resolved itself after that.

The NAACP letter to Captain McKenzie in mid-December 1972 requesting discovery documents also asked "that funds be made available to the defense to hire an investigator to assist the defense in making its investigations like unto the assistance received from the government and from the Naval Investigative Service Office."[32]

As in virtually all criminal cases, civilian and military, the defense is at a distinct disadvantage when it comes to resources. That was certainly true with the *Kitty Hawk* cases. The Navy had already spent untold man-hours in its investigation of the incident over the preceding months. Our defense team was just getting started.

Recognizing that disparity between the parties, the *Manual for Courts-Martial* provides that defense counsel can request funding from the government to retain expert witnesses and consultants. The requests are to be made directly to the convening authority,[33] and authorization is expected if the requisite statement of reasons is given for the request.

In our situation, twenty-three defendants were being defended against a total of almost one hundred charges arising out of a chaotic melee that lasted several hours. Our defense team asked only for sufficient funds to retain a single investigator to assist in our defense.

By an unlikely coincidence, the same day our discovery request letter was sent to Captain McKenzie, he was in court testifying he would be receptive to my future contacts with him on behalf of my clients.

> Q: What, sir, what is your attitude with respect to Mr. Truhe's contacting you personally with respect to further matters in these cases? . . .
>
> A: Mr. Truhe can have equal access with all counsel to me as far as these matters are concerned. There is no prejudice in my mind, whatsoever, to Mr. Truhe.[34]

That testimony by Captain McKenzie was given in response to my motion hearing in which I was trying to get him removed as convening authority.

Two weeks later, Captain McKenzie responded to our funds request, "Your request for funds to hire an investigator is denied."[35] That was it. No comment, no reason, and no explanation. Once again, I recognized my failure to have Captain McKenzie removed as convening authority would remain as a major obstacle to our ongoing defense of our clients.

———————

The *UCMJ* grants defendants the right to request JAG counsel "of their own choosing," in addition to their initially Navy-designated JAG counsel. The only qualification is that the IMC counsel be "reasonably available."[36] Recognizing the consequences of a court-martial conviction, the Navy typically makes every effort possible to grant IMC requests.

Often that means flying in counsel from outlying duty stations and making them available for the duration of the court proceedings.

At the outset of the trials, fourteen *Kitty Hawk* defendants requested IMCs. Their list of named JAG officers included two commanders, one lieutenant commander, and eleven lieutenants.[37] Those requests had to be directed to, that's right, the convening authority. How did Captain McKenzie carry out his legal obligation to ensure our clients had all the resources necessary to receive a fair trial?

He took a full month to respond, and eleven of the fourteen IMC requests were rejected out of hand, so only three of them ever served as IMCs.[38] Most were rejected with a simple declaration, and no explanation, that the requested JAG officers were "Not reasonably available."[39] Incredibly, because McKenzie had delayed so long in his response, one IMC request was effectively denied because, by then, that defendant had already been tried.

Military law obligates the convening authority to make witnesses available to defense counsel. That includes the right to compulsory process, that is, issuance of subpoenas.[40] During the *Kitty Hawk* trials, I made only one request to Captain McKenzie for a witness. As required, I submitted a letter—in fact, two letters—to him detailing the reason for the request. Ironically, my witness request was made to support my motion to have McKenzie removed as convening authority.[41] No clearer example could be shown of why a convening authority should never serve in that capacity if he has a personal interest in a proceeding, much less one in which his actions can directly influence the outcome.

Moreover, the witness I had requested was not just anyone. He was a fellow JAG officer who had been recently transferred from San Diego to carrier duty. He had witnessed the aftermath of McKenzie rebuking me and would corroborate my testimony. Several days after I submitted the letter, I received a short response from McKenzie: "After due consideration of your request, and in concurrence with the First Endorsement thereto, your request is denied."[42] Again, no comment and no explanation.

I appealed his denial to the only judge available to hear the matter, Captain Bobby Day Bryant. After a hearing, he likewise summarily denied my request, suggesting my witness testimony was unnecessary to support my motion to have McKenzie removed as convening authority.[43] It was the first time I ever had a judge tell me what evidence I needed, or didn't need, to support my own case.

With the latest denial, the pattern had been set for how our defense team would be treated with any and all requests to Captain McKenzie. We requested that McKenzie release our clients from the brig. Request denied. Our clients requested IMCs. All but a few denied. We requested disclosure of all evidence in the hands of the government. Request ignored. After learning of the investigative report, we requested its production. Request delayed for weeks, and then only a portion of the report was produced. Our request for investigator funds was denied, and, finally, a request for a JAG officer as a witness was denied.

Captain McKenzie had testified that, "Mr. Truhe can have equal access with all counsel to me as far as these matters are concerned." Perhaps he simply meant he would treat all defense counsel the same— with utter disregard.

The hearing on our motion on withheld evidence spanned four days of trial and included multiple witnesses. Judge Bryant had an efficient way of dealing with all that testimony. At the conclusion of our case, immediately following my cross-examination of the ship's legal officer, the judge asked him just one question, "Have you ever during this, since 12 October, intentionally kept any evidence from the defense?" Lieutenant Martin responded, "No, sir."[44]

That was good enough for Judge Bryant. Motion denied.

Shortly after, we learned that the stack of documents given to our defense team in late January 1973 contained only a fraction of the full investigative report, which was five inches thick.[45] A substantial number of eyewitness statements were withheld from the outset, and never provided to us throughout the trials.[46] We only knew that because those witness statements were exhibits to the investigative report and were consecutively numbered.

The withheld evidence was addressed during an NAACP press conference in New York City in late February. The *New York Times* reported, "In New York City, NAACP officials said at a news conference that the Navy had withheld an 'exculpatory' investigation report that would have resulted in acquittal of the blacks tried so far."[47]

Ben James, who was cocounsel with me on many of my cases, also voiced his opinion on how our defense team was being treated. He was quoted in a *San Diego Union* article with a headline declaring, "Navy Accused of Injustice":

> There has been so much injustice in the Kitty Hawk cases that it reminds me of the famed Scottsboro trials of the 1930s. . . . The Navy has withheld statements made by witnesses as well as photographs, [James] said. As a result, while it is assumed that a man is presumed innocent until proven guilty, we have found that we must prove the man's innocence beyond any reasonable doubt. . . . James called the conviction of Seaman Cleveland Mallory of rioting and the sentence to a bad conduct discharge a "miscarriage of justice."[48]

The cumulation of all the injustices perpetrated against our young clients made me a very unhappy and angry lawyer. Before the *Kitty Hawk* cases, I prided myself on a calm and professional demeanor, never raising my voice or becoming argumentative with others, and remaining very deliberate and thoughtful in the courtroom. But I soon found myself arguing with opposing counsel and others, and too often venting my frustration and anger.[49]

I took some solace in knowing I was not the only one who succumbed to the pressures of the *Kitty Hawk* trials. On more than one occasion I witnessed trial counsel and other defense counsel arguing outside the courtroom,[50] something that I had never seen before the trials.[51]

Shortly after the story surfaced about my possible court-martial, an NAACP defense lawyer told me he was very concerned I would be thrown out of the Navy. He mentioned the court-martial rumor and my aggressive actions against senior commanders such as Captain McKenzie. He hastened to tell me he agreed with what I had been doing, but nevertheless was genuinely worried.[52] I thanked him for his concern but tried to reassure him that his fears were unfounded.

15

UNDERCOVER TRIUMPH

Date: 1 February 1973
Time: 1400H
Location: San Diego Naval Station Law Center

After seemingly endless weeks of frustration and disappointment, something happened to instantly lift my spirits. Billy Hicks, our undercover agent, called us with some great news. He had been at Laurie's apartment the night before, worn a wire, and hit a solid double. We finally had the first break since Mallory's conviction a month earlier. Hicks had taped Laurie saying he hated Black people, invariably using the crudest of ethnic slurs. Laurie also talked freely about his drug use.[1]

Our defense team was impressed with how quickly Hicks had exposed Laurie. He obviously had a special talent. A few of us got together with him, and he played his tapes. They were shocking and revolting, but we all knew Laurie's statements of racial bigotry would not be enough to overturn Mallory's conviction. Nothing short of his admitting to lying under oath would probably accomplish that. Hicks warned us of the risk of blowing his cover if he tried to push Laurie into talking about his trial testimony. It certainly wasn't the type of conversation that came up naturally. Nevertheless, we decided it had to be done, regardless of the risk.

Just a few days later, Hicks again delivered. This time it was a home run. On 7 February 1973, he taped Laurie explicitly admitting he lied at Mallory's trial.[2] Hicks had succeeded far beyond our expectations.

With those damning tapes in hand, our next step was to get them transcribed as quickly as possible. Hicks flew to San Francisco and took the tapes to Lipset Service, the investigative firm that was his employer during his undercover work for us. That office immediately began transcribing the tapes, with Hicks's assistance.[3]

Time was of the essence. I had to get the transcripts to Captain Merryman, the appellate authority, before he completed his review of Mallory's conviction, as those tapes might well tip the scales in our favor. On 16 February, Hicks called and said the transcripts were completed and would be on a United Airlines evening flight to San Diego.[4] He then asked something that took me by surprise.

"Are you going public with the transcripts?"

"Not me Billy. The transcripts will be part of my appellate pleadings, but those documents won't be made public."

"That's not what I meant. Will the transcripts and my affidavit be given to the press?"

I told him they would, since Nathaniel Jones planned to schedule a New York City press conference to expose the perjury, at which time he would make copies of the transcripts available to the media.

There was silence at his end of the line for a minute. And then, "I was afraid of that."

"Why, does it matter?"

"Actually, it does. I'm worried, Marv, that Laurie and his friends might come looking for me and my wife. I already moved back to my old apartment, but they could probably track us down."[5]

I was taken aback and couldn't think of a response. Hicks then told me he taped Laurie bragging about how he and his buddies had brutally assaulted Black sailors during the October incident. I then understood why he was concerned about what Laurie's reaction might be when he learned who Hicks really was. The transcripts would expose Laurie to potential criminal charges for perjury, assault, and drug use, and Hicks had made it all happen.

Even though I was talking to a former marine officer and FBI agent, Hicks made me realize that some undercover work came with significant personal risk. He knew, of course, what he had signed on for, but that didn't lessen his obvious concern for himself and his wife's personal safety.

"I've been through this before," he said, "and I may be worrying about nothing, but I just want to be careful."

"I'm sorry, I had no idea. Unfortunately, I can't control what the NAACP does. They paid for your work and can use the transcripts however they want. I will ask them, though, to alert you before they go public."

I then asked what he might be able to do to protect himself and his wife when his undercover role was blown. He said he didn't want to leave San Diego while still attending law school but said he would check into possible police protection. He explained that follow-up police protection was routinely given when he worked undercover for the FBI but didn't know if that protection would exist with him working in his private capacity.

After our conversation, I thought of all the TV and movies I had seen about undercover agents, not having a clue what that meant in real life to those willing to take it on.

That same evening, I drove to the San Diego airport, picked up the tape transcripts, and took them back to my office.[6] As I read through them, I found them much more revealing, incriminating, and disgusting, than I had anticipated. They ran the gamut from statements and admissions of racism, to extensive drug use, perjury, and more.

The transcripts were comprised of four separately bound documents totaling forty-seven pages, each identified by the recording date and listing others present at the time of recording, in addition to Billy Hicks and Michael Laurie.[7] The first transcript was dated February 1973.

BH: Well, you're not really prejudiced against them.

ML: [Expletive] no. I think everyone should own one.
      (Laughter)

BH: But you really are. You really are right?

ML: Right. Oooh, I hate 'em!

BH: You hate 'em? Well, how would—why would you hate 'em?

ML: I don't know, I just hate 'em.[8] . . .

BH: They ask if you're prejudiced or anything [on the witness stand]?

ML: Yeah.

BH: You can't tell them the truth can you?

ML: No.[9] . . . I just say, look, you know, quit harping on me, I ain't prejudiced.

BH: Can you say that with a straight face?

ML: Yeah[10] . . . There's one [expletive], man, I swear to God, squirrelly.

BH: Who's that? Is he the prosecutor or the defense?

ML: Defense.

BH: Black or white man?

ML: Black . . . He's a real [expletive] [*n*-word], too.[11] . . . I wish I would've had a gun that night. . . I swear to God I would have shot at least thirty of them [expletive]. I wish I could relive that night tomorrow night. . . I'd get me a [expletive] lead bar about four feet long, weighing about 65 pounds.[12]

When Hicks asked Laurie if he was using drugs during the times he testified at the trials, Laurie said he was "tripped out on smack."[13] He was taped saying he got his drugs at San Diego's Ocean Beach, was taking hits of "acid," and that he would "rather smoke dope than smoke cigarettes."[14]

ML: The, uh, I've been through the scene and back, you know, a couple of times.

BH: Cocaine. Cocaine blues.

ML: Yeahhhh.

BH: What is it? What's it like? Is it a high like marijuana or what?

ML: It isn't even a high really. . . . First of all, you know, you get your nostrils all cleared, you know, and snort the cocaine.[15] . . .

BH: Have you—have you tried the whole bit—smack and everything?

ML: I just got to that lately—over at—overseas. . . . That stuff over there is pure . . . the only (Inaudible) way is to cut it. . . . Pull the needle when you know you're messed enough."[16] . . .

BH: Have you got some coke here? . . .

ML: Yeah, I got some. I got about sixty dollars' worth.

BH: Sixty dollars' worth of cocaine![17]

Despite all his talk about prejudice and drug use, however, we were most interested in what Laurie said about his testimony at Mallory's trial.

ML: We exaggerate a little bit.

BH: What? You exaggerate a little bit?

ML: Yeah. Like, I say, you know, there was six guys that I
       saw around Unland, you know, beating him up and
       stuff, but I didn't actually see any of the blows connect,
       you know, or anything, but, you know, I say [expletive],
       like, yeah, I saw—definitely I saw blows connect.

BH: So, you're really just lying?

ML: Um hmm. (Affirmative) Granted. . .

BH: You—you haven't gotten caught in any of those lies,
       have you? Huh?

ML: No, we do it so you can't get caught. . . . Man, I never
       get caught doing nothing.

BH: Yeah, but they could catch you in some kind of [exple-
       tive] lie somehow or other, couldn't they?

ML: They could, but I'm too [expletive] smart. I think about
       everything before I say something.[18]

I was overwhelmed with the success of Hick's undercover work and
began thinking of how our defense team could use the transcripts most
effectively. From a strictly legal standpoint, the tapes and transcripts
could qualify as new evidence, since they further incriminated Mallory's
only direct accuser. The recognized legal procedure when dealing with
new evidence is to file a motion with the trial court judge asking for
a reconsideration of his verdict or retrial. I strongly believed, however,
that despite the compelling nature of the new evidence, Judge Bryant

would simply reject the motion out of hand because I would be asking him to consider new evidence that directly impugned his original verdict.

Therefore, I decided to bypass Judge Bryant and submit the new evidence directly to the appellate review authority. Precedent existed for that course of action, but only in a narrowly defined set of circumstances. I did not really care whether our situation qualified; I was going down that road regardless. I prepared a supplemental appellate pleading and included the transcripts as exhibits along with an authenticating affidavit from Billy Hicks.

The NAACP had been pressing me to delay submission of the transcripts to the Navy until after their New York City press conference. I had responded by telling Ben James that I did not want to risk the Mallory verdict being affirmed before I submitted the transcripts.[19] If that happened, our next level of appeal would probably take months, and I did not want Cleveland Mallory to suffer any more than he already had.

Date: 20 February 1973
Time: 1300H
Location: San Diego Naval Station Law Center

I was at an impasse with the NAACP for several days. Finally, on Tuesday, 20 February, I told James I could wait no longer and was going to deliver the transcripts, along with my pleadings, to COMFAIR's office later that same day. He did not resist and he let Nathaniel Jones know of my plans.

Before making the trip over to the North Island Naval Air Station to deliver the tapes, I decided to give the other Mallory trial participants a heads up. I wanted to tell them about the tapes before they heard it from the media. I must admit, that was not just a professional courtesy. I wanted to see their reactions to the dramatic news.

I first called the ATC who had prosecuted Mallory's case.[20] He was home at the time, and didn't seem particularly surprised at the news, probably because Laurie's trial testimony was so unbelievable.[21] I then invited the trial counsel in Mallory's case to my office.[22] After he was seated, I began reading portions of the transcripts to him. He then asked to look at the transcripts and began leafing through them. We then talked about the possibility of other government witnesses being complicit in the perjury.[23] At that point in time, we had no way of knowing.

I next went down the hall to talk to Judge Bryant and gave him an overview of the transcripts. He didn't react like I thought he would; in fact, he didn't really seem to react at all.[24] He was really playing it close to the vest, so I could only imagine what was going through his head. When I told him I would be taking the transcripts directly to the reviewing authority, he concurred. Neither of us mentioned the obvious option of my filing a retrial motion directly with him. He probably welcomed the chance to bypass the publicity, and awkwardness for him, of that course of action.

I then shared the transcripts with the other *Kitty Hawk* defense counsel in the law center's defense wing. As far as I was concerned, Laurie's testifying days were over. We found Laurie listed as a witness on four of our uncompleted cases. Billy Hicks's delivery of the tapes was timely, as all but one of those cases was scheduled for trial within three weeks.

Ten minutes later, I was crossing the Coronado Bay Bridge on my way to Lieutenant Commander Rapp's office where I had delivered my original appellate brief three weeks earlier. When I arrived, his secretary said Nathaniel Jones had just called, asking to talk to me before I spoke to Rapp. I gave her my supplemental appellate brief and the transcripts, then took the call in an adjacent office. Jones told me he was in New York City with Roy Wilkins, the NAACP'S executive director.

Jones wanted to coordinate his plans for the transcripts with mine. I told him I appreciated that courtesy. He said their press conference would be held in three days, on Friday morning, February 23, and they would be making a direct appeal to the secretary of the Navy, John Warner. They would ask him, in that very public way, to reverse Mallory's conviction.[25]

They also intended to ask the SECNAV to put a halt to the remaining *Kitty Hawk* trials, pending a full-scale investigation into the perjury issue raised by the tapes. How widespread was the perjury? Who else might be involved?

I asked him to hold off his press conference for a few additional days because I was concerned that his public appeal to SECNAV might interfere with our legal appeal. After further discussion, I conceded my feelings were mixed on the issue, and since he was quite eager to go public with the transcripts, I did not protest further. His Friday press conference would go ahead as scheduled.

I did not have mixed feelings on another important issue. I told Jones that even recognizing the strength of the transcript evidence, we should not push that issue too far. For example, we should not suggest a Navy-wide conspiracy of falsified testimony when we had no evidence of that. He quickly agreed.[26]

My telephone conversation with Jones lasted longer than I planned. When I returned to Rapp's office, he said he had not yet read my new pleadings because he was fixated on the transcripts. He then made a very interesting comment. "This stuff is just too good to be true."

"Glad to hear you say that."

"This Laurie actually admits to perjury."

"I know, that's why I wanted to get the transcripts here before you ruled on the appeal."[27]

My words "you ruled" were not a slip of the tongue. I guessed that someone with Rapp's experience as a career JAG officer would have a strong influence on the appeal even though Captain Merryman would be signing the actual decision.

"Do you know if these transcripts are completely accurate?" he asked.

"I can't swear to it, but I can get you the original tapes."

"No, I'm not asking that. Let me put it this way, how well do you know this guy?"

"The undercover guy?"

"Yeah. Who is he?"[28]

He obviously had not yet read Hicks's affidavit showing his background in the Marine Corps and FBI. I sorted through my pleadings and handed him the affidavit. He read it and looked up and smiled. I told him Hicks was in town and had been over to my apartment the night before. I offered to have him come over, but Rapp said that wouldn't be necessary. He then assured me their review would be impartial. Knowing him, I had no reason to think otherwise, but it was good hearing him say it anyway.

I next brought up a touchy subject. I told him of my conversation with Jones and his plan at the press conference to ask Secretary Warner to reverse Mallory's conviction. Rapp noticeably grimaced, knowing as I did that the legal appeal could end up being preempted in the political arena.

"I don't know if that would be a good idea," he said. "We can take care of that better right here." That was music to my ears. Knowing he had read my original brief, and now the transcripts, I strongly sensed he was letting me know he intended to recommend reversal of Mallory's conviction.[29]

He then said something that really surprised me. He said perjury charges against Laurie would have to be brought by the convening authority—that is, Captain McKenzie, and not by his office.[30] That was further music to my ears, as I had never mentioned the subject of perjury charges against Laurie.

As I left his office, it occurred to me that NAACP's direct appeal to SECNAV might actually prompt Lieutenant Commander Rapp and Captain Merryman to expedite the appeal. All things considered, my trip across the Coronado Bay Bridge seemed like time well spent.

I then remembered my promise to Billy Hicks that he would be alerted before the transcripts were publicly released. I called Ben James who assured me he would let Hicks know. That same day, arrangements were made with the San Diego Police Department for squad cars to patrol Hicks's residence, beginning the day of the scheduled NAACP press conference.[31]

Ben James also told me that Milt Silverman was preparing a federal district court action against SECNAV and others, along with a writ of habeas corpus asking for the release of all defendants from the brig. At the morning press conference the following Friday, Nathaniel Jones and Roy Wilkins revealed the tape transcripts and asked for a full-scale investigation of the entire *Kitty Hawk* affair.

On that same day, Milt Silverman filed the NAACP Complaint in the United States District Court for the Southern District of California in San Diego.[32] He named sixteen of the *Kitty Hawk* defendants as petitioners, including Cleveland Mallory. The respondents in the lawsuit included the SECNAV Warner, Captain McKenzie, the legal officer Lieutenant Martin, and Airman Laurie.

The lawsuit alleged the respondents had violated the defendants' Constitutional rights under the Civil Rights Act. Among more specific allegations, it sought relief arising from Laurie's perjured testimony in Mallory's trial. The lawsuit also asked for a court order compelling SECNAV to make "a complete and impartial investigation of the Oct. 12 and 13 incidents on the carrier *Kitty Hawk*."[33]

The NAACP press conference and federal lawsuit unleashed a torrent of nationwide news, including a lengthy article by Earl Caldwell in the *New York Times*. He cited several transcript statements about Laurie's perjury, and then mentioned the shipboard investigation: "The transcript excerpts also quoted Mr. Laurie as saying that Navy Lieut. John [sic] Philip Martin. . . was racially prejudiced. He 'didn't even ask us white sailors if we fought back because he knows we did.'. . . Roy Wilkins, executive director of the NAACP, termed the Navy's handling of the affair a 'despicable perversion of justice.'"[34]

When Earl Caldwell, a Black reporter, came to San Diego to cover the *Kitty Hawk* trials for the *New York Times*, he had already made a name for himself in his coverage of civil rights matters. He was the only reporter present when Martin Luther King Jr. was assassinated and filed a memorable firsthand account. He also covered the racial upheavals in the cities in the late sixties, and the Chicago "riots" during the 1968 Democratic National Convention.

Caldwell began covering the *Kitty Hawk* incident in November 1972 when he reported on the ship's arrival back in San Diego[35] and was still covering the story six months later when the trials were completed.[36] He could always be counted on to present a fair and balanced story, and was especially focused on the experiences of the accused, and our perspectives as defense counsel. He sought me out as a source early on, and we spoke often. In mid-March 1973 he began working on a feature story about the entire *Kitty Hawk* affair and came to my apartment, where we visited until the early morning hours.[37] By then I had come to greatly appreciate and respect his reporting on the injustices perpetrated against the *Kitty Hawk* defendants.

———————

Date: 27 February 1973
Time: 1400H
Location: San Diego Naval Station Law Center

The NAACP's press conference was held on Friday, February 23, 1973, and four days later a newspaper reporter called to tell me that Mallory's conviction had been reversed.[38] I was elated, of course, and immediately called Mallory to give him the great news. He was speechless. I invited him to join me and my wife that evening for a steak dinner. A short while later, I called his mother in Pittsburgh, and she, too, was over-joyed. Since she had not yet heard from her son, I told her I would have him call her.

Lieutenant Commander Rapp had taken just six days from our meeting to draft that reversal for Captain Merryman's signature. I couldn't help but think that the quick decision had been prompted by the NAACP press conference and federal lawsuit.

I received a copy of the decision that same day, which read, "In the foregoing case of Seaman Cleveland (NMN) Mallory, U.S. Navy, 185-40-1386, the sentence is disapproved and the charges are dismissed."[39] That decision was in the form of an official order compelling its implementation. The decision stated that Mallory would be returned to his former rank as seaman, his bad-conduct discharge withdrawn, and his records expunged of all information about the trial.[40]

Captain Merryman was quoted saying that the perjury tape transcripts played no part in his overturning of the conviction. "The Navy said the conviction has been overturned in the normal process of judicial review and not as a result of the evidence in the tapes."[41] The stated basis for the decision was that the trial record did not support the guilty verdict. In other words, we had a full-blown reversal "on the facts." I was relieved by that statement because by excluding reliance on the taped conversations, the government could not contest the reversal by contending that the tapes were never made part of the court record. In fact, the reversal decision was so compelling that the government never even bothered to challenge it on appeal.

When I filed the appeal, I knew that a reversal on the facts was virtually unheard of but felt that if any case deserved such a reversal, Mallory's did. The reversal was a stern declaration that Judge Bryant's verdict was totally unsupported by the evidence. He was later asked by a local reporter for his reaction to the reversal and said he had judged over a thousand cases and this was the first time he had ever been reversed on the evidence.[42]

Nothing could have better underscored the rarity of such reversals, or the clear injustice of his original verdict.

———————

Date: 27 February 1973
Time: 1530H
Location: San Diego Naval Station Law Center

The reversal of Mallory's conviction was front-page news, and local TV reporters wanted to interview Mallory and his defense team. Attorney Ben James and I were interviewed on local TV the same day that news of the reversal broke.

Newscaster:	What is your reaction to the reversal of the conviction of Cleveland Mallory?
James:	Total elation. I think justice has triumphed.
Truhe:	Very happy, very happy.
Newscaster:	Now I understand Lieutenant Truhe, that you presented a lengthy document on the basis of which, at least partially, this reversal was made possible.
Truhe:	I just wrote an appellate brief, in which I pointed out the portions of the trial itself in which we felt the evidence was insufficient for conviction.[43]

I then mentioned the seven government eyewitnesses who had not seen Mallory at the scene. Ben James talked about the uniqueness of the reversal on the facts, saying it was not only unusual in the Navy; it was unusual anywhere. "It simply means that there were insufficient facts to support a conviction."[44]

Ben James used the television platform to say something which I believe was intended primarily for the benefit of other government witnesses. "The perjury evidence . . . we intend to use that in other cases. [Our] investigation was rather comprehensive, the person whom we caught in perjury was not the only witness investigated. There were a number of other witnesses investigated and we'll be prepared to come forward with whatever evidence is necessary at the appropriate time. And I might add, that the investigation is continuing."[45]

I believe James intended to leave the impression that the NAACP had other undercover agents at work, seeking out possible perjury by other witnesses. That in itself might cause potential witnesses to rethink the certainty of their testimony, especially their eyewitness identifications of alleged assailants. I never knew if other undercover work was ongoing, however, and I never asked.

Cleveland Mallory was an outstanding and honorable young man, and his television interviews the next day proved that without question. San Diego Channel 10 News was the first to secure an interview with him.

> TV studio newscaster: As we reported yesterday, the San Diego Fleet Air Commander has reversed one of the convictions in the ongoing *Kitty Hawk* courts-martial proceedings. . . . At the same time, an investigation has been ordered into the testimony of the key witness in the case, Seaman Michael Laurie. Mallory . . . talked today about his feelings when the conviction was handed down.[46]

The coverage then switched to an on-site reporter who was with Mallory. She asked for his reaction to the initial court-martial conviction.

Mallory: It came as a sudden shock to me, you know. I was surprised cause I was just waiting for him to say not guilty, 'cause I knew in my heart that I hadn't done nothing, and that he couldn't justifiably prove me guilty. And when he came down with a guilty verdict, it just tore all my hooks up, 'cause I know what a bad-conduct discharge and a court-martial could do to your record, and I would have to live with it for the rest of my life.

Reporter: It has been indicated in a suit filed by the NAACP that the eyewitness' testimony presented in your case was perjured. Do you think that was a deliberate effort on the part of the witness or do you think the Navy was involved in some way?"

Mallory:	It's kind of hard to say . . . 'cause really I can't say that the Navy actually planned it that way; it's just that the guy, he has something against Blacks. He was just trying to get back at 'em, and he did it the best way he could—was to lie on the stand.
Reporter:	Do you think he's just an individual and it's not the Navy in general is prejudiced?
Mallory:	No, I don't believe exactly the Navy in general is prejudiced. The Navy has prejudiced people in it. In general, I don't think it's actually prejudiced.[47]

A television reporter from another TV station asked about his pretrial incarceration and his future.

Newscaster:	How long were you in the brig charged with riot and assault?
Mallory:	Nearly three months.
Newscaster:	What are your feelings toward the Navy now?
Mallory:	Well, my feelings towards the Navy is I can't say I have exact resentment against it. I just resent the people that's prejudiced against you, the people that try to use you for a reason of their own.
Newscaster:	With your court-martial being reversed and you're about to be restored to active duty, do you intend to stay in the Navy?

| Mallory: | Well, I haven't really made up my mind fully, whether I wanted to stay in or become discharged. Just I still have three years to go, and I'm not sure whether [to] spend three years . . . or just go ahead and get out now, and take my chances with life now.[48] |

Date: 27 February 1973
Time: 1930H
Location: Boathouse Restaurant, San Diego

Later that evening, my wife and I took Cleveland to the Boathouse Restaurant for his promised steak dinner. We spent the next two hours celebrating the victory and enjoying each other's company. During our meal, a waiter came by and said I had a telephone call. A fellow JAG officer told me the six defendants still in the brig had just been released.[49] That was great news, and I immediately thought it was no coincidence that just four days earlier the NAACP had released the perjury transcripts and filed its federal lawsuit.

The next day, I learned it was, in fact, no coincidence. I was with Ben James and Milt Silverman when we called Nathaniel Jones in New York City.[50] He told us that the NAACP's actions had raised alarm bells in Washington, DC, and Secretary Warner had dispatched Rear Admiral Merlin Staring to San Diego to see Captain McKenzie and find out just what on earth was going on. Staring was the most senior Navy JAG officer, and he arrived in San Diego on 27 February, the same day Mallory's conviction was reversed. It was also the same day charges were dismissed against another defendant because the sole government witness had retracted his eyewitness identification of the accused.[51]

According to Nathaniel Jones, Admiral Staring told Captain McKenzie in no uncertain terms, to "clean up his act."[52] Since Jones was on a first-name basis with both Secretary Warner and Admiral Staring, I assumed he got his inside information from one of them. That same day, McKenzie ordered the release of the six defendants still in the brig.[53] Pleased as I was by their release, I could not help thinking that Admiral Staring and Secretary Warner had it within their power months earlier to order their release when first approached by Nathaniel Jones.

At the time of their eventual release, those six defendants had each served 114 days in pretrial confinement, all while legally presumed innocent of their charges.

16

UNEQUAL JUSTICE

R acial injustice can take many forms, many of which are subtle, and thus difficult to spot. The racial injustices perpetrated against the *Kitty Hawk* defendants, however, were not even remotely subtle. Those were succinctly encapsulated in a quote reported in *Nation* magazine: "'Anytime you have a so-called race riot and you lock up 25 blacks,' one black Navy official noted caustically . . . 'that has to raise some questions.'"[1]

During the American Civil War, Congress adopted the Fourteenth Amendment to the Constitution, which ensured "equal protection" of laws, without regard to race or any other classification.[2] What does that mean in the context of the *Kitty Hawk* incident? Quite simply, the punitive articles of the *UCMJ* are to be applied equally. With twenty-five Black sailors charged in October 1972, and not a single white sailor, no one could seriously suggest that the *Kitty Hawk* defendants were afforded "equal protection" under military law.

Likewise, the unequal treatment of the *Kitty Hawk* defendants during the onboard investigation was clearly on display, as Airman Laurie bragged while being secretly taped by Billy Hicks.

BH: You got a little on the side?

ML: We all went out there and stomped some ass.

BH: You stomped some ass?

ML: Some people saw us out there, too."[3]

ML: Yeah, we were all together (inaudible).

BH: Anybody have any pipes or chains or anything, any (inaudible).

ML: Yeah, I had a lead pipe about six feet long.

BH: Oh, you did.

ML: I cleaned up a couple. I don't remember who. One of the guys had a CO_2 bottle. . . . We were out there fighting with wrenches and stuff and then we worked our way over to a fire hose, broke out the [expletive] fire hose. . . .

BH: I'm surprised they didn't mess around and try to charge some of you all then.

ML: Well, we, we did it without gettin', without getting caught. . . . They haven't even asked us if we fought back or anything.

BH: Uh, did the legal officer inter—even interview y'all?

ML: Yeah, he interviewed us.

BH: But he wasn't interested in prosecuting you?

ML: He didn't even ask us if we fought back cuz he knows [expletive] well we did. . . If it happens again and I'm around when it happens I'll kill me some [expletive] [*n*-word]s. It's gonna be in self-defense too.[4]

Shortly after the *Kitty Hawk* trials began, a couple of us defense lawyers challenged the Navy's actions, as reported in a local newspaper, "A motion by Glover's lawyers, Lt. Marvin D. Truhe and Dennis Kelly, a civilian, contended that the government practiced 'selective prosecution'—that it singled out [Black sailors] in the face of evidence that whites also committed assaults."[5] Our selective prosecution motion was not a defense on the merits, but an assertion that the law was applied unequally.

The US Supreme Court has held that "the decision whether to prosecute may not be based on an unjustifiable standard such as race, religion, or other arbitrary classification."[6] Selective prosecution is a violation of the Due Process Clause of the Constitution's Fifth Amendment. If our motion were to succeed, the remedy would be the dismissal of all the defendants' cases. Accordingly, we set out to establish, in the words of the Supreme Court that, "similarly situated individuals of a different race were not prosecuted."[7]

In support of our motion, we called witnesses and presented evidence on how the Navy conducted the shipboard investigation.[8] That investigation began a few hours after dawn broke on Friday morning, 13 October, and its first priority was identification of assault victims. To do that, the investigators began a review of the fifty-one medical reports issued following the night's incident.

Each medical report, signed off by the ship's chief medical officer,[9] noted the time, place, and nature of the injuries, as well as the medical treatment. A section of the reports included each patient's statement of how he received his injuries. Finally, the reports indicated the post-treatment status of the patient: returned to duty, held for observation, or flown off the ship for further treatment.

Medical reports were issued for just nine of the many Black sailors treated in sick bay, and included two with head lacerations, one with a possible fractured hand, and one with three broken ribs. All nine Black sailors reported they were victims of unprovoked assaults by marines or other white crew members. Only three of those patient victims were even interviewed, and no follow-up investigations were made on any of their reported assaults. Shockingly, six of those nine victims were themselves later charged with rioting and assaults.

No record indicates who made that decision to treat the Black victims as assailants; however, we do know Captain Townsend's feelings on the subject: "Again no whites were involved in any rampaging. The injury statistics bear this out. Three of the blacks treated in Sick Bay were later accused of assault. The others were treated for minor injuries arising out of the resistance to the Marines on the hangar deck."[10] Among much else, Townsend even misstated how many were charged. As noted, six of the nine Black victims were charged, not three.

Townsend obviously believed none of the seriously injured Black sailors could possibly be victims of assaults, so all must have sustained their injuries as assailants.

How many other injured Black sailors were bypassed in the investigation? The records show many more were injured who never sought medical attention. They include, for example, the handcuffed Perry Pettus and Durward Davis, who was attacked in the passageway by five white assailants. In addition, as previously noted, the majority of the Black sailors treated in sick bay never had medical reports issued for them. As previously noted, one of several hospital corpsmen said he personally treated ten or eleven Black sailors. The total number of injured Black sailors is unknown, but it undoubtedly far exceeded those nine with accompanying medical reports.

From the outset, complaints were made that only white crew members were being interviewed by the investigators. Commander Cloud brought that to the attention of the ship's legal officer, Lieutenant Martin. "I implored him, of course, that the work he was doing and the ship's investigators . . . certainly had to be unbiased in nature; and if there was . . . going to be any curtailing of evidence or information, either for or against an individual because they were white or black, that I personally would like to know about it."[11]

That plea fell on deaf ears. The onboard investigation generated 136 sworn statements. A full three months after the incident, our defense team finally received copies of ninety-six of those statements, but only two of those ninety-six were from Black sailors.[12] A senior first class petty officer was openly critical of the investigation. He said, "Investigators were beating a path back and forth to sick bay soliciting statements from white victims . . . [so] I asked them why they were not getting statements from blacks who were also injured and I was told they got one statement from a black."[13]

The investigators also took extensive oral testimony from crew members. As with the sworn statements, however, that testimony came almost exclusively from white crew members. Commander Cloud said complaints were made "that the preponderance of the witnesses . . . that had testified before Captain Haak's investigation were all white, in excess of a hundred, with only maybe two or three, at the most, blacks being allowed or invited to testify."[14]

Only one Black assault victim was allowed to testify, and his complaint was never followed up on. During my pretrial interviews of witnesses, I also learned of three Black petty officers who had been eyewitnesses to assaults because they had been ordered by division officers to break up altercations. The investigators did not take statements from any of them even though they may well have been able to identify assailants and victims in those altercations.[15]

The virtual absence of written statements or oral testimony from Black crew members was inexplicable, given that the onboard confrontations occurred exclusively between Black sailors and white sailors and white marines. It became clear from the outset that investigators were not interested in Black crew members' accounts of those incidents. One defendant told a newspaper reporter, "Black sailors, even though they knew the identity of assailants, were not permitted to file charges against whites."[16]

While secretly taping Airman Laurie, Billy Hicks asked him why no charges were brought against white sailors.

> BH: Did they even accept any complaints from [the Black sailors] after the big fight? Did some of [them] try to make complaints?

ML: Yeah, they, they don't listen to 'em.

BH: They don't listen to 'em. They say . . . there's the door?

ML: Yeah.[17]

As indicated, the few complaints that Black sailors were even allowed to make, were completely ignored. If that were not enough, even those complaints were the subject of outright fabrications by those in authority. In January 1973 attorney Ben James sent a letter to Captain McKenzie asking for all records of complaints made by Black sailors.[18] Captain McKenzie's official letter in response stated, "There are no written or oral complaints by blacks that whites participated in the riot."[19]

What possible reason would McKenzie have to falsify his response and purposely mislead our defense team? The most obvious answer is that he wanted to put us off track so we would stop investigating the entire sordid coverup of white sailors and marines assaulting Black sailors during the October incident.

A total of about 130 white sailors made sworn statements, but I testified in late January 1973 that not a single one had been given Article 31 warnings before being questioned.[20] That article of the *UCMJ* requires that a warning of the right to remain silent, for example, is to be given to potential suspects.[21] Those warnings are especially crucial during assault investigations because, at the beginning of questioning, it is unknown who is the assailant and who the victim. Often, each of the parties claims to be the victim.

Thus, when I noticed that none of the white sailors had been given Article 31 warnings before being questioned, I was highly suspicious. That meant from the very outset of the investigation, not a single white sailor was ever considered a potential suspect.

Cleveland Mallory's experience is representative of how Black sailor's complaints of assaults were handled. After his conviction was reversed, he was interviewed by a television reporter. He said he was not involved in any of the shipboard assaults on others but had himself been assaulted.

Reporter:	I understand that you were injured?
Mallory:	Yes, I was. I sustained three broken ribs that night. . . . I was attacked myself that night.
Reporter:	Who attacked you? What were the circumstances?
Mallory:	Well, I was working up in the store at the [officers' oh three] level of the ship, and I was opening up my store that night when three white guys came running up through the passageway, they seen me in there, so they all came in and one had a pipe. They jumped on me, and I hit one, he fell down and I turned around to face the other two and all of a sudden I got hit upside the ribs with a pipe.[22]

The afternoon after the incident, Mallory went to the ship's legal office and told investigators he wanted to make a complaint about the assault. He was refused. By then, investigators had been interviewing white sailors for several hours and recording their sworn statements. Mallory was simply handed a form and told to fill it out. His handwritten statement describing the assault was only three sentences long.[23]

The only "investigation" into his assault immediately followed his completion of the form.[24] Mallory said he was in the investigator's office "about five minutes," and was handed a year-old *Kitty Hawk* "cruise book," which were published annually.[25] They contain pictures of only a fraction of the crew members and air squadron personnel.

Inexplicably, the investigator asked Mallory to look at only a couple of pages of pictures, and then dismissed him. At no time was he ever shown any mug shots nor any lineup of potential suspects, even though he told the investigator he thought he could identify his assailants. In fact, he described his three assailants in detail, saying all were his height or taller, no beards or mustaches, no glasses, and so on. Following his five-minute "investigation" he was never questioned by anyone.[26]

We had two separate hearings before Judge Bryant on our selective prosecution motion. I called Lieutenant Martin, the ship's legal officer, as a witness in both of them since his office was responsible for responding to all complaints.[27] During my cross-examination of Martin, he said he never spoke to Mallory, nor did any of his investigators.[28]

In his handwritten statement Mallory mentioned his attackers were wearing yellow deck jerseys. Martin acknowledged that information alone identified the assailants as belonging to the ship's air division on the O-3 level, the same level where Mallory was assaulted. He further acknowledged there were "in the neighborhood of 65" airmen in that particular division.[29] Since airmen wore one of seven distinctively colored jerseys, each one identifying their duty assignment,[30] knowing the jersey color narrowed the list of suspects to perhaps ten.

I asked the legal officer about any follow-up on that:

> Q: Do you recall whether any of your investigators or you, yourself, ever talked to [Mallory] regarding the description of the assailants of Cleveland Mallory?

> A: Well, if no one talked to him, I don't think we asked for details.[31]

Three days before Lieutenant Martin testified that no investigation was made of the assault on Mallory, I received a letter from Captain McKenzie stating that "SN Cleveland Mallory's complaint was also thoroughly investigated."[32] In that same letter, he stated, "There are no pending investigations concerning alleged assaults by whites upon blacks aboard the Kitty Hawk."

In his testimony, Martin admitted he never had any photographs taken of any white sailors during their entire investigation of the night's incident. He readily conceded, however, that photographs were taken of virtually all the Black sailors who were eventually charged.[33] Those photographs were shown to alleged white victims for identification purposes. Martin even admitted he knew about several assaults on Black sailors that were never investigated, including those sailors requiring medical treatment.[34]

During my cross-examination of Martin, he said that Captain Townsend decided that no one would be charged for their actions on the hangar bay. That, of course, ruled out all the unprovoked assaults by marines on Black sailors. He also testified that Townsend told him the marines "were acting pursuant to lawful orders" and "the assaults which resulted which may have included one or two examples of use of excessive force by Marines were just the result of the further confused situation."[35]

In other words, the "excessive force" that left many Black sailors with serious injuries, including bleeding head and facial wounds, was just the result of a "confused situation."

Lieutenant Martin readily acknowledged that some Black sailors assaulted on the hangar bay could identify their white marine assailants.[36] He also admitted some Black sailors who were assaulted after the hangar bay incident could also identify their white assailants.[37] Those included the petty officer who had subdued the pistol-wielding marine,[38] and the white petty officer accused of striking a Black sailor in the aft mess incident.[39] Despite that, no investigations were made of any of those incidents, and no charges were issued.

Commander Cloud was personally present when several white assailants were identified by their Black victims. He was also present when several Black sailors identified a white master-at-arms who had assaulted them. The XO took the MAAs' security badge and told the sailors "I will look into the matter and I will let you know . . . that seemed to have placated the blacks right there, that we were definitely going to do something about the situation."[40] No record exists of anyone following up on that promise.

Lieutenant Martin also admitted that he personally knew of at least four other assaults by white sailors that were never investigated. I asked him about a Black airman apprentice who made a complaint about a white sailor striking him on the head with an oxygen cover.

> Q: Are you aware [of] that . . . complaint?

> A: No.[41]

I knew better, so I repeated the question.

> Q: You don't recall [him] making a statement in which he said he was hit in the head by an oxygen cover by a white?

> A: Let me try and recollect that. I can recall the statement by [him] on an injury report indicating he had been hit on the head with an oxygen cover. I may have seen a statement . . . to that effect; I can't recall.[42]

I asked Martin similar questions about statements made by three other Black sailors who were assaulted by white sailors. He admitted that no investigations had been made of any of those assaults. Further, he admitted, reluctantly, that shortly after he received those complaints, all three complainants were themselves charged with assaults on white sailors.[43]

I then asked Martin why no charges were brought against the white petty officer who was identified in the hangar bay mezzanine incident.

> Q: Were you aware that there were statements that a first class . . . was hurling racial epithets, a white first class from the mezzanine level, during this skirmish?

> A: Yes, I was.

> Q: And were you aware that statements had been made by blacks that they could identify him?

A: Yes, they did identify him.

Q: And as a result of that, were any charges brought against [him]?

A: No.

Q: Was this under the general guise again of no charges being brought against anybody in the hangar bay?

A: No. It was under the guise that no charges were to be brought for a speech alone: Disrespect, and provoking words and gestures.

Q: There was a general rule that no charges should be brought against anybody for speech alone?

A: Yes. . . .

Q: In your investigation of what was alleged that first class [petty officer] might have said, do you think that in your legal opinion that that could have constituted inciting a riot?

A: I did not.

Q: It could not have?

A: It could not have.

Q: Are you sure?

A: Yes. . . . He was yelling in a very excited manner; certainly used the word "bastard." It's very debatable whether he used the [n-word] or not.[44]

However, Commander Cloud himself had testified to the contrary earlier in that same hearing.[45] The XO also said the white sailors on the
mezzanine were "taunting" the Black sailors, "hurling verbal abuses,"
and "egging the marines" on in the altercation below.[46]

Those actions were a textbook violation of the *UCMJ* offense of
inciting a riot. The white petty officer, as well as others with him, could
have been charged with "committing a tumultuous disturbance of the
peace in a turbulent manner in concert with others."[47]

As I tried to continue questioning Lieutenant Martin about his
investigation of the hangar bay incident, Judge Bryant summarily shut
me down.

> MJ: I hate to interrupt this again, but I am going to stop
> this line of questioning at this particular point. There
> was a witness yesterday, the Executive Officer of the
> *Kitty Hawk*, who was brought in by defense counsel;
> who testified concerning these matters. I don't think
> there is any question as to what happened there and
> as to what this witness thought I think is irrelevant; I
> think we are wasting time.
>
> DC: Referring not only to the statement made by persons on
> the mezzanine level, but it is irrelevant as to anything
> else that went on in the hangar bay?
>
> MJ: Yes. I ruled you were precluded from asking questions
> about anything that happened on the hangar bay. You
> have already asked questions concerning the hangar
> bay.[48]

I was dumbfounded. Judge Bryant had just ruled that our challenge to
the investigation of the precipitating incident for the night's violence
was now off-limits. And he had done so for no valid legal reason. If
that were not enough, he made his ruling *sua sponte*, that is, on his own
initiative, and not in response to government counsel raising an objec-

tion to my questions. Had I just stepped into a surreal world where any notions of justice no longer applied? Or was I just getting too close to the truth about the entire sham investigation?

Having no recourse from his ruling, I moved on to other matters. I asked Lieutenant Martin about his statement that no one was to be charged for speech alone.

> Q: There was a general rule that no charges should be brought against anybody for speech alone?

> A: Yes.

> Q: Are you aware of a sailor that went to trial here about two weeks ago?

> A: That was a communicating a threat charge. . . .

> Q: And that is a verbal assault?

> A: Yes.[49]

That charge was brought against a Black sailor. Lieutenant Martin also filed a speech charge against one of my clients, a Black petty officer. He was charged with using "provoking words" against an airman the night of the incident.[50] "In that [the accused] did, on board the USS *Kitty Hawk* . . . wrongfully use provoking words, to wit: 'Come on Whitey,' and make provoking gestures."[51]

Martin had personally drafted speech charges against two Black sailors, even while testifying that "no charges were to be brought for a speech alone."[52] If that were not enough, that was his stated excuse for not charging the white petty officer who was directing taunts and racial slurs from the mezzanine.

I then asked Martin if any white sailors had been charged with any offenses whatsoever as a result of his investigation. He said none had been, but then said they were "investigating" a complaint made against a white sailor. I was taken aback by his statement.

I was questioning him more than three months after the issuance of the final report on the Navy's investigation of the October incident, and now, in the middle of my cross-examination of him about his one-sided investigation, he claimed they were investigating a complaint against a white crew member. His office had sworn out charges against nineteen Black sailors within eight days of the incident, and the last six, shortly after.[53] But an investigation into a white sailor was still ongoing?

The next obvious move was to ask Martin how long his purported investigation had been going on.

> A: [The complaint was] first investigated in October. [The] investigation continued through the month of early November . . . and the paperwork did not flow up the channel to COMFAIR, San Diego until sometime in December.
>
> Q: Let me get this clear; In other words, there were more than 20 blacks charged, and [the] one white . . . is not yet charged?
>
> A: Well, the convening authority is not CO of the *Kitty Hawk*. The decision over whether to refer it to trial will be made by [the convening authority].[54]

Captain McKenzie became the convening authority in November 1972, when the first of the defendants arrived at the North Island Naval Air Station, and Martin was testifying in late January 1973 that no charges had been filed against a white sailor because of an alleged ongoing investigation. I had the distinct feeling that Lieutenant Martin had just made a decision, while sitting in that witness chair, that it might be a good idea to charge a white sailor with something, anything, to counter our motion based on only Black sailors being charged.

In our selective prosecution motion, we had strongly emphasized the completely unprofessional nature of the investigation. That unprofessionalism was manifested in many different ways.

A cardinal rule in any civil or criminal case is that witnesses must be kept apart at all times, both before and after their testimony. Trial witnesses, for example, are given strict instructions not to talk to other witnesses about their testimony and must remain out of the courtroom until called to testify.

Witness separation is a precept firmly embedded in the American judicial system, and the *Manual for Courts-Martial* specifically addresses it. One rule, "Excluding Witnesses," applies to a courtroom situation and states that upon request, or on his own, "The military judge must order witnesses excluded so that they cannot hear other witnesses' testimony."[55]

Those constraints are intended to preclude witnesses from being influenced by other witnesses, even unintentionally. This is especially true of eyewitnesses to events. The strictures are also in place to prevent intentional collusion, that is, witnesses "getting their stories together." The constraints would certainly be known to a lawyer, say a JAG officer aboard a carrier.

Apparently not.

We called a listed government witness to testify who was an alleged assault victim. I asked the white airman apprentice about group meetings of potential witnesses in the ship's legal office. He said he was among a group of half a dozen white sailors who were summoned and questioned individually by the legal officer, Lieutenant Martin.[56] They were called back a second time because Martin "wanted us to get together and get it straight" and "wanted better statements"[57] about an alleged assault by Black sailors who entered a berthing compartment and assaulted a white sailor.

I questioned him about that second meeting with the legal officer.

Q: And did Lieutenant Martin call you in for that group meeting?

A: Yes, sir.

Q: And in that particular meeting were you in one at a time or were you sitting as a group?

A: As a group. . . .

Q: And how many of you were there at that time?

A: Six or seven. . . . We discussed what had transpired in the compartment [where the assaults occurred].

Q: Was it—Could it be classified as a group discussion?

A: (The witness nodded his head in the affirmative.)

Q: How else might you classify it?

A: A rap session.[58]

He then testified that each of them, in the presence of the others, told about what they recalled of the assaults. The witness said Lieutenant Martin was asking questions throughout and taking notes, and that particular group session lasted "I'd say 45 minutes to an hour." He said they talked about which Black sailors were mentioned by others to be involved in particular incidents. Martin also showed them "15 to 18" photographs of Black sailors with names on them, those "that were supposed to take part" in the assaults.[59]

The witness also acknowledged that during the group meeting, they already knew that some of the Black sailors they were talking about had already been charged.[60] The witness said they were then asked about a Black sailor who was pointed out to them from a group photograph.

Q: And specifically, what did Lieutenant Martin ask you about that photograph you have just mentioned?

A: He asked if any of us had seen him do anything.

Q: Did he say that that man had done anything?

A: I'm not sure of that. I can't remember. He said something to the effect that there were charges on him, or something.[61]

That white witness who was testifying had been listed as a victim of an assault by a Black sailor, even though he never said the sailor had assaulted him. He only learned later that he was listed as a witness when the accused Black sailor brought it to his attention prior to trial. The airman told the sailor that he would correct the situation by going with him to the legal office and have himself removed as a government witness.

I questioned the airman about what happened next in the ship's legal office.

Q: Had you ever said that [the Black sailor] had hit you?

A: No, sir.

Q: What was your reaction to that? What did you do?

A: I said, "Let's go get this straightened out," I guess. So we went on down and told them. And they said, "Well, it would come out in the trials."[62]

In other words, the airman would remain as a prosecuting witness, and the Black sailor would remain as a defendant, even though the airman hadn't accused the sailor of anything. Were those in the legal office hoping the airman would change his mind? Be convinced otherwise during another group meeting of white witnesses?

During my interview of sailors who were at the group meetings, another one told me they were being shown photographs of Black sailors, when someone said, "These are the photos of people we know were rioting. We want to see if you can pick any of them out."[63]

Lieutenant Martin freely admitted that he showed photographs of Black sailors to potential witnesses in his office for identification purposes. He acknowledged the photographs had the sailors' names on them and that those individuals already had charges sworn out against them.[64]

I then asked Martin:

Q: Did you have any control group, that is, of non-accused blacks?

A: You mean, were there any non-accused in the photos?

Q: That is correct.

A: Yes, there were.

Q: From the standpoint of non-suspects?

A: Yes.

Q: And how many non-suspects were there in that group?

A: I believe four.

Q: And how many total photographs?

A: Twenty-one.[65]

I was stunned. A JAG officer had conducted a photo lineup to help identify suspects in a manner that utterly defied logic or even fundamental fairness. Only one suspect should be in a lineup of perhaps five or six individuals. Instead, Martin conducted photo lineups which included seventeen suspects and only four nonsuspects! He virtually guaranteed anyone picked out of the lineup would be an existing suspect, some of whom were already charged. And he had testified to that with total aplomb, as if to say, "So what?"

I then asked:

Q: And did you show these photographs in group fash-
     ion; that is, hand the stack of photographs to the
     individual[s]?

A: Yes, sir.

Q: And did you ever show these photographs in the pres-
     ence of several witnesses at once?

A: Yes, I may have.

Q: Did you ever have group discussions conducted in your
     office by eyewitnesses?

A: No discussions. I questioned—I had groups in my office
     that I questioned individually.

Q: Were the other ones there in the room?

A: With other witnesses present, yes.[66]

By now, I was beyond stunned. The ship's legal officer had blatantly violated several cardinal rules of identification. He failed to separate potential witnesses. He conducted photo identifications without a proper control group. And he had group discussions about possible suspects, letting everyone hear what others said about the individual and each incident. Each and every one of those identification practices would strongly influence participants to personally identify alleged assailants, even if in doubt at the time, simply because others in the group had picked them out. After hearing others describe the alleged assaults, they would then be likely to testify to those details, perhaps not even realizing they hadn't actually witnessed those particulars.

By this time in the hearing, I had no reason to doubt the government witness who said he was told, "These are the photos of people we know were rioting. We want to see if you can pick any of them out."

———

During my trial preparation, I reviewed the Charge Sheets of all the defendants, and in particular the list of witnesses the government intended to call in each of the trials. In my review, I noticed one incredible coincidence. Among almost two hundred government witnesses, three white crew members were listed as witnesses in no fewer than nineteen cases. Those three witnesses included the perjurer Airman Laurie.

The disproportionate weighting of three prosecution witnesses appearing in nineteen cases could not be ignored. What were the odds that, collectively, three sailors out of thousands of crew members had personally witnessed virtually all the alleged assaults by Black crew members that occurred throughout the massive carrier that evening? That "coincidence" staggered the imagination.

What could that possibly mean?

I got an inkling of the answer when I discovered yet another shocking detail about the cases and the investigation. Two of those three witnesses were then working in *Kitty Hawk*'s legal office on board the ship, and the third, Laurie, was working in the legal office of Captain McKenzie, the convening authority at the Naval air station.

And just what investigative or clerical skills did the three white witnesses possess that led to their being chosen to work in the legal offices? Two of them were aviation ordnance men, responsible for bombs, rockets, and other munitions. The third, Airman Laurie, was assigned to the aircraft ordinance shop. None had any legal or yeoman training, yet their assigned duties included finding potential witnesses, and helping prepare witness statements. In that role, they could freely discuss the incidents with every witness that entered the legal offices. A more blatant violation of the principle of witness separation could hardly be imagined. Plus, what possible reason existed for them to be working in those legal offices? I asked the *Kitty Hawk*'s legal officer about it.

Q: Lieutenant Martin, has Petty Officer Unland ever worked in your legal office?

A: You mean, has he even been assigned there?

Q: Has he ever worked in your office?

A: Yes, he has.

Q: And has Airman Webber ever worked in your office?

A: Well, they have done work in my office; yes.

Q: And to the best of your knowledge, how many cases is Unland listed on as a Government witness?

A: Seven.

Q: And Webber, how many?

A: Seven.

Q: Now, when defense counsel wanted to get witnesses from the ship . . . did he not have to go through the legal office?

A: Yes.

Q: And if they wanted to come aboard for. . . getting evidence or pictures . . . were they not supposed to go through the legal office?

A: Yes.

Q: Why was the reason that these two particular witnesses were working in your legal office?

A: They happened to be there when the phones ring and my other two yeoman were gone; and I asked them to pick up the phone, see what it was . . .

Q: You mean they just happened to be there on one occasion?

A: Oh, no. They were—they—Well, in which they worked for me, one or two occasions. They would come down probably three or four times a week. . . .

Q: What do you consider the . . . propriety of having these Government witnesses working in your legal office?[67]

At this point, the trial counsel objected to my question:

TC: Your Honor . . . this appears to question Lieutenant Martin's integrity in the way it's asked. . . .

MJ: Objection sustained.

DC: Your Honor, I [by] no means want to impugn the integrity of Lieutenant Martin. Perhaps if I ask the question in this fashion: Did you think it was right to have witnesses who were involved in seven cases each working in the legal office that were handling other witnesses and handling defense counsel requests? . . .

TC: Your Honor, I still believe the question is argumentative in its nature and I [interrupted]—

MJ: Objection sustained."[68]

Kitty Hawk's legal officer never had to answer my clearly appropriate inquiry into his blatant breach of the rules of witness separation. He had implied that the airmen did not work in his office, they just happened to drop by "three or four times-a-week" to help out.

But what about Airman Laurie working in the legal office of Captain McKenzie, the convening authority? Was Laurie just dropping by to help out? We had a chance to find out when one of our defense team questioned Laurie at a later court-martial hearing. Laurie was asked, on an unrelated matter, about his air squadron. He replied, "I was not attached to my squadron at the time. I was TAD to the legal office at NAS North Island."[69]

TAD stands for "temporary additional duty," meaning a duty assignment made for a specified period. Again, the question must be asked, why was an airman, a nineteen-year-old airman at that, working in the legal office of the convening authority? Not just any teenager, but a key government witness listed on five separate Charge Sheets?

I never had an opportunity to ask who gave Laurie his TAD assignment. Nevertheless, he continued to work in Captain McKenzie's legal office during the majority of the *Kitty Hawk* trials.[70]

As mentioned, we defense counsel were obligated to go through *Kitty Hawk*'s legal office to secure witnesses to interview. As a result, the prosecutors could speculate about our intended trial tactics. If that were not enough, since key government witnesses were now working in the ship's legal office, we had yet another infringement into the privacy of our defense efforts.

JAG Defense Counsel Glenn Haase represented a Black sailor accused of assaulting a white sailor in a small compartment on the ship. In his sworn statement, the victim claimed his assailant was jumping up and down and yelling, "Here's another whitey, lets beat him up."[71] The defendant had denied the assault and told Lieutenant Haase the compartment where the alleged incident had occurred had a very low overhead.

Accordingly, Haase wanted to go aboard *Kitty Hawk* to take a picture of the compartment and measure its height to counter the claimed details of the alleged assault. He later testified that he called the ship's legal office and the person answering the phone insisted he tell why he wanted to come aboard. Haase hesitated, but knowing he needed permission, complied. He told him, "I would like to look at that part of the ship in which Unland was allegedly beaten up so I can take some measurements."[72] Haase said he wanted to use the information at the trial to challenge the testimony of the alleged victim, Unland. At that point, the person on the other end of the line said, "That is who you are talking to."[73] It was Petty Officer Unland.

During his testimony about the incident, Haase was asked about the size of the ship's crew complement.

> Q: Do you know how many men are aboard the USS Kitty Hawk?
>
> A: I suppose 5,000.[74]

That drew an objection from the trial counsel.

> TC: Your Honor . . . I don't believe that this is necessarily relevant . . . we seem to be drifting off.[75]

The judge then apprised the prosecutor of the relevance of the question, much to his chagrin.

> MJ: I suppose they are showing that out of those 5,000 there were two that were in the legal office and there could have been 4,998 others . . .[76]

Justice dictates that criminal investigations be impartial and unbiased. Likewise, a prosecutor's obligation is to see that justice is done, regardless of the outcome of any criminal case he prosecutes. If those two precepts are honored, justice prevails. Or at least, it has a fighting chance of prevailing. Without them, the system breaks down completely.

Another basic tenet of criminal justice is the obligatory separation of investigative and prosecutorial functions. Those two roles must remain scrupulously independent of each other. Without that independence, an overzealous prosecutor might impinge on the impartiality of the investigator. Or vice versa.

That separation is the reason the *Manual for Courts-Martial* provides, "No person shall act as trial counsel or assistant trial counsel . . . in any case in which that person is or has been . . . an investigating or preliminary hearing officer."[77] That *MCM* rule leaves no wiggle room. An investigator is disqualified from later acting as a prosecutor on the same matter, period.

With that in mind, we return to my cross-examination of Lieutenant Martin.

> Q: Did you ever tell [civilian defense counsel] Mr. Silverman that you had expressed a desire at some time to prosecute these cases or be an assistant in helping to prosecute these cases?
>
> A: I may have indicated to him a message . . . to the effect in which the Captain [McKenzie] requested I be designated assistant trial counsel. I think I may have brought that up in the presence of [Captain McKenzie's staff judge advocate and Lieutenant Bradley].
>
> Q: Did you ever tell Mr. Silverman that you had asked to be assistant on the prosecution of these cases?
>
> A: I don't believe I said, "I asked to be." I believe I said, "The Commanding Officer has requested I be assistant."
>
> Q: Just a minute. Are you saying you did not say that to Mr. Silverman?

A: I do not recall.

Q: It could have happened?

A: It's possible.[78]

Lieutenant Martin had just admitted he may have initiated the discussion of his serving as a prosecutor. How impartial could he have been as an investigator with his eye on ultimately prosecuting the very people he was investigating? He testified that the convening authority had initiated the discussion of his serving as prosecutor. In either event, his serving in that role would have blatantly violated the law prohibiting an investigator from later serving as prosecutor.

In my closing argument, I stated why I believed only Black sailors were charged immediately after the incident:

> We submit, Your Honor . . . the Government drew the conclusion from the very beginning that blacks were responsible for rioting and assaulting aboard the Kitty Hawk. . . . What we have shown is that the intent on the part of the Government at various levels existed to selectively prosecute blacks. . . . They drew the conclusion that blacks had rioted aboard that ship and at that point were totally blinded to any other possibility. And that was the reason, Your Honor, we have the vast preponderance of white statements. We have the fact that no rights were ever given to any whites and we have the fact that all of these incidents involving blacks were never investigated. . . . [The] obliviousness on the part of many individuals that took part in this . . . resulted in this type of selective prosecution . . . this type of attitude on the part of the Government from the very beginning that led to these charges against 21 blacks, and then the only charge being brought against a white being a delayed charge.[79]

The hearing on our selective prosecution motion took four days with eight witnesses, including *Kitty Hawk*'s XO, Commander Cloud. The trial transcript ran to 247 pages. Immediately after I finished my closing argument, the military judge issued his ruling.

> I think that . . . in the initial phase of the investigation, there was some lack of professionalism shown, that may be understandable also. However, . . . I don't think [that] goes to the crux of the matter, and the motion to dismiss because of selective prosecution is denied.[80]

There you have it in a nutshell. No selective prosecution of Black sailors. No racial bias in the investigation. No racial discrimination in leveling charges. Just a perfectly "understandable" and entirely excusable "lack of professionalism."

PART IV

TRIAL OUTCOMES
AND BEYOND

17

FINDING JUSTICE

A ll's well that ends well." We've heard that uplifting phrase of
encouragement often enough, but does it apply in real life?

The accused in the military justice system are brought to trial fairly
quickly, usually within a few weeks after charges are sworn out against
them. The *Kitty Hawk* trials were an exception because of the sheer
number of defendants and the complexity of their cases. The first trial
began in late December 1972, and the last one ended in early April
1973. Ten different judges presided over the trials and 165 witnesses
were called.[1] Seventeen witnesses testified in the Cleveland Mallory trial
alone.

Mallory's case was the second one to go to trial. Because of his unjust
conviction by Judge Bryant, in all remaining cases the defendants elected
to have jury panels decide their fate. No more judge alone. The Mallory
case also had a lasting impact on our defense team. Our outrage over
that injustice made us vow that nothing like it would happen again.
We defense lawyers often felt like the entire military justice system
was arrayed against us and our clients. And who could blame us, with
our clients locked up in the brig for months and with all the obstacles
thrown in the way of our defending them?

Those barriers included selective prosecution of twenty-five Black
sailors and only one white sailor, a strongly biased and one-sided investigation, the withholding of critical evidence from our defense team, a

265

military judge who had denied every one of our motions, and a convening authority who bucked us all the way following his threat to remove me as defense counsel.

Despite all those obstacles, in retrospect, I feel that some semblance of justice ultimately prevailed. That only happened because of the efforts and dogged determination of the entire defense team, and because our clients trusted us and worked with us every step of the way.

Twenty-three Black sailors faced special courts-martials in San Diego—the original twenty-one who were flown in, plus two more who were charged after *Kitty Hawk* arrived.

Seven of them entered into plea agreements and pled guilty to one or more reduced charges. In return, the government dismissed all other charges against them and agreed to minimal sentences.

The remaining sixteen pled not guilty.

Six of them were totally exonerated—three had all charges dismissed before their trials, two were acquitted of all charges at their trials, and Cleveland Mallory had his conviction reversed on appeal.

The remaining ten were found guilty of one or more offenses, but every one of them also received a minimal sentence.

As previously stated, a bad-conduct discharge is the most severe of possible special courts-martial sentences. None of the defendants, however, received a BCD except for Mallory, and his was reversed.

Just as each of the *Kitty Hawk* defendants was unique in his own way, each of their courts-martial cases followed its own course to resolution.

Falling Dominoes

Many antiwar protestors blamed the Vietnam quagmire on the "domino theory" voiced by many politicians in the 1960s. The "hawks," the prowar advocates, advanced the theory that if America allowed one country to fall to communism, others would inevitably follow. Therefore, they argued, we must keep every country, large or small, out of communist hands. The hawks held sway over the "doves" in national politics for most of the sixties, and millions of young Americans were sent off to Vietnam and put in harm's way.

Sometimes, however, falling dominoes can be a good thing, as they were in some *Kitty Hawk* courts-martial cases. The initial toppling domino was the NAACP's national press conference in New York City the morning of February 23, 1973. Its disclosure of the Laurie perjury tapes unleashed a rush of nationwide news. Little did we know that the perjury tapes would have repercussions far beyond our most optimistic expectations.

———

Date: 23 February 1973
Time: 1300H
Location: San Diego Naval Station Law Center

Airman Perry Mason was from Los Angeles and had been aboard *Kitty Hawk* about two months at the time of the incident. He was an airman attached to the ship's permanent company—that is, not part of the temporarily deployed air wing. Before the incident, he reported he was assaulted by a white sailor who knocked his food tray out of his hand. Another time, his shoes were thrown overboard by a white petty officer. The response? In his words, "nothing happened."[2]

After the 12 October incident, Mason was charged with rioting and with assaulting Aviation Ordnanceman Third Class Unland in the hangar bay, the same incident that gave rise to charges against Cleveland Mallory. The only government witness against him was the alleged victim, Unland. Mason's trial was set to begin the afternoon of 23 February, just hours after news broke of Laurie's perjury tapes. Mason's defense counsel, Lieutenant Glenn Haase, was visiting with him in his office just before the trial when he received a call from the prosecutor. All charges against Mason were being dropped. Haase was understandably surprised, and Mason was elated.[3]

Haase later learned that the charges were dropped because Unland retracted his prior statements just before the trial was to begin, saying he was no longer sure of his identification of Mason as his assailant.[4] Was it just a coincidence that Unland was a good friend of Airman Michael Laurie,[5] who committed perjury?

The first of the dominoes had toppled.

———————————

Date: 27 February 1973
Time: 15300H
Location: Naval Station Correctional Center

Four days later, Admiral Staring, the Navy's top lawyer, arrived in San Diego to have a serious talk with Captain McKenzie. He was sent because of the just-disclosed perjury tapes and the NAACP's federal lawsuit. By coincidence, he arrived the same day that Mallory's conviction was reversed and Mason's charges were dismissed. That sequence of events undoubtedly helped trigger the release later that day of the six defendants still in the brig.

The second of the dominoes had fallen.

———————————

Seaman Apprentice Willie Faison was a young Black man from Alabama, barely out of his teens when the *Kitty Hawk* turmoil erupted. He was assaulted that night by a white marine, an assault he duly reported. No follow-up ensued, however, even though he said he could identify his attacker. He was not accused of committing any offense himself, and so remained aboard the ship when it sailed for San Diego.

However, as the carrier pulled into the North Island Naval Air Station on 27 November 1972, Willie Faison committed an offense that Captain Townsend considered so reprehensible it could not be ignored. *Time* magazine reported on the story:

The aircraft carrier *Kitty Hawk* nosed into the waters of San Diego harbor last week to end a marathon 9½-month tour at sea and to face a bitter post-mortem on one of the worst race riots in modern naval history. The sights and the sounds of the homecoming were mostly friendly, with helium-filled OPERATION WELCOME balloons lifting off the pier and mothers of crewmen's children born since the ship sailed waving from a special stand. But as the giant vessel came to port, two black crewmen, framed against the disk of the radar screen, lifted their fists in the black power salute.[6]

One of those Black crewmen was Seaman Apprentice Faison. Much to his dismay, the *Time* magazine article included that photo of the two men with raised fists. The rest of the article was not kind to Captain Townsend, and he was not happy about seeing two of his sailors flashing Black power salutes from the deck of his ship.[7]

When the ship pulled into the dock, Captain Townsend was quoted by a reporter: "There was no evidence of racial discrimination aboard the Kitty Hawk."[8] The very next day, however, Townsend summoned Willie Faison to a captain's mast and found him guilty. The charge? Lieutenant Martin testified Faison disobeyed a general order because the photo showed he was "out of uniform."[9]

A newspaper reported that several sailors around Faison were also wearing dungarees, and that "Mark Meyers, free-lance photographer who took the picture on assignment for *Time* magazine, said Lieutenant Martin asked him for a blow-up of the photo but he refused."[10]

The *New York Times* published more details:

> Officially . . . Willie Faison was convicted in a captain's mast proceeding for violation of a lawful order, the Navy said. It was alleged that he wore dungarees when the ship's plan of the day called for "a proper blue uniform" in areas visible to the public, and that he was in a restricted, dangerous radar area. News pictures when the carrier entered port showed Capt. Marland W. Townsend, commander of the *Kitty Hawk*, and behind him against a radar

dish were several sailors with fists raised. The Navy said that Seaman Faison was not tried on any charge relating to a salute.[11]

The absurdity of the charge, and the actual reason for it, was not lost on Faison. Since he was tried at a captain's mast, he was not entitled to counsel. Captain Townsend fined him, busted him in rank, and gave him thirty days' brig confinement.[12]

Unfortunately, Faison's troubles were just beginning. On the following day, new criminal charges were preferred against him,[13] this time because of an offense he allegedly committed two months earlier while being questioned about the *Kitty Hawk* incident. He was charged with committing perjury based on his testimony at a pretrial hearing.[14] What had he allegedly lied about? He said he witnessed white sailors attacking Commander Cloud that evening. The XO had in fact testified he had been knocked down after a "collision" with a group of white sailors during which he was threatened.[15]

I was assigned to represent Faison and, during a later hearing, I had a chance to question Lieutenant Martin about the remarkable sequence of events over that three-day period. First, Faison's photo in a national magazine, then captain's mast for being out of uniform, and then court-martial charges for perjury dating back to the previous October.

> Q: On the 13th of December he was referred to court-martial out of an offense arising on 12 October?

> A: Yes.

> Q: And that was just a coincidence that that happened right after the mast?

> A: Yes.[16]

Within a few days of being charged with perjury, Faison had yet another charge leveled at him. The new one also dated back to the

October incident. A white sailor gave a sworn statement on 10 February 1973 that Faison had assaulted him four months earlier during the October incident. My cocounsel Mike Pancer[17] looked at the new charges and said, "They're looking for Faison."[18] I did not disagree. Faison was clearly being targeted because of his raised clenched fist in the *Time* magazine photo.

Faison's trial was scheduled for the afternoon of 7 March 1973, two weeks after the perjury tape bombshell hit the streets, and while that story was still getting regular media play. The morning of the trial, Pancer and I were in my office waiting to talk to the sole government witness on the assault charge. We wanted to ask why he waited four months to come forward with his accusation against our client. He was very nervous when he arrived, and initially kept evading my questions. When I asked him what was going on, he finally blurted out, "I can't identify Faison!" He said he was never sure it was Faison from the beginning and now realized he couldn't testify that it was him.[19]

Pancer told him it was not a problem, just testify to what you know. But that didn't settle him down. He explained that he identified Faison as the assailant three previous times. The first, at the XO's screening mast; then, at captain's mast; and finally, in his early February sworn statement. He said Captain Townsend asked him during the captain's mast if he could find any more witnesses to back up his identification.[20] He couldn't.

Even with that additional information, we still didn't understand why he was so nervous. Finally, he asked, "Can they get me for perjury?"[21] Now it all fell into place. He must have heard the news of Laurie's perjury. He was concerned if he testified at trial that his identification was in doubt, he might be charged with perjury for contradicting his prior sworn statements.

Pancer and I just looked at each other in disbelief. I told the witness he needed to immediately talk to the prosecutor, as our trial was about to begin. He did so, and within thirty minutes the prosecutor told us all of Faison's charges would be dropped.[22] I saw the witness as he was leaving the law center, and he said the prosecutor was not happy with him.[23]

The third domino had toppled.

Seaman Apprentice James Allen was from the small town of Louisville in Alabama. Its population of five hundred was about evenly split between Black and white residents, and in small-town Alabama in the 1950s, evenly split was probably an apt expression. Segregation prevailed. When Allen was two years old, Martin Luther King Jr. became pastor of the Dexter Avenue Baptist Church just up the road in Montgomery.

Allen came aboard *Kitty Hawk* in early 1972 and, after the incident, was charged with rioting and three assault counts. His defense attorney was NAACP-retained Dennis Kelly who had just completed his JAG Corps tour of duty. With that background, Kelly knew just what buttons to push. He advised the prosecutors he planned to file another selective prosecution motion, a motion my cocounsel and I had pursued twice before without success. We had called Commander Cloud and Lieutenant Martin as witnesses, but Kelly told the prosecutors he intended to call Captain Townsend personally as a witness and challenge his onboard decision to charge only Black sailors.[24] At the same time, the prosecutor decided not to have Airman Laurie, one of Allen's accusers, testify.[25] It was clearly no coincidence that the Laurie perjury tapes had been released to the public just a few days earlier. Shortly after, all charges against Allen were quietly dismissed.

The fourth domino had fallen.

Plea Agreements

Pretrial plea agreements in the military are different from those in civilian criminal courts. In civilian courts, a plea agreement case usually ends with the judge handing out the sentence agreed to in the plea. In the military, however, the defendant has the option of proceeding to a sentencing hearing after he enters his guilty plea. The jury is told of the guilty plea but is not told a plea agreement even exists.

The plea agreement caps the maximum sentence the defendant will receive. After the jury hands down its sentence, the defendant gets the benefit of the lesser of that sentence or the terms of his prior plea agreement. Thus, if the jury sentence is a bad-conduct discharge and a $500 fine, but the pretrial agreement limits any fine to $750 and precludes a BCD, the defendant receives a $500 fine and no discharge.

The government may offer plea agreements for a variety of reasons. For example, they may do so to obtain convictions when they are nervous about their prospects at trial, or to move cases quickly through the system with a minimum of time and effort.

Defendants have their own reasons to accept plea agreements. They include pleading guilty to lesser charges in exchange for the withdrawal of more serious charges and capping maximum sentences. The *Kitty Hawk* defendants had two additional compelling reasons to enter into plea agreements.

The first reason was that Mallory's case was the second one to go to trial. At the end of all the evidence, he was found guilty in what everyone thought would be a slam-dunk acquittal. Well, everyone but the judge. If Mallory could be convicted despite an airtight alibi and completely discredited witnesses, what chance would other *Kitty Hawk* defendants have in their cases? They feared that they might also suffer an unjust conviction.

The second reason was equally compelling. Most had been languishing in the brig for months awaiting their trials, and if a proffered plea agreement included immediate release from incarceration, and a minimal sentence, it was hard to resist. In fact, the first defendant to enter into a plea agreement even agreed to plead guilty to rioting.

One airman was offered an irresistible deal by Captain McKenzie. In exchange for a guilty plea to rioting, he would be immediately released from his seventy days and counting of brig incarceration and receive an early out and a ticket home with an honorable discharge.[26] Why did McKenzie make such an offer? By doing so, he did not risk an acquittal at trial, and he got a conviction on a riot charge, which the press dutifully reported. The local newspaper also quoted one of our defense team saying the defendant "pleaded guilty to riot because he was so fed up that he would do anything to get out of confinement and obtain his honorable discharge."[27]

Seaman Apprentice Durward Davis was originally charged with rioting and an assault on a white sailor in a berthing compartment.[28] After his arrival in San Diego, three additional assault counts were added to his Charge Sheet. As previously noted, Davis was the sailor attacked by five white sailors as he was walking down a passageway but who was then rescued by fellow Black sailors.

At his special court-martial trial, he was represented by his initial counsel,[29] and also by an individual military counsel, JAG Lieutenant Bruce Locke. Locke secured a pretrial agreement in which Davis would plead guilty to the original single assault, and a breach of peace. In return, the government dismissed the other three assaults and the riot charge.[30]

In the sentencing phase of Davis's trial, the white sailor he had struck testified that the assault took place in a darkened berthing compartment as a group of Black sailors came through. By coincidence, the victim knew Davis from before. Earlier, the victim had served time in the ship's brig and was released on a work party where Davis worked. During their time together, Davis was very kind to him, even buying him cigarettes and Cokes.[31] The victim testified that Davis's actions during the assault were so out of character that something must have set him off. He did not know of the assault earlier that evening that Davis had suffered at the hands of the white sailors, an assault that was never investigated.

The three-member jury panel returned a sentence of forty-five days' restriction, a fine of $408, and reduced Davis in rank from E-2 to E-1. He was offered an early out but chose to finish out his tour and later served honorably aboard the carrier USS *Oriskany*.[32]

I represented two other clients who accepted plea agreements that guaranteed them a very light sentence and a promised early out of the Navy with an honorable discharge.

One was a third class petty officer[33] who agreed to plead guilty to two assaults, and his riot charges were dismissed. At his sentencing hearing on 5 February 1973, he received additional time in the brig. However, he was then given an early out and returned home to Colorado with an honorable discharge.[34]

My other client was the seaman recruit who testified he spent a hundred days in maximum security, with over half of that time in solitary.[35] He pled guilty to two assaults, one against a brig marine guard who was forcing his friend into an adjacent cell.[36] After his 12 February 1973 sentencing hearing, he was released from the brig and, three weeks later, went home to Pennsylvania with an early out, clutching his honorable discharge.[37] He had been on active duty just over a year.

Not Guilty Pleas

Third Class Petty Officer Hiram Davis[38] was the first of the *Kitty Hawk* defendants to go on trial. His civilian attorney, Alex Landon, said Davis experienced racism on *Kitty Hawk* at a level he had never experienced growing up in Los Angeles. That included being on the receiving end of racial slurs and other personal insults. He often felt helpless and threatened during those encounters, especially since he received no support from his superiors.[39]

The evening of the October incident, Davis was walking through the ship and encountered a white crew member. What ensued was the subject of conflicting testimony between the two sailors. Davis was charged with rioting, assault, and unlawful detention of the white sailor. The alleged victim was never charged.

Davis stood trial on 29 December 1972 and elected to go "judge alone," with Judge Bryant, the same judge who heard Cleveland Mallory's case a few days later. Just before the trial, the law center director said he considered Davis's case the weakest of the *Kitty Hawk* cases and questioned why he was even charged.[40]

Judge Bryant acquitted Davis of the riot and assault charges but found him guilty of "unlawful detention." Davis was given a $450 fine and reduced from pay grade E-4 to E-3. Unlawful detention under the *UCMJ* provides that "any person subject to this chapter who, except as provided by law, apprehends, arrests, or confines any person shall be punished as a court-martial may direct."[41] Davis never arrested or confined anyone, but did he "apprehend" his alleged victim?

Davis's attorney, Alex Landon, commented on the unexpected and inconsistent verdict in a posttrial television interview:

> I was unhappy that he was found guilty of unlawful apprehension, the military judge found him not guilty of assault which basically was surrounded by the same incident that the unlawful apprehension comes from. It's sort of a shame on the facts that were presented. . . . The only testimony that he apprehended the individual was that of the witness, . . . and [his] testimony was not believed for purposes of the assault, so a . . . logical extension of that would be a not-guilty finding on the apprehension.[42]

Seaman Arnold Petty was a soft-spoken nineteen-year-old from Philadelphia. He joined the Navy within weeks of graduating from high school. His timing wasn't the best, as he came aboard *Kitty Hawk* just a month before the incident.

His was one of the first cases to come to trial, on 11 January 1973. He had been charged with rioting and a single assault on a white sailor. Petty flatly denied the assault. The alleged victim testified he was attacked in a small ship's compartment by Petty. He claimed Petty aggressively jumped up and down during the assault.

His lawyer was Lieutenant Haase, who had earlier contacted the ship's legal office to arrange to come aboard, only to find himself talking to the alleged victim. Haase showed the jurors pictures of the compartment in question, which had a very low overhead. He then had Petty stand up, all six foot five of him. Seaman Petty was acquitted of all charges.[43]

After a dozen trials had concluded, our defense team was feeling very optimistic. One of our defense team members told me, "Sure, we're getting tired, but I think we're wearing [the government] down, too, and they'll give up before we do."[44] I had to agree, as I dictated that day in my personal record, "All the [prosecution] cases are slowly crumbling."[45]

Airman Apprentice Vernell Robinson worked aboard *Kitty Hawk* in a small cubicle one deck below the hangar bay. He was in charge of the aircraft parts inventory, which he signed out to aircraft maintenance personnel. The night of the incident, he locked up his cubicle and went to the aft mess to eat. Afterwards, he stuck around to play a card game, bid whist, with his buddies. When he left, he witnessed a Black sailor and a white sailor scuffling in the passageway.

He thought they were just horsing around, but then he saw more of the same from others and realized fights were breaking out. When Commander Cloud ordered the marines and Black sailors to opposite ends of the ship, he knew the fighting must be widespread. He never saw any weapons, never saw any double-teaming during the assaults, but he heard plenty of profanity and ethnic slurs. He was never personally assaulted and thought it was because the white sailors recognized him, or because he was several inches shorter than most.[46]

After he returned with the ship to San Diego, he was inexplicably charged with rioting and with assaults on two white sailors during the October incident. He had three lawyers in his corner, with Lieutenant Tom Phillips as his lead counsel.[47] He was the lawyer who quelled the brig confrontation when the defendants first arrived at the Naval station brig.

Phillips was immediately impressed with Robinson and found him to be mature for his twenty-one years, well mannered, and very likable. After hearing Robinson's version of the night's events aboard *Kitty Hawk*, Phillips was convinced he was defending an innocent man. Phillips said they relied on two defenses: First, an alibi. Robinson was playing cards with his buddies in the aft mess when the assault occurred. Second, they raised what he called his SODDI defense—Some Other Dude Did It.[48]

His case went to trial on 4 April 1973 and was heard by a jury panel of three Navy officers and presided over by a marine lieutenant colonel.[49] At the outset, the marine military judge kept referring to "Captain Phillips" when addressing Lieutenant Phillips. The mistake was understandable because the rank insignia of both Marine captains and Navy lieutenants are similar. Navy captains, however, sport four stripes, not just two. Phillips could see that being called "captain" rankled the Navy officers on the jury who were senior to him. He approached the bench, the judge apologized, and everything sailed along smoothly after that.

Robinson's seventeen-year-old wife came to San Diego from Chicago and sat behind him during the trial.[50] His defense team filed a pretrial motion to dismiss the charges because of an alleged delay in prosecution, since he was being tried more than five months after the incident. That motion was denied.[51] However, one of the government eyewitnesses identified someone else as the assailant in one of the assaults, and they were off to a running start.

The alleged victim in another assault did identify Robinson as his assailant, but on cross-examination he revealed his feelings about Black people. Robinson remembers the victim insisting he was not racially prejudiced, but then volunteered he would never live next door to a Black person.[52]

Robinson took the stand and testified that he was playing cards at the time of the assault, and then his lawyers played their own trump card. They produced another Black *Kitty Hawk* sailor who came into the courtroom—not to testify, but only to be seen. He bore a resemblance to Robinson so striking that it completely discredited the government's eyewitness identification testimony.

Phillips and his cocounsel also called several of Robinson's card-playing buddies to support his alibi. His division officer then testified that Robinson consistently received the top 4.0 ratings on all his fitness reports, and Robinson's young wife testified as to his good character.

According to a subsequent newspaper report, the jury panel returned their verdict in eighteen minutes.[53] Not guilty. At that point, Robinson shook the hands of his defense team, walked up and shook the hands of each of the jurors, and then even shook the hands of the prosecutors.[54] The military judge and court reporter must have felt left out.

Robinson wanted to return to the *Kitty Hawk* but was denied that option, with no explanation given, even though he was acquitted of all charges. Instead, he was offered an early out with an honorable discharge, or transfer to an undesirable duty station. He took the early out and returned home to Chicago.[55]

Airman Apprentice Ronald Glover had an unbelievable night aboard *Kitty Hawk*. And to top it all off, he was court-martialed. I represented him at his trial.

Glover had been assaulted by the marines on the hangar bay. He was struck in the head and face with a nightstick, and with his mouth and forehead bleeding, stumbled into Commander Cloud's compartment. The XO sent him to sick bay, where his troubles multiplied. He was the sailor who tried to leave the treatment room to keep from having needles stuck in his head. As he struggled to leave, a marine struck him in the face with a nightstick, opening up another bleeding wound. Glover grabbed a broom handle and started swinging it blindly before ending up on the floor, where the marine corporal said he "bit [Glover] as hard as I could on the leg"[56] so he could identify him later.

One week later, while he was still recovering from his injuries, Glover filed a formal request to be discharged from the Navy. He was so desperate to get out he was willing to accept an undesirable discharge. In his request, he said, "I joined the Navy . . . mostly as a way to see the world. I have an older brother who was in the army. . . . My family consists of my mother, five brothers, and five sisters."[57]

Glover then described the injuries he received during the night's incident: "I got hit on the head so hard that it took eight or nine stiches to close it. . . . Getting put in the sick bed with my head split open, and a hurt back where someone pounded me with a stick is enough punishment. . . . The whole experience has made me afraid and bitter, and I do not expect that my attitude will change. I just do not want to have anything more to do with the Navy, even if it means I get an undesirable discharge."[58]

His request was sent up through the chain of command where it was summarily recommended for denial at every level, including by Captain McKenzie.[59] The denial letter stated, "I do not believe that the approval of your request would serve the interests of justice, or the best interests of the parties concerned. Accordingly, your request is denied."[60]

Glover was charged with rioting, three assaults in a berthing compartment, and two assaults in sick bay, including an assault on the marine corporal who bit him. No one was ever investigated or charged with inflicting Glover's injuries. During my trial preparation, I interviewed several white sailors who were present during the berthing compartment incident. Three of them knew Glover personally.

One said Glover was "nice, quiet, well liked, and never said anything against whites."[61] Another said Glover was "not the type to ever get in a fight. I never saw him do anything [during the berthing incident]." That government witness testified that Glover actually tried to help him during the incident.[62] A third white sailor told me he had known Glover since he came aboard and said Glover "always had fun and jokes a lot and everyone got along with him." He said Glover was "not the type you would expect" to commit an assault.[63]

At his 1 March 1973 trial the jurors acquitted Glover of rioting and also found him not guilty on all but one of the five assaults. They found him guilty of striking a corpsman in sick bay as he was blindly flailing about but acquitted him of an assault on the marine who bit him.[64] They sentenced him to reduction from E-2 to E-1, a $342 fine, and one month of additional brig time. He had already served 112 days in pretrial confinement.[65] Mercifully, he was offered an early out and, within two weeks of his trial, left the Navy with an honorable discharge.[66]

Airman Apprentice James Jackson had been aboard *Kitty Hawk* a little over a year at the time of the incident, having enlisted at age nineteen. After the incident, he was charged with rioting, two counts of assault, and one count of disrespect. His defense counsel argued that the rioting charge should be dismissed, as being overly broad and vague. The military judge agreed and dismissed that charge.[67] Jackson's trial began 2 February 1973.

JAG Lieutenant Jim Bradley prosecuted the Jackson case and remembers it well. He was one of the two JAG officers who had flown out to the *Kitty Hawk* along with Milt Silverman.[68]

A petty officer testified that several Black sailors, including Jackson, came into his berthing compartment and began accosting white sailors in their racks.[69] A white sailor responded by squaring off with Jackson, striking him in the head with his fist. That sailor testified that Jackson left, returned, and threw a metal pump handle at another sailor, fortunately missing him.[70]

Bradley brought a similar pump handle into the courtroom to use as demonstrative evidence. He carried it concealed in a brown paper bag, leaving many to wonder what was in it. They soon found out when the bag accidentally fell off the table onto the floor, startling the judge and jury. Defense counsel were convinced he dropped it on purpose for dramatic effect.

The jurors ultimately found Jackson guilty of two counts of assault and the charge of disrespect, which is committed if someone "behaves with disrespect" toward a superior commissioned officer.[71]

The jury sentenced Jackson to fifteen days' restriction, a $600 fine, and reduction from E-2 to E-1. However, the military judge suspended the fine and rank reduction, so he effectively received just two weeks' restriction.[72] By then, however, Jackson had already suffered through more than three months of pretrial confinement in the brig.

One *Kitty Hawk* trial that resulted in an outright acquittal deserves special mention. That case is unique for two reasons: one, because of the identity of the accused; and two, because of the identity of the prosecutor.

The accused was Airman William Boone. An assault allegation had been made against him immediately after the incident, and he appeared at a captain's mast on 31 October 1972. Captain Townsend took no action on the case and three months passed before Boone was formally charged with the assault and his case referred to a special court-martial.[73]

The Boone case was prosecuted by JAG Lieutenant Mike Sheehy, who arrived in San Diego in January 1973. He had come directly from Naval Justice School, and when he reported to the Naval Station Law Center he was assigned to the prosecution wing. It was virtually unprecedented that a prosecutor assignment be given to a newly arrived JAG officer. In fact, none of us other JAG officers could recall a single time it had ever happened. As mentioned, the Navy believed in on-the-job training for first-time JAG counsel—but only by representing defendants, not the government.

When Sheehy was assigned to prosecute the Boone case, half a dozen *Kitty Hawk* cases had already gone to trial. Each had been accompanied by extensive publicity and an overflowing courtroom spectator section. Under those circumstances, and with no trial experience, Sheehy recalls the "overarching pressure" of being assigned to prosecute a *Kitty Hawk* case.[74]

He expressed his concern but was told not to worry, that he would do just fine. He then asked who would be prosecuting the case with him, as he knew all prior *Kitty Hawk* trials had at least two prosecutors, and sometimes three. To his considerable surprise, he was told he would be the sole prosecutor. He was on his own.

During the next three weeks, Sheehy handled several uncontested plea agreement cases, none of them *Kitty Hawk* trials. The Boone trial began on 12 February, and the defendant had pleaded not guilty. Sheehy recalls it as his first contested case in his then very short prosecutorial career.

Sheehy's strongest memory of the trial was the speed with which the jury returned its verdict of not guilty. They had been out mere minutes. He remembered feeling that the jurors had only enough time to walk back to the jury room, take a vote, and return.[75]

The Boone case was unique for one other very important reason: the defendant was the only white sailor referred to trial in the entire *Kitty Hawk* affair.[76] How fortunate that the sole white sailor's case was prosecuted by the newest guy on the block who had no experience in contested cases and no supporting cocounsel. Few were probably surprised that a not-guilty verdict was returned in minutes.[77]

Equal justice anyone?

Final Tally on the Riot Charges

Twenty-three Black *Kitty Hawk* sailors were charged with rioting. Two were tried aboard the *Kitty Hawk* in November 1972, and both were acquitted of their riot charges. Only two of the remaining twenty-one sailors charged with rioting were found guilty in contested case trials.[78] One received a $700 fine and a reduction in rank.[79] The other just a $600 fine.[80]

With only two out of twenty-three found guilty of rioting in contested cases, it would be hard to imagine a sterner rebuke of the decision to charge all the sailors with rioting.

Early in my representation of my clients, I came to believe the riot charges were a complete overreaction to what actually occurred the night of the incident. I felt the defendants should have been charged only with assaults. Had that been done, their cases could have—should have—been disposed of on board at captain's masts as had been done by Captain Townsend in all assault cases he presided over before the incident.

One final irony of Townsend's decision to swear out riot charges cannot go unmentioned. The only two defendants convicted of rioting following their contested cases received sentences that Townsend himself would undoubtedly consider lenient if he had handled their cases at captain's masts. And he would have avoided all the adverse publicity that ensued.

The outcomes on the riot charges were not really surprising, given that a riot conviction required proof that the accused was a member of an assembly of three or more persons who mutually intended to unlawfully commit a "tumultuous disturbance of the peace" in a violent or turbulent manner. They further required proof that the accused's actions terrorized others or that they were intended to cause alarm or terror.[81]

In short, a riot conviction required proof of a unified effort with a specific intent to incite terror. The randomized assaults that evening hardly met those criteria. JAG Lieutenant Smith, one of the defense counsel who was flown aboard *Kitty Hawk* shortly after the October incident, challenged the riot charges at a pretrial hearing on the ship:

> The government has a responsibility here, I believe, as it does at every pre-trial investigation, to winnow out the baseless charges. I think that . . . this is going to take some extra work by the government and that extra work is certainly demanded by a system that operates on equal justice under the law. . . . Defense submits that hearsay, rumors, gossip, certainly surround these events, and has a tendency, very unfortunately, to blow them up into something bigger than they are, which Defense submits is a breach of the peace, that is, individual fights scattered around the ship. Certainly no evidence has been submitted by the government of a furtherance of a common purpose, which is one of the elements of a riot. . . . What went on seemed so disorganized, so randomized around the different parts of the ship, it seemed to really be more of a reaction to confrontations between the MAA force and between the Marines and between individuals.[82]

No better summation could be made of how the Navy overreacted and overcharged the young Black sailors, and Lieutenant Smith's words continued to resonate throughout the subsequent trials.

I saw one very positive outcome of the entire *Kitty Hawk* affair, and it came from none other than Chief of Naval Operations Admiral Zumwalt. The man was a larger-than-life figure who at age forty-nine became the youngest CNO in history. Appointed in 1970, he championed modernizing the Navy fleet and "humanizing" the lives of sailors in order to bolster the retention of young sailors.[83] He also declared from the outset that he saw "significant discrimination" in the Navy, and immediately instituted several minority and human relations programs. Many of his revolutionary changes came about through his "Z-grams." In an early one, he declared, "Ours must be a Navy family that recognizes no artificial barriers of race, color or religion. There is no black Navy, no white Navy—just one Navy—the United States Navy."[84]

Before long, however, Zumwalt expressed dissatisfaction that his race relations programs were not being carried out. His frustration grew and finally reached a breaking point in the wake of the incident aboard the *Kitty Hawk*, and an occurrence three weeks later involving *Kitty Hawk*'s sister ship, the carrier USS *Constellation*.[85] In that incident, 120 protesting Black crew members sat down on the dock at the North Island Naval Air Station and refused to board the ship because of grievances very similar to those expressed by Kitty Hawk's Black sailors.[86]

Zumwalt's top advisor on race relations stated, "Tensions are approaching the flashpoint because reforms are not keeping pace with the rising expectations of blacks in the Navy."[87]

Zumwalt assembled a group of Navy admirals in the Washington, DC, area for what might be considered a "dressing down" on the race relations issue. He told them the Navy had made "unacceptable progress" in race matters and "the reason for this failure was not the programs but the fact they were not being used" and that "equal means exactly that, equal."[88]

And he was just getting started.

Zumwalt then issued an "unprecedented order telling all commands that, in effect, their careers may depend on how quickly they move to improve conditions for the growing numbers of blacks now serving in the fleet."[89] Never one to mince words, he stated that he "invites Navy officers who do not view improved race relations as their critical duty right now to retire from the service."[90]

18

PERJURY ON TRIAL

Date: 20 September 1973
Time: 0635H
Location: San Diego Naval Station Law Center

Dawn was just breaking over our Linda Vista apartment, but I had already been up and about for over an hour. I had trouble sleeping. Today would be my last day in court in the *Kitty Hawk* saga. Not as a lawyer this time but as a witness.

The trial would also be the end cap of the Mallory trial nine months earlier. Had it really been that long? It was. Mallory was wrongfully convicted on 4 January 1973, Billy Hicks had gone undercover two weeks later, and three weeks after that Hicks had taped Airman Laurie admitting to perjury.

Mallory, Hicks, and Laurie. Where were they now? Mallory was back home in Pittsburgh with his mother and younger twin siblings. Hicks had graduated from California Western School of Law and was just starting his legal career. And Laurie? Well, I was going to see Laurie this morning, for the first time since Mallory's trial. And that is why I had trouble sleeping.

The NAACP's New York City press conference was on 23 February 1973, and immediately after wrapping up they sent a telegram to Captain McKenzie informing him of the perjury tapes.[1] That evening,

286

Ben James called me to say he talked to McKenzie and asked him to charge Laurie with perjury, using the tapes as evidence.[2] He said McKenzie responded politely, but firmly, saying he didn't think his office had jurisdiction to bring perjury charges.

Besides, he told James, Laurie was on leave.[3] Really? How could the CO of the Naval air station have known the present duty status of a single sailor among perhaps a thousand under his command? He could if he, or someone on his staff, was still in direct contact with Laurie.

McKenzie's stated lack of jurisdiction was absurd, given that his office had sworn out perjury charges against my client Willie Faison several months earlier. As convening authority for the *Kitty Hawk* trials, he had complete authority over the cases, wherever that might lead.

Shortly after, I began my own efforts to get someone—anyone—to bring perjury charges against Laurie. I talked with a law center prosecutor who had no connection to the Mallory trial, knowing he had no conflict of interest. He demurred, saying it wasn't his decision to make.[4] Since military prosecutors don't personally swear out charges, he was technically correct. However, we both knew prosecutors sometimes influenced who was charged and at what level. They were the ones, after all, who had to take those charges to court.

I then decided to go directly to the source and contacted Captain McKenzie. As he had done with Ben James earlier, he politely but firmly said he doubted his jurisdiction over Laurie's perjury. I reminded him that he had sworn out perjury charges against my client Willie Faison. That didn't faze him in the least. Then, to add insult to injury, he suggested I take the perjury case to the San Diego County District Attorney's office.[5] He was well aware that a civilian county prosecutor's office lacked jurisdiction over a crime committed on a federal military base.

I next approached two other JAG officers who might convince McKenzie to charge Laurie. I talked to McKenzie's staff judge advocate and also to the San Diego Naval Station Law Center director. Both also demurred, claiming the undercover agent's testimony about Laurie's admissions would be uncorroborated, and thus inadmissible.[6] They were referring to a quirk in US law known as the "two-witness" rule that applied to crimes of perjury. Broadly stated, an accused can be convicted of a major crime such as murder on the testimony of a single witness, but one cannot be convicted of perjury, at least not without other evidence.

In military and civilian law, however, a single witness with other "corroborating" evidence will support a conviction. That rule is explicitly stated in the *Manual for Courts-Martial.*[7] In Laurie's case they had Billy Hicks's testimony, as well as Laurie's taped admissions. When I pointed that out to the two JAG officers, they still resisted, this time claiming the perjury tapes had too many lapses with unintelligible conversations.[8] I was surprised and disappointed at the director's response, in particular, because up until then he had supported our defense team.

I even struck out with Captain Merryman, the commodore who had reversed Mallory's conviction. Surely, he would be sympathetic. To my exasperation, not even he would touch the case, even though he could have sworn out charges by simply taking on the role of a convening authority.[9]

If ever there was a time to be paranoid about what was going on behind the scenes in the Navy hierarchy, this was certainly it. I was now convinced that at some level of authority, word had come down that Laurie was not to be touched. Was someone concerned that if he was charged, he might reveal something best kept under wraps about his perjury, about his totally inappropriate duty assignment to the convening authority's legal office, or even something else?

As I made the rounds of the Navy's senior brass trying to get someone to charge Laurie, I must have struck a chord somewhere. Much to my surprise, I learned that the Naval Investigative Service (NIS)[10] had begun quietly pursuing an investigation into Laurie's perjury. In March 1973 the NIS agents questioned the two Mallory prosecutors. Both submitted sworn statements saying they were completely unaware that Laurie had committed perjury when he testified.[11] Under the circumstances, I had absolutely no reason to doubt them, especially since I personally knew both to be honorable men.

It took another month before the NIS questioned Lieutenant Martin, *Kitty Hawk*'s legal officer. In his 6 April 1973 NIS statement he said, "I personally believe that Laurie did not perjure himself."[12] Martin gave that sworn statement seven weeks after the Laurie perjury tapes had been made public.

Yet another month passed before the NIS agents questioned Airman Laurie. They read him his legal rights and advised him he was suspected of perjury in the Mallory court-martial trial. They took three separate sworn statements from him over the ensuing weeks, but he proved to be a moving target. Each time he swore under oath to the truth of his statements, his story had changed from before.

In one sworn statement on 16 May 1973, he only answered questions about his suspected drug use. He denied ever using narcotics, and said he only "experimented" with marijuana two or three times. He did admit to telling Hicks that he used hard drugs. He claimed, however, he had "just decided to give him a story," and that his admission of hard drug use was fabricated.[13]

In another sworn statement that same day, he claimed that all his testimony at the Mallory trial was true. He again insisted he met Mallory in the Hong Kong Bar and had seen him assault Unland. When shown the transcripts of his taped conversations, he freely admitted to making those contradictory statements. He claimed, however, that he suspected Hicks was an undercover agent and so started "putting him on" by giving him the "answers that he seemed to want to get."[14]

Another month passed, and on 18 June 1973, Laurie was again called in by the NIS, this time to take a polygraph test. While waiting for the test results, probably quite nervously waiting, he decided to make yet another "confession."[15] This time he admitted to lying during the trial but claimed "there was never any deliberate attempt on my part to perjure myself at the court-martial of Mallory." He did admit he had not seen Mallory in the Pussy Cat Bar and had not seen Mallory commit the alleged assault.[16]

Laurie tried to justify his perjury by saying, "I wanted to stick with [my prior statements implicating Mallory] even though it was not true because I was somewhat afraid to change my statement."[17] He further claimed he lied at the trial "because of the persistence of the ship's legal officer and investigators in asking me for positive statements or positive identifications even though I was not sure."[18]

This was the statement of someone who just admitted to committing perjury at the trial, after earlier telling the NIS he told the truth at the trial. With his latest version of his story, he tried to cast blame on others for his crime. Given what I knew by then about Laurie, I did not believe that Lieutenant Martin, nor anyone else, had actively suborned Laurie's perjury. He had proved himself quite capable of that without anyone else's help.

Sometime during the NIS investigation, Captain McKenzie was replaced as the commanding officer of the North Island Naval Air Station.[19] Even after Laurie admitted to his perjury, however, it took that replacement CO another five weeks before he swore out charges against Laurie on 23 July 1973. He referred the case to a special court-martial. Laurie's Charge Sheet included three counts of perjury in the Mallory trial and at another hearing,[20] and two counts of making false statements to the NIS agents.[21]

Captain McKenzie had insisted to the bitter end that he did not have jurisdictional authority to convene a court-martial against Laurie. His successor in command, however, knew full well he did have that authority.

The NAACP had earlier asked that Laurie be confined to the brig pending his trial. That was not to be. Not even for a day.[22] Cleveland Mallory, the innocent sailor he had falsely accused and helped convict, had served sixty-nine days in confinement awaiting his trial.

Laurie's trial was held on 20 September 1973 before a military judge,[23] and a five-member jury panel. The trial was not convened to determine Laurie's guilt or innocence. He pled guilty to the perjury and false statements charges at the opening of the proceedings; therefore, the jury's only function was to determine his sentence.

I was the only witness to appear for the government as Cleveland Mallory had already returned home to Pittsburgh. I testified about the devastating effect that Laurie's false accusations had on Mallory and how he broke down crying in my office. I told the court that shortly after his conviction, Mallory was given leave to return home to Pittsburgh while his bad-conduct discharge was being processed. I testified about the conversations I had with his mother regarding his conviction. She had told me that his conviction and bad-conduct discharge were front page news back in Pittsburgh. She said it was extremely upsetting to her and affected how her son was treated by his friends and neighbors when he returned home while awaiting the outcome of his appeal.[24]

The defense called four witnesses in mitigation, the last of whom was Laurie. He testified that before identifying Mallory as the assailant, he was shown a picture of him by Lieutenant Martin and told that Mallory had been identified by others as being at the scene.[25] Of course, as the Mallory trial showed, only Laurie placed Mallory at the scene.

He then expressed contrition for his perjury, said he harbored no antagonism toward Mallory, and was not prejudiced against Black people. He said his wife was expecting a baby in January, that he wanted to remain in the Navy, and asked not to be given a bad-conduct discharge as he wanted to make a career of the Navy.[26]

The hearing continued into the following day when the prosecutor gave his closing statement to the jury. He talked about the impact that Laurie's perjury had on Mallory and ended by saying:

> Evidence before the court is largely brought forward by people who are swearing under oath to tell the whole truth—to tell the truth, the whole truth, and nothing but the truth. Earlier today the members of this court took an oath as well as myself, as well as the defense counsel, as well as the Military Judge and court reporter, have all taken oaths to uphold the military justice system. . . . We rely upon the truth of statements that are elicited from witnesses. Where such witnesses perjure themselves, it undermines the whole system, and the severity and gravity of such perjury should be readily evident.[27]

The closing statement by Laurie's JAG defense counsel did not downplay the gravity of the offense, but painted Laurie as a naive teenager from a broken home and a high school dropout "who doesn't have a particularly high GCT."[28]

The jury of commissioned and noncommissioned officers[29] deliberated for over two hours before reaching their sentencing decision.[30] Their verdict? A reduction in rank to E-1, one month's brig time, and a bad-conduct discharge.[31] The jurors obviously recognized the seriousness of Laurie's offense. His perjury had led to the conviction of an innocent sailor who spent over two months in the brig awaiting his trial. Finally, justice was served.

Or was it?

Later that same day, we learned that Laurie had been offered a sweetheart pretrial agreement by the convening authority. In return for a guilty plea, he had been promised that a jury sentence of a bad-conduct discharge would be automatically suspended. In addition, he was promised he would not be reduced in rank more than one pay grade. As a result, the jury sentence of a bad-conduct discharge and reduction to E-1 were both nullified.[32] The hearing had lasted two days, and the five jurors had spent over two hours deliberating a sentence that was meaningless.

For me, that was the last straw. The perjurer who had helped convict an innocent man, and who had bragged about brutally assaulting Black sailors, had just escaped justice. And he had done so with the complicity of a senior Naval officer who gave him a pretrial agreement that defied all logic, and fundamental fairness. As a result, the final chapter in the *Kitty Hawk* affair could be chalked up as yet another flagrant injustice.[33]

19

REFLECTIONS

S ignificant events, historical or otherwise, are often best chronicled following the passage of time, when they can be viewed dispassionately and objectively. That is undoubtedly true of some aspects of the *Kitty Hawk* incident and its legal aftermath. The perspective that comes with time, however, does not alter the reality of the blatant injustices perpetrated against the *Kitty Hawk* defendants, which are just as indefensible and abhorrent today as they were fifty years ago.

Nevertheless, some questions about the incident invite further scrutiny. They include the underlying reasons for the outbreak of violence and the actions of those in response. Take, for example, Captain Townsend's treatment of his Black crew members in the weeks leading up to and after the *Kitty Hawk* incident. His actions were questioned and challenged, and rightfully so, but that never seemed to faze him in the least. He had a ready answer for whatever came his way, including from congressional subcommittee members. One question he could not seem to shake off, however, was, *Why didn't you go to general quarters and put a quick end to the night's tumult?*

When Condition I, better known as GQ, is called, all crew members rush to their battle stations, putting the ship in its maximum state of readiness. GQ may be called if a ship is under attack or in some other emergency condition. The order will come over the ship's intercom, usually from the ship's commanding officer, "General Quarters! General Quarters! All hands man your battle stations!"[1]

Sailors learn from basic training onward to immediately react to a GQ order. Don't try to find out what's going on, just move! In order to avoid collisions as the crew members rush to their preassigned battle stations, they follow the FUSDAP rule in using starboard or port passageways—Forward: Up and Starboard, Down: Aft and Port.

From the outset, many questioned why Townsend did not call GQ to immediately break up all groups and disperse them throughout the carrier. The ship's chief master-at-arms, in charge of security, also questioned why GQ wasn't called. "Maybe the first inkling of an incident we should go to general quarters before it gives them a chance to arm themselves."[2] A marine first sergeant said, "I'd have gone to GQ right off the bat. You have to consider people automatically do that. . . . They just do that by instinct. Like when GQ goes, a guy jumps out of the rack and habit takes over."[3]

Neither the chief nor the sergeant had probably commanded a Naval vessel, but someone who had did question Townsend's judgment. Admiral Clarey, the commander in chief of the US Pacific Fleet, commanded 290 ships and almost a quarter-million personnel. He said, "My first statement when I heard about this situation . . . was 'Why didn't they go to general quarters?' It is a perfect device we have aboard ship where everyone has a station and this is a general alarm order which gets people to go to their stations and all the watertight doors are closed until this thing has diffused."[4]

Captain Townsend responded to his critics, "One of the things that precluded my going to GQ that night, at the times I had an option to go, was that the cry on the part of the ones I called the criminal leaders was that, 'They are killing our brothers, they are killing our brothers,' and my simple argument was, 'Show me somebody being killed! Show me!'"[5] By "criminal leaders," he was referring to Black sailors who he alleged led the night's upheaval. But how was that response an answer to his critics? Did he mean the situation wasn't as dire as some were thinking?

He gave a second response that was equally perplexing because it contradicted his first response: "Whether I should have moved back to the bridge and gone to general quarters is a good question. I felt it unsafe to do that. I felt we would have had people killed if we went to GQ. I still hold to that."[6] Despite that comment, just minutes later he told the subcommittee that in the future, under the same circumstances, "We will at . . . the very earliest possible stages, go to GQ."[7]

For some, the term *mutiny* conjures up images of Marlon Brando's dramatic portrayal of First Lieutenant Fletcher Christian in the 1962 movie *Mutiny on the Bounty*. Frequently, the term is loosely tossed around in connection with the *Kitty Hawk* incident. Often, the reason is to sensationalize the account, as in the following: "The USS *Kitty Hawk* riot is the first mass mutiny in the history of the Navy and were it not for military law, the incident might be passed off as a demonstration."[8]

Even old-school Navy men could be heard talking of mutiny in connection with the *Kitty Hawk* affair. "You call it a riot, you say, but the charges were too harsh. Well, do you know what the people out here are saying, the retired Navy men on the golf course? They're not talking riot. They call it mutiny. They say they should have been charged with mutiny."[9]

During the *Kitty Hawk* trials, newspapers couldn't resist a catchy headline. A *Los Angeles Times* banner trumpeted, "*Kitty Hawk* Riot: Mutiny or Reaction to Racism?"[10] "Mutiny" spices up headlines and publication titles, but the reality of the *Kitty Hawk* incident is more mundane. Captain Townsend summarized it succinctly, "At no time was there anything that looked like a mutiny."[11] In fact, a majority of the ship's company were unaware anything was amiss at all that evening. Townsend testified to the situation, "The initial reports of the incident indicated that it was a large fight between blacks and whites, which was not true, and that made the crew very unhappy, because it was simply not accurate reporting. And, of course, the majority of the crew, as you can tell from the statements I have given you so far, simply didn't know anything was going on at all. I would say 3,000 people didn't have any idea of what was happening. There were limited people involved out of a crew of 5,000."[12]

The sheer size of *Kitty Hawk* was one reason the majority of its crew members were unaware of the incident. Just like any community of several thousand, what happened in one neighborhood might never be known in the next. In addition, communication between the carrier's "neighborhoods" was often limited.

A petty officer said many junior officers were mostly unseen throughout the evening, and for an understandable reason. He said that when the late-night confrontations erupted, most were already in their O-3 berthing spaces three levels above the hangar bay. Also, since the 1-MC, the ship's mass communication system, is muted to many berthing spaces, they wouldn't have heard the XO and CO's intercom announcements. Accordingly, "A lot of them slept right through it."[13]

The confrontations were also limited to a relatively small area of the ship. After the initial marine assaults on Black sailors in the hangar bay, virtually all other assaults occurred one and two decks below on the mess and berthing levels. That isolated the incidents in the lower, nonoperational decks. Captain Townsend said. "The way the carrier is laid out we have long fore and aft passageways on the second deck, those were the avenues of communication. A majority of the things happened in that area."[14]

That isolation of incidents was key to *Kitty Hawk* being able to continue its late-night and early-morning operational schedules. Several commanders and department heads confirmed combat operations continued uninterrupted. Flight quarters were secured at 2030 the evening of 12 October,[15] and air strikes commenced on schedule at 0800 the next morning.[16]

The operations department head stated, "After the evening meal . . . approximately 1800H on 12 October, I commenced my normal routine . . . going between strike operations . . . air operations and combat information center. . . . I saw no visual sign of disorder. It was not until the early morning hours of 13 October that I was fully aware of the disorder. . . . At NO period of time was I in doubt as to the Captain being in full command and control of the ship."[17]

That sense of control even extended to the *Kitty Hawk*'s bridge, although Captain Townsend was absent from that nerve center most of the night. The ship's navigator assumed control of the bridge at Townsend's direction. He said:

> [The Captain trusted me to] operate the ship in accordance with the established routine and his operating policies which are quite well known to me. . . . There was a confrontation between blacks and Marines and then blacks and isolated whites. The extent of these involvements was not made known to the Bridge in real time probably due to the presence of the Captain and Executive Officer in the disturbance areas.[18]

All squadron commanders of the attached Attack Carrier Air Wing Eleven likewise reported that none of their operations were affected by the disturbances in the lower decks. Their offices and berthing areas were also on the O-3 level, three levels above the hangar bay. The senior commander of the air wing was already in his berthing space and awaiting his 0445 wake-up for the scheduled morning Alpha strike when he heard Captain Townsend on the 1-MC saying the situation was in hand, so he turned in again. He said flight operations were conducted routinely the next day with no time lost because of the incident.[19]

One of the squadron commanders said that none of the aircraft were touched, even those located far forward in the hangar bay. He confirmed that at no time was the operational readiness of his squadron affected by the night's tumult. Notably, he extended praise to his squadron's Black personnel who worked full shifts, at their own request, even though they were told they were excused from work until noon the next day.[20]

Another squadron commander said no attempt was made to destroy property or aircraft belonging to his squadron and its readiness was not degraded.[21]

Judging from some sensationalist accounts of the *Kitty Hawk* incident, one might believe the ship suffered wholesale damage and destruction. The reality borders on uninteresting. Commander Cloud reported that no damage was sustained by aircraft, ordnance, or support equipment. The only damage to any compartment or space was during the initial aft mess deck incident. The XO reported damage to mess deck tables and chairs, the salad bar, and a coffee urn. The final damage tally for the entire ship came to $1,395.94.[22]

Despite many reports of a "ship-wide riot," a limited number of crew members, white and Black, were involved in the tumult. Opinions of the number of Black sailors causing disturbances varied between 15 and 110. Captain Townsend made the largest estimate: "Keep in mind we saw about 110 people maximum . . . involved in this thing throughout the whole night out of 295 Blacks aboard ship, and I sincerely believe 75 to 85 of the Blacks . . . involved . . . were very much afraid not to be there."[23]

What did he mean by "afraid not to be there"? He believed a small group of militant Black sailors had coerced other Black crew members to assemble throughout the night. Asked how many were "coercing," Townsend replied, "I would say 10, no more than 10 or 12."[24]

The pistol-wielding marine estimated thirty-five Black sailors were roaming that night.[25] A white airman who suffered severe injuries mentioned an even smaller number. "It was . . . at the most, 15 or 20 people that were actually involved. . . I honestly believed . . . that everyone else just thought, 'Well, this is the thing to do, follow it.'"[26] One conclusion that can be safely drawn is that the overwhelming majority of Black crew members did not participate in any of the night's tumult.

Those that describe the *Kitty Hawk* incident as an uncontrolled riot, or violence run amok, are faced with another cold reality. With only a couple of exceptions throughout the evening, whenever armed Black or white crew members encountered those in authority, they immediately obeyed orders to stand down and get rid of makeshift weapons.

Captain Townsend testified, "Everywhere I went on that ship and demanded people give me weapons or stop, regardless of who they were, they responded. They would give me whatever weapons they had." He also said that when large groups had gathered in the mess decks a second time, he told them, "'You are going back to the forecastle, you are not going to stay here. I am going to run this ship today,' and they responded nicely. At no time was there anything that looked like a mutiny, because every order I gave was basically followed."[27]

Commander Cloud was likewise successful in his meeting with 150 or more Black crew members on the forecastle early in the evening. After he calmed them down, they all lay down their weapons and dispersed quietly. He was again successful with the armed white sailors in the berthing compartment who were about to head out and assault Black crew members. Those white sailors, estimated at between 100 and 150, were initially unruly and disrespectful. They even leveled death threats at him. Yet the XO was eventually able to calm them down and avert any more confrontations between Black and white crew members.[28]

As previously noted, one senior officer personally broke up two confrontations between Black and white sailors in the ordnance handling compartment. In both instances the sailors obeyed his dispersal requests.[29] The CO of the Marine Detachment also testified to the acquiescence of Black and white crew members when he asked them to surrender their weapons. "I would approach a group and ask them for their weapons, or if they saw me they would drop their weapons."[30] A lieutenant commander said his encounters with armed sailors were always peaceable. "Nobody was abusive to me. Anytime I went to a man and said 'I want that wrench out of your hand'. . . I got them away from them. I didn't have fear for myself."[31]

That compliance with orders by both Black and white sailors also negates any suggestion of a mutinous uprising aboard the *Kitty Hawk*. Military law provides that a person is guilty of mutiny if, in concert with anyone else, he attempts to override military authority by refusing to obey orders, or who "creates any violence or disturbance . . . with intent to cause the overthrow or destruction of lawful . . . authority."[32] The allowable punishment includes the death penalty.[33]

On only two or three occasions were orders to cease and desist disobeyed, and by individual sailors only, certainly not by anyone acting in concert with others to overthrow the ship. In short, no evidence whatsoever exists to support a claim that a mutiny, attempted or otherwise, took place that evening.

So why did crew members, white and Black, arm themselves in the first place? Undoubtedly, some did so with the intent to commit assaults on others. That would include Airman Laurie and other armed white sailors who assaulted Black sailors, including Cleveland Mallory outside his store and Durward Davis in a passageway. It would also include Black sailors who assaulted white sailors in their berthing areas.

However, a closer review of the evening's incidents suggests that the vast majority of sailors, Black and white, armed themselves strictly for self-defense.

The first report of a Black sailor picking up a makeshift weapon occurred when the marines confronted that sailor on the hangar bay. A marine reported that as his squad was struggling to apprehend him, the sailor grabbed a hammer, but was disarmed.[34] Others gave accounts of Black sailors arming themselves with hangar bay tools in self-defense as the marines confronted them, or to help defend fellow Black crew members who were being forcibly subdued.

Many sailors, both Black and white, started picking up makeshift weapons right after the hangar bay incident. The ship's chief criminal investigator testified, "I think that the overall opinion of the people I have talked to, if you weren't black that night you were afraid. There were a lot of black people who were afraid as well."[35] One was the bleeding and hysterical Black sailor who burst into the XO's cabin exclaiming, "They are going to kill us all!"

The record is replete with accounts of Black sailors continuing to fear the marines, as well as other white crew members, throughout the evening. And with good reason. Captain Townsend had assured them after the incident on the aft mess that he would handle the situation and they no longer had to fear the marines.[36] Commander Cloud said that assurance by Townsend left the Black crew members feeling "that there would not be a problem with the Marines."[37] Within minutes after they left the aft mess, however, they were confronted and assaulted by the marines on the hangar bay.

Commander Cloud again reflected on the situation after the hangar bay incident, saying Black crew members no longer trusted the two most senior officers on the ship. "The situation at that point, I felt, was out of hand. Great numbers of people at that point did not believe me, did not believe the captain, and did not believe our sincerity, primarily because we had told them that they would be all right."[38]

The situation was exacerbated, of course, by the rampant rumors that "Marines are killing blacks and throwing them overboard," that marines were being flown in armed with M-16s, and by sailors yelling, "They are killing our brothers!"

As the hangar bay incident was winding down, Townsend apologized to the assembled Black sailors. As recounted, he told them, "That is an error, a mistake on the part of the Marines, there is no intent on my part to ever have you broken up in groups of three."[39] He told them, "You blacks disperse and the marines I am going to put away right now."[40] Not long thereafter, the marines showed up in force in the passageway outside sick bay, and more aggressive confrontations ensued. That was when the Black sailor implored a senior officer, "I gotta get off this boat, can you get me off this boat?"

Even Captain Townsend acknowledged that Black sailors feared white crew members that evening, but he claimed their fear was based simply on their "leaders" telling them that they were in danger. Significantly, however, Townsend did admit that the Black sailors were "watching really as much as anything, defending themselves if necessary, and ready to take any actions to defend themselves if what their leaders were telling them [about being in danger] were true."[41] It was undoubtedly true. One Black sailor said the marines attacked first on the hangar bay, and after that "we were fighting for our lives."[42]

Many accounts of the *Kitty Hawk* affair mention Captain Townsend's harsh criticism of Commander Cloud's conduct that evening. The first of those incidents occurred early in the evening when Townsend entered the aft mess and saw the XO trying to calm the situation. "When I walked in, I found a situation badly out of control. . . . The XO was . . . operating as a black to a black rather than as XO to blacks, which was a mistake. I took a look at that and decided I am either going to have to throw the XO out now or walk out and leave this . . . because my authority is eroded."[43]

Townsend did give some credit to his XO, but accompanied by a threat. "The XO . . . used some very bad techniques, totally unacceptable, but everything he did was in sincere good faith and good will. I told him that morning if he ever did anything like that again, any more black-power salutes or anything like that, he was off the boat, I could not work with him."[44]

Captain Townsend had been especially harsh on his XO after Commander Cloud issued his dispersal order over the ship's intercom. "I certainly had no way of knowing why the XO was taking over the ship."[45]

What led to the incident aboard *Kitty Hawk* the evening of 12 October 1972? Many witnesses before the congressional subcommittee were asked that question. Captain Townsend dismissed any notion that Black crew members were reacting to racial discrimination exhibited by him. When questioned about racial bias in his masts, he said, "They know damn good and well my record is fair."[46] He even testified, "There were no black resentments resulting from the Subic in port period and there was no unusual tenseness about the ship."[47]

He made similar comments to the press. As reported in the *New York Times*, "Under questioning by newsmen, the captain said that there was no evidence of racial discrimination aboard the *Kitty Hawk* and that 'things are just fine the way they are.'"[48] He had taken the same tack when asked by a congressional subcommittee member whether he saw any relation between his arduous work schedule and the incident. He responded, "No, sir, if that were the case, it would have been a mixed-bag riot, which it was not. . . . [It was] all black. Totally black."[49]

Those remarkable statements by Townsend are directly contradicted by his personal meetings with Black sailors that evening when they strongly voiced their grievances about racial discrimination on his ship. Townsend even denied that the defendants themselves harbored feelings of discrimination. "Furthermore, the blacks charged as a result of the incident had no known grievances."[50]

The subcommittee parroted those comments by Townsend in the findings of its report, stating they were "unable to determine any precipitous cause for rampage aboard U.S.S. Kitty Hawk." Incredibly, they also stated that there was "not one case wherein racial discrimination could be pinpointed."[51] Those statements are completely at odds with their challenging Captain Townsend to explain why he took no disciplinary action in captain's masts against white sailors who assaulted Black sailors, and Commander Cloud telling the subcommittee that the marines confronted only Black sailors when carrying out their dispersal orders. Of course, we must also remember that the subcommittee heard no testimony whatsoever from any Black sailors from the lower enlisted ranks, any number of whom could have given examples of indisputable racial discrimination aboard the ship.

Chief of Naval Operations Admiral Zumwalt took direct issue with Captain Townsend and the subcommittee's denials of the role that racial discrimination played in the incident. "The principal contributing factors seems to be the indefinite, extended deployment of *Kitty Hawk* and the resultant separations from home [and] the belief on the part of a few young blacks that there was racial prejudice on *Kitty Hawk*, and the belief by a few others that there had been injustice in handling of mast cases.[52]

Admiral Zumwalt later added that the Kitty Hawk incident, and a later racial incident on another carrier, were "not the cause of racial pressures; rather, they are the manifestations of pressures unrelieved. . . . This issue of discrimination must be faced openly and fully."[53]

Commander Cloud also singled out racial discrimination when asked about the cause of the upheaval that night. He said, "Well, it was an accumulation of many things, just like it is an accumulation of many things in society off the ship."[54] He then focused on the strong feelings by Black sailors of racial inequality and injustice shown by the *Kitty Hawk* command. He didn't mention Captain Townsend by name, of course, when he said, "There was an indication that [the Black sailors] could not place any faith or allegiance in the validity of what we, his supervisors and leaders were telling him, in terms of the fact that the laws apply equally one and all in the military. That the administration of justice will be applied equally one and all in the Navy. And then more specifically, if you adhere to the rules which we outline that you will be treated fairly and squarely."[55]

Captain Townsend was asked if he thought the night's incidents had been preplanned and answered, "I think it was completely spontaneous."[56] He said the onboard investigative report reached the same conclusion.[57] He also offered another important concession about the marines' culpability in the aft mess incident, when he admitted the marines were acting without valid orders. "That was one of the things that caused the problems in the aft mess decks."[58]

Commander Cloud had also placed blame on the marines, saying their aggressive confrontation of Black crew members on the hangar bay "started the altercation."[59] He also agreed with Townsend that nothing was preplanned.[60]

The ship's chief medical officer said he believed "there was a darned sight more in the way of hoodlumism that night on the part of certain individuals than a black-white race riot."[61] He downplayed the racial aspect of the night's incident, but that element clearly existed since there were no reports of assaults by sailors upon others of their own ethnicity.

On the other hand, clearly not all the incidents, both before and during the night's tumult, were racially motivated. When confrontations occurred between Black and white sailors, an understandable reaction was to treat them as "racial" incidents. But some of them may have been simply "interracial" incidents unrelated to the ethnicity of the participants. Take, for example, the three mess deck incidents in which Black sailors had confronted white sailors. They included the white mess man picking up a glass that was still in use, the Black sailor being refused a second sandwich, and the Black sailor who had his foot stepped on. All three encounters were "interracial," but were they racially motivated? Perhaps not, since none of those incident reports said ethnicity was mentioned during the confrontations, such as the use of racial slurs.

Thus, might not each of those encounters be the result of the Black sailors' anger at the *actions* of the white mess men, and not because they happened to be white? For example, wouldn't a sailor respond negatively to being refused a second sandwich by any mess man, regardless of his ethnicity?

Admiral Zumwalt made a similar observation: "It is self-deception to consider all issues involving blacks and whites solely as racial in motivation. They are not. . . . I believe many incidents are characterized as racial only because that is their most visible aspect. They have, in fact, many causes. Men at sea for months on end, working extended hours seven days a week, with aging equipment, and escalating demands, face pressures almost inconceivable to those who have not known them."[62]

The distinction between "interracial" and "racial" incidents came into play in one of my *Kitty Hawk* trials. I was defending the Black airman recruit who had assaulted the white mess man for prematurely picking up his glass. During my cross-examination of the mess man, he said that while the incident might have had "racial overtones,"[63] he thought a more likely reason for my client's outburst was something else altogether. "I did notice other persons aboard the Kitty Hawk were also somewhat high strung during that particular period of time. In my opinion, I think that the people were mostly just tired because we were working, like, twelve-hour days, some people longer. . . . I did witness other persons, as a result of that, being high strung and getting involved in name calling and whatnot on the mess decks."[64]

I had explored that line of questioning to show that my client's actions were not racially motivated, but merely his anger at having his drinking glass taken away as he was eating and simply taking a break from his unrelenting work schedule.

On the other hand, the *Kitty Hawk* affair provided quite a few examples of actions that may have been racially motivated, even though those persons may have truly believed they carried no such prejudices.

As noted, just after Judge Bryant handed down his conviction of Cleveland Mallory, attorney Ben James said that one of the more insidious forms of racism can come from those who sincerely believe they are free of any racial bias. He made that statement just two days after

Judge Bryant was quoted in a local newspaper: "As far as I know, I am not a racist and I harbor no grudge or prejudices towards blacks."[65]

Well-meaning people of all ethnicities, all beliefs, and all persuasions, who would never for a minute consider themselves to harbor any racial or other prejudices, are a product of their environments, upbringings, and life experiences. As such, they can hold prejudices without any inkling of how their statements or actions may come across to others. In those situations, which may never manifest themselves overtly, their true character and feelings are revealed.

In addition to Judge Bryant's actions, other examples from the *Kitty Hawk* cases come to mind. A member of the congressional subcommittee asked one of the ship's investigators why the two groups of white sailors, while armed, were eventually talked out of assaulting Black sailors.

> Congressman: Why, in your judgment, have the whites remained passive to this point and not retaliated?
>
> Chief Johnson: I think it is because we [that is, white people] have faith in the system. We have been told the system will take care of people like this. You know, there is the judiciary, the courts, and the judiciary system is the way to handle this sort of thing and these people will be punished by the courts in a legal manner. And we have faith in the system. . . . I think the average white man has a better education and a better understanding of the system and is more willing to accept the system's way.[66]

So why didn't the Black sailors have a similar faith in the white man's system? Could it possibly have anything to do with their witnessing Captain Townsend's particular brand of justice in captain's masts over the preceding few months? Or their witnessing the dispersal order being used only against Black sailors? Or perhaps the collective experiences of all the Black sailors over their entire lives and their perception of white man's justice?

Both the white congressman and the white chief petty officer telegraphed their sincere bewilderment, some might say obliviousness, as to why the Black sailors just didn't believe in the system. Unfortunately, that outlook might be expected from those who truly believe the system is fair to all, and Black people just don't get it. Again, obliviousness.

Other examples are Townsend's apparent lack of self-awareness when he talked about "people" not congregating in groups like Black sailors do; his bringing charges against only Black sailors following the incident; his ignoring the unprovoked assaults by white sailors against Black *Kitty Hawk* crewmen on his ship and in Subic Bay; and his totally disparate treatment at captain's masts of Black and white crew members. This is the same man who told the subcommittee, "There is equality in mast procedure,"[67] and, "They know damn good and well my record is fair."[68] Sadly, he may have actually believed what he said.

Since racial bias, subtle or overt, is not limited to any single ethnicity, I came to appreciate the wisdom of Ben James when he said that those who are oblivious to their own prejudices are guilty of one of the more insidious forms of racism. Ben James was not the only one to have drawn those conclusions about racial discrimination and bias.

In April 1972, six months before the *Kitty Hawk* incident, Secretary of Defense Melvin Laird appointed a special task force to address the issue of racial disparity in the military justice system. He asked the group to examine racially related patterns and factors contributing to disparity of punishment under the military code.[69] The Secretary appointed as cochairs an Army lieutenant general, and the NAACP's Nathaniel Jones, and directed the task force "to determine the nature and extent of racial discrimination in the administration of military justice."[70]

The DOD task force findings confirmed that the disparity in disciplinary treatment between Black and white crew members was not unique to the *Kitty Hawk*, nor to the Navy, for that matter. On

5 October 1972, before the formal issuance of those findings, Nathaniel Jones gave a preview of them at a conference of Judge Advocate General of the Navy Admiral Staring.[71] By incredible coincidence, his conference comments were given exactly one week before the interracial confrontations erupted aboard *Kitty Hawk*.

His statements were astonishingly prescient of the entire *Kitty Hawk* affair. "To give credibility to the military justice system, we must assay the steps to be taken to deal with complaints against it. . . . It is generally conceded that large numbers of black servicemen perceive the military justice system to be discriminatory and unjust. . . . Of the two levels of military justice, judicial [courts-martial] and nonjudicial [captain's masts], the greatest area for distrust is the latter. For it is in the nonjudicial area that we find the greatest amount of discretion being exercised and, in my view, it is the area in which the greatest abuses occur."

When Jones mentioned nonjudicial captain's masts, he could have been speaking directly to Captain Townsend and his unequal treatment of interracial mast cases in the months leading up to the October incident.

Jones also said, "I give the court-martial system fairly good marks for the protection it affords a defendant," but then added comments about how decisions are often made on whether to refer cases to courts-martial trials. "The decision to refer to trial is, to many observers, the place where racial discrimination may lurk. The decision often involves subjective evaluations and emotional reactions to a specific set of facts. How a commander reacts may depend upon his background and experiences. . . . Thus, it is not enough for military commanders and lawyers to content themselves with the fairness of formal machinery. It is imperative that they carefully weigh the subjective factors that operate prior to the initiation of charges."[72]

Jones's reference to "subjective factors" was not to overt racism, as such, but instead, as Ben James mentioned, to more subtle factors that might lead to decisions such as those made surrounding the *Kitty Hawk* affair. Those decisions include Captain Townsend's inequitable handling of masts and his charging of only Black sailors. They also include Lieutenant Martin's one-sided investigation, Captain McKenzie's pretrial incarceration of the defendants, Judge Bryant's Mallory verdict, and on and on. While some of those decisions may have been consciously discriminatory, is it perhaps more likely they were the product of sub-conscious racial biases and prejudices?

As Jones explained, "None of us is born into a vacuum. We are creatures of the forces of society. To a large extent, racism exists in society. It is like a virus. When a person reaches the military phase of his life, he brings with him that infection."[73]

Admiral Zumwalt made quite similar comments. "It is self-deception to think that the Navy is made up of some separate species of man—that Navy personnel come to us fresh from some other place than our world—that they come untainted by the prejudices of the society which produced them. They do not."[74]

When the *Kitty Hawk* trials were finally wrapping up, Earl Caldwell of the *New York Times* wrote a feature article about the entire affair. That article included an interview with me:

> The issue of prejudicial treatment is being raised by some who have made the charge before, but also by at least one young white military lawyer who says that until now he had always considered the system fair. In a recent interview, he said that the blacks accused of the *Kitty Hawk* riots simply "were not treated fairly." "Maybe it was because the system was never confronted with anything like this," he said. But he added that the handling of the cases was "appalling to me as a mili-tary lawyer." "And it should be noted," he said, "that of the first 21 cases to go up, there was not a single bad-conduct discharge." The reason? "Because most of them shouldn't have been charged," he said.[75]

Before the *Kitty Hawk* cases, I really had always believed in the fair-ness of the military justice system. However, the *Kitty Hawk* cases proved the exception to the rule. That began on board the ship with a one-sided investigation and only Black sailors being charged. Their unjust pretrial confinement was next, followed by my threatened removal as defense counsel. It culminated with the government improperly withholding evidence from our defense team, and, most dramatically, Cleveland Mallory's conviction on perjured testimony.

I served another fourteen months in uniform following the *Kitty Hawk* trials, the last year as a military judge. During that time, I had a chance to reflect on what had happened, and concluded that the outcome of the trials ultimately proved a vindication of sorts, after taking into account all the acquittals, dropped charges, and relatively lenient sentences. Most importantly, all the defendants left the Navy with honorable discharges. Nevertheless, no one could give back to the young sailors the months they spent in totally unjustified pretrial confinement. Nor would they easily forget what they experienced that October night in 1972 off the coast of North Vietnam.

20

WHERE ARE THEY NOW?

With the passage of fifty years, some who played a role in the *Kitty Hawk* story have passed on. Those remaining are now senior citizens, and most have since retired. I connected with many of them who graciously shared their *Kitty Hawk* experiences and their lives thereafter.

Kitty Hawk Sailors

Seaman Apprentice Durward Davis accepted a plea agreement and received a relatively lenient sentence. Davis was offered an early out but remained in the Navy and next served aboard the carrier USS *Oriskany*. After completing his service and receiving an honorable discharge, he returned home to live with his mother. He worked for the Pepsi company for several years and then spent seventeen years in a maintenance position at Barnes-Jewish Hospital in St. Louis. During that time, he struggled with drugs and alcohol, but he sought treatment and eventually recovered. He has three children and eleven grandchildren. During one of our visits about his *Kitty Hawk* trial, he told me, "Thank my lawyer. He was in my corner. I was so scared. He was there for me, and I'll never forget that."[1] Davis's lawyer was Lieutenant Bruce Locke.

Seaman Apprentice Vernell Robinson was acquitted of all charges at his trial. He could have remained in the Navy by transferring to the carrier USS *Midway* but accepted an early out with an honorable discharge.

He returned home to South Chicago and had an enjoyable and rewarding career at McDonald's. After thirty years, he left as a regional manager. His next job was managing a parking garage at a condominium apartment complex. Unfortunately, in 2014, he suffered a stroke and had to retire at age sixty-three. After a first marriage ended in divorce, he remarried and they had two children. His second wife died in 2005, a year after his mother died, and their passing is still very hard on him. Robinson is a strong Christian, however, and says his faith keeps him going.[2]

Airman Perry Pettus loved being in the Navy and had an illustrious military career. He was never implicated in any of the October night's incidents. He left the *Kitty Hawk* in 1974 and reported aboard the soon-to-be commissioned, nuclear-powered supercarrier, USS *Nimitz*. He served as fly one director of aircraft on the foremost part of the flight deck. He was a second class aviation bosun's mate when he re-enlisted, but then had to take an early out with a medical disability. He returned to Kentucky and settled in Louisville. Pettus spent most of his post-Navy career working for the US Postal Service, eventually serving as postmaster at Fort Campbell, Kentucky. He also worked as an internet manager for auto dealerships and was an admissions counselor at a business college when he retired in 2010. Pettus has four daughters and ten grandchildren.[3]

Seaman Cleveland Mallory returned home to Pittsburgh in 1973, having accepted an early out with an honorable discharge, and initially lived with his mother and younger twin sister and brother. His sister remembers "Butch" as a very friendly and caring older brother who was well liked by all. He loved basketball and his bicycle, which he rode everywhere. Cleveland had girlfriends over the years but never married. He was a loving son who called his mother every day until her death in 2013. Cleveland had two long-term jobs, first with Greyhound Lines, and then working concessions at Three Rivers Stadium and at the arena for Pittsburgh's NHL team. He was still working full-time when he died in 2017 at age sixty-three. While riding his bicycle, he was struck by a vehicle. Cleveland was laid to rest at the military cemetery in Bridgeville, Pennsylvania. He was proud of his Navy service to the end, and his obituary picture shows him in his Navy Service Dress Blues.[4]

Senior Officers

Captain Marland Townsend's service as commanding officer of the *Kitty Hawk* ended on 15 November 1973. He had been at the helm for eighteen months and never again captained a ship. He was never promoted to admiral as would have been expected with his Service Record—that is, his record before the *Kitty Hawk* incident. After retirement from the Navy, he had a career with ARAMCO in Saudi Arabia and in the States. He eventually settled in California, where he served as mayor of Foster City, California, and passed away in July 2020, at age ninety-two.[5]

Executive Officer Benjamin Cloud continued to serve on board *Kitty Hawk* following the trials and was next assigned to Prairie View A&M University in Texas, where he commanded the Navy ROTC program. He then served in Naples, Italy, as commanding officer of the US Naval Support Activity. His last assignment was as chief of staff to the commander at the Pearl Harbor Naval Station.[6] He retired in 1984 to live in El Cajon, California. He served on the board of directors for the San Diego Air & Space Museum and his records at the museum state, "The fallout from a race riot onboard the [*Kitty Hawk*] slowed Cloud's career." That is unfortunate, because I believe he, more than anyone, deserves credit for helping put down the tumult that October evening in the South China Sea. He passed away peacefully at his Southern California home in August 2021, at age eighty-nine.[7]

Captain Robert McKenzie, the convening authority, began his military career as a Navy pilot. He was appointed Commander of the Naval Air Station North Island following his service as operations officer for the US Seventh Fleet. After the *Kitty Hawk* trials, he was promoted to rear admiral (lower half) in April 1973.[8] He remained in the Navy until 1982 and was commander of Key West Naval Forces in the Caribbean upon his retirement.[9] He passed away in Jupiter, Florida, in March 1990, at age sixty-five.[10]

Judge Bobby Day Bryant continued to serve at the law center after the *Kitty Hawk* trials. I began serving as a special courts-martial judge at the law center in June 1973, so our times on the bench overlapped.

We maintained a professional relationship but never had any meaningful conversations about the trials or the *Kitty Hawk* affair. Although I disagreed with virtually all of his rulings and findings in the *Kitty Hawk* cases, I give him credit for being the only military authority who agreed with our defense team that the defendants did not belong in pretrial confinement. After completing his military career, he returned to his home state of Georgia. He passed away in Decatur, Georgia, in October 1980, at age fifty-four.[11]

Undercover Agent

Billy Hicks was originally from Texas. He graduated from California Western School of Law in San Diego in 1973, just months after his undercover work on the *Kitty Hawk* cases ended. He moved to Prescott, Arizona, where he practiced law until his death in May 2010, at age seventy-one. He was survived by his wife and three children.[12]

Kitty Hawk Lawyers

Thirteen of the *Kitty Hawk* lawyers shared their recollections of the trials and of their clients with me for inclusion in this narrative. The civilian lawyers were Clifton Blevins, Dennis Kelly, Alex Landon, Mike Pancer, and Milt Silverman. The JAG officers were Paul Black, Jim Bradley, Harry Carter, Bruce Locke, Bob Pearson, Tom "TJ" Phillips, Mike Sheehy, and Dick Smith.

Following are some of the lawyers, beginning with our "defense team," a term I use throughout this book because our defense of the *Kitty Hawk* sailors was truly a team effort.

Civilian Defense Lawyers

Ben James was practicing law in San Francisco when the NAACP came calling and was one of the first civilian lawyers to commit to our defense team. Ben was a stalwart and welcome cocounsel with me on four of my cases, and, at age forty, one of the more senior members of our defense lawyers' group. After Mallory's conviction, when James vowed to devote the rest of his life, if necessary, to finding justice for our client, I never doubted him for a minute. Once the trials concluded, he returned to his law practice at Williams & James in San Francisco. He passed away in November 2006, at age seventy-four.

Alex Landon represented Hiram Davis, the first defendant to go to trial. Landon was an outspoken opponent of the Vietnam War and a strong supporter of civil rights. Standing up to injustice came naturally to Landon. His German-born father and grandfather were sent to the Buchenwald concentration camp by the Nazis in 1938. His paternal grandparents perished during the Holocaust, but his father was able to get out of the camp, emigrate to the United States, and serve with honor in the US Army during World War II. Landon was active in the ACLU and volunteered to defend two of the *Kitty Hawk* sailors, without compensation. He still practices criminal law in San Diego and also teaches at the University of San Diego School of Law.[13]

Milt Silverman had a reputation as an aggressive cause lawyer and coordinated the efforts of the NAACP's legal team. He was my unwitting cohort, some would say coconspirator, in creating the firestorm that erupted following his flight to the *Kitty Hawk*. His background wouldn't have suggested a future challenging the Navy in its treatment of the *Kitty Hawk* defendants. His father was a US Naval Academy graduate and career Navy man, and Silverman once considered a military career himself. Instead, he entered college and while there, and later at UCLA Law School, became committed to civil rights and social justice. He practiced criminal law in San Diego until his retirement in 2020.[14]

Dennis Kelly was sitting as a military judge at the law center when he was asked to head up the prosecution team for the *Kitty Hawk* trials. He was about to end his Navy tour of duty, however, and accepted what he considered a better offer from the NAACP to help defend three of the accused as a civilian attorney. His father sat on the Michigan Civil Rights Commission, and Kelly learned early on to stand up for the oppressed. He entered the JAG Corps after graduating from the University of Michigan Law School, and later volunteered for Vietnam duty, serving at the Da Nang Naval Law Center. He says he greatly respects the military justice system, but his *Kitty Hawk* experience left him deeply disappointed with some of the Navy's senior leadership. He says it was "a good system went very much awry because of some very flawed individuals." He retired in 2020 after practicing law for over fifty years in San Diego and is now an ordained Anglican priest.[15]

NAACP General Counsel

At the time of the *Kitty Hawk* incident, Nathaniel Jones had been general counsel for the NAACP for three years. He served in the US Army Air Corps during World War II and witnessed, firsthand, racial segregation in the military. He served on President Johnson's Kerner Commission, which studied civil unrest and rioting in US cities. That commission issued the oft-quoted pronouncement, "Our nation is moving toward two societies, one black, one white—separate and unequal." As noted, he also cochaired the DOD Task Force on Military Justice. He served on the federal Sixth Circuit US Court of Appeals for twenty-three years and passed away in January 2020, at age ninety-three.

JAG Defense Counsel

Lieutenant Glenn Haase was an outstanding defense lawyer with a humble demeanor. He represented six of the defendants and was fearless in their defense, never hesitating to square off with Navy authorities when the situation warranted. He was the attorney who called the *Kitty Hawk* legal office only to discover he was talking to a key government witness. He grew up in Toledo, Ohio, and excelled scholastically in college and Duke University School of Law.[16] He was a senior counsel for the Firestone Tire Company, specializing in domestic and international litigation. He passed away in January 2013 of complications from Parkinson's disease at age sixty-seven.

Lieutenant Bruce Locke represented defendant Durward Davis and remembers him as a "soft-spoken, honest, nice guy." He grew up in Massachusetts and graduated from Bowdoin College, where he joined the US Navy Reserves. He later attended the US Navy Officer Candidate

School and was granted a military deferment to attend Boston University School of Law, where he served on *Law Review*. He practiced law in Houston, Texas, for thirteen years and was a federal public defender in Sacramento, California, when he retired in 2018.[17]

Lieutenant Tom Phillips was the attorney who stepped into the Naval station brig confrontation. He represented Vernell Robinson and recalls him as "a good man, a good and innocent man. I was glad to have met him." After Robinson was acquitted of all charges, Phillips said, "The system worked in his case." He had graduated from the University of Notre Dame and the University of Michigan Law School. After his Navy service, he practiced civil litigation law for twenty-five years in Traverse City, Michigan, and then served eighteen years on the bench as a district court judge before retiring in 2018.[18]

Lieutenant Dick Smith's father was a career officer in the US Public Health Service Commissioned Corps. He received his own commission by way of a highly competitive JAG program offered to college seniors. After his graduation from Harvard Law School, he reported to the Subic Bay law center wearing his father's dress blue officer uniform. It fit perfectly. Smith represented the *Kitty Hawk* defendants who stood trial aboard the carrier and also was cocounsel with me in the San Diego trial of Airman Apprentice Glover. He practiced corporate and environmental law in Miami, Florida, before retiring in 2011.[19]

Myself, Lieutenant Marv Truhe. Immediately after the trials, I received another interesting assignment, but this one lasted just a few weeks. I was sent to the Subic Bay Naval Base, where I defended sailors who had staged a sit-down strike on a mine clearing ship off the coast of North Vietnam.[20] My last year in uniform I served as a military judge for special courts-martial trials. When I completed my Navy service in 1974, my wife and I returned to my home state of South Dakota, where I served as an assistant attorney general and head of the trial division in the South Dakota attorney general's office. I then went on to practice law in Rapid City, South Dakota, for thirty years, specializing in corporate, mining, and environmental law. After I retired in 2008, we moved to Colorado to be close to our son's family and our two grandchildren, Blythe and

Blake. I was very fortunate in finding a profession that I loved, beginning as a twenty-five-year-old Navy lawyer and ending all those years later.

Trial Counsel

Lieutenant Jim Bradley prosecuted seven of the *Kitty Hawk* cases. He came from a Navy family, with his uncle serving in World War I as President Wilson's telegrapher in Rome. When he entered the JAG Corps, his older twin brothers were Navy line officers serving at sea. He received bachelor of arts and bachelor of electrical engineering degrees from the University of Notre Dame, and a juris doctorate degree from Southern Methodist University Law School. He practiced patent and intellectual property law in Dallas, Texas, and upon his retirement in 2016 was managing partner of the Dallas office of a national law firm.[21]

Lieutenant Mike Sheehy prosecuted the only white *Kitty Hawk* defendant. Sheehy had been in the Navy ROTC program at Marquette University in Wisconsin, received his officer's commission at graduation, and was granted a delay in reporting for active duty to attend Georgetown University Law Center. He had an exemplary end to his JAG career, teaching military law at the US Naval Academy. His post-Navy career was primarily in the federal legislative branch of government, including service as the staff director and chief counsel to the House Intelligence Committee, and as national security adviser to the Speaker of the House of Representatives.[22]

USS *Kitty Hawk*

Kitty Hawk had a long and distinguished career. From its commissioning in 1961 to its decommissioning forty-eight years later in 2009, she served the US Navy well. Her final berth was at the Navy's Inactive Ships Maintenance Facility in Bremerton, Washington. The USS *Kitty Hawk* Veterans Association tried for years to turn the ship into a floating museum, but without success. The final chapter in its storied history was decided on 29 September 2021, when the Navy sold *Kitty Hawk* to International Shipbreaking Limited in Brownsville, Texas. Its destiny was the scrapyard, and the selling price was a penny.[23]

NOTES

Preface

1. "Court-Martial Opens for First of 21 Blacks on Carrier," *New York Times*, December 29, 1972.
2. *Report by the Special Subcommittee on Disciplinary Problems in the US Navy*, 92nd Cong., 2nd sess., 1973, H.A.S.C. 92-81, Section II, B. 1.

1. In the Beginning

1. CAPT William Newsome was a JAG officer, as were all lawyers assigned to the Naval Station Law Center.
2. Author tape transcript, 18-3. Throughout the *Kitty Hawk* trials the author dictated many of his daily activities, conversations, and reflections. The eighteen transcribed chapters of his tape recordings are referenced herein by chapter and page.
3. USS *Kitty Hawk* Quartermaster Notebook, Navigation Department Head CDR Wayne House Jr. statement, 22 October 1972, Haak Investigation, Exhibit 115. Carrier Task Group 77.7 was a part of Carrier Task Force 77.
4. USS *Kitty Hawk* Quartermaster Notebook.
5. USS *Kitty Hawk* Ship Roster, 20 October 1972, Exhibit 1a of Formal One-Officer Investigation to Inquire into the Circumstances Surrounding an Incident of Racial Violence Which Occurred on Board USS *Kitty Hawk* (CVA-63) on the Night of 12 October 1972. Captain Frank Haak was onboard during the incident and conducted this investigation, hereinafter Haak Investigation.
6. Carrier Wing Eleven Command History, 9 June 2010.
7. Quartermaster Notebook, CDR House statement, 25 October 1972, Exhibit 115; Fuel Officer LT Etheridge, author tape transcript, 13-1, 13-2.

8. "Report of the Task Force on the Administration of Military Justice in the Military," November 30, 1972, Vol. II, 94–95.

9. "Report of the Task Force," Vol. II, 96–97.

10. "Report of the Task Force," Vol. II, 101.

11. Later known as the Gulf of Tonkin Incident.

12. The Easter Offensive was the crossing of the Demilitarized Zone into South Vietnam by the People's Army of Vietnam.

13. ADM B. A. Clarey, commander in chief of the US Pacific Fleet, in his testimony, page 858, in the Hearings Before the Special Subcommittee on Disciplinary Problems in the US Navy of the Committee on Armed Services, House of Representatives, Ninety-Second Congress, Second Session, H.A.S.C. 93-13. The online record of those hearings, held in November and December of 1972, will be cited herein as "Cong. Sub."

14. Clarey, Cong. Sub., 858.

15. Clarey, Cong. Sub., 860.

16. Report during testimony of ADM Elmo Zumwalt Jr. at hearing. Cong. Sub., November 20, 1972, 34.

17. 3 April to 22 May of the second line period immediately following the spring Easter Offensive.

18. *Kitty Hawk* deployment schedule, statement of CDR Malcolm Guess (operations department head), Haak Investigation, 22 October 1972, Exhibit 112. The total days are through 4 November 1972, the last day of *Kitty Hawk's* seventh line period.

19. CAPT Marland Townsend. Cong. Sub., December 6, 1972, 515.

20. ADM Elmo Zumwalt Jr., Cong. Sub., 4.

21. Letter of Commendation from CAPT O. H. Oberg, 16 March 1972.

22. Capt Nicholas Carlucci, Cong. Sub., 6 December 1972, 608.

23. Cpl Anthony Avina, Cong. Sub., 8 December 1972, 720.

24. *Kitty Hawk* Ship Roster, 20 October 1972, Haak Investigation, Exhibit 1a.

25. Traditionally, officers have "ranks" and enlisted men have "rates." However, that distinction is fading. See, *The Bluejacket's Manual, US Navy, 2017*, 110. For simplicity, "rank" will be used herein for both officers and enlisted personnel.

26. *Kitty Hawk* Ship Roster, Haak Investigation, Exhibit 1a. An E-1 who was part of the ship's crew held the rank of SR (seaman recruit), an E-1 in the embarked air wing was an AR (airman recruit); and a marine was a private (designated Pvt).

27. An E-2 held the rank of SA or AA (seaman apprentice or airman apprentice) or marine PFC (private first class). An E-3 held the rank of SN or AN (seaman or airman), or marine LCPL (lance corporal). Enlisted ranks in ascending order also include E-4 through E-6 which are, respectively, third class, second class, and first class petty officers. E-6s through E-9s are chiefs, senior chiefs and master chiefs. Officer ranks in ascending order from O-1 through O-6 are ensign, lieutenant junior grade, lieutenant, lieutenant commander, commander, and captain. Ranks O-7 through O-10 make up the four admiral ranks.

28. ADM Elmo Zumwalt, Cong. Sub., 20 November 1972, 39.

29. CPO Virgil Enochs, chief master-at-arms, Cong. Sub., 655.

30. Capt Carlucci, Cong. Sub., 602.

31. Carlucci, Cong. Sub., 601.

32. The launch to recovery time for each pilot's sortie was typically eighty to ninety minutes. Author interview, June 29, 2021, with former carrier A-6E jet pilot.

33. CAPT Townsend, Cong. Sub., 515.

34. Townsend, Cong. Sub., 517.

35. Townsend, Cong. Sub., 516.

36. Air Wing Eleven also had McDonnell Douglas F-4 Phantoms that were also twin engine, all-weather, long-range supersonic jets. The F-4 two-member crew sat in tandem, whereas the A6-E pilot and bombardier/navigator sat side by side.

37. A rack is the term used by sailors to refer to their sleeping space, otherwise called a bunk.

38. ADM Zumwalt, Cong. Sub., 20 November 1972, 4.

2. New Commanding Officer

1. CAPT Townsend obituary, US Navy Stars and Stripes, 28 July 2020.

2. All commanding officers of Navy ships are called "captain" regardless of their rank. The Bluejacket's Manual, US Navy, 25th ed., 188.

3. "Benjamin Cloud Personal Papers," San Diego Air & Space Museum, accessed April 25, 2022, https://sandiegoairandspace.org/collection/item/benjamin-cloud-personal-papers.

4. Obituary for Benjamin W. Cloud, San Diego Union-Tribune, September 5, 2021, https://www.legacy.com/us/obituaries/sandiegouniontribune/name/benjamin-cloud-obituary?id=16817148.

5. Presidents John Kennedy and Lyndon Johnson.

6. "Deep selected" means CDR Cloud was selected over other officers with higher rank or more time in grade.

7. Capt Nicholas Carlucci, Cong. Sub., 608. A Marine captain is the equivalent rank of a Navy lieutenant. A Navy captain, on the other hand, is three ranks superior to a Marine captain.

8. Carlucci, Cong. Sub., 599–600.

9. CDR Benjamin Cloud, Cong. Sub., 6 December 1972, 551. CAPT Owen Oberg had served as CO for just fourteen months.

10. Cloud, Cong. Sub., 551.

11. The *UCMJ* is a federal law enacted by Congress in 1950 and, as amended since, is the governing criminal law for the US military.

12. Article 15, *UCMJ*.

13. Article 15(b), *UCMJ*.

14. Investigator MM2 William McNeill testimony, Haak Investigation, 59.

15. CAPT Townsend, Cong. Sub., 520–521.

16. MM2 McNeill testimony, Haak Investigation, 59.

17. AA Terry Avinger and SN Melvin Newson. SKI Clifford Thompson testimony, Haak Investigation, 55.

18. MM2 McNeill testimony, Haak Investigation, 59–60.

19. BMCS Virgil Enochs testimony, Haak Investigation, 53.

20. CAPT Townsend, Cong. Sub., 521.

21. CDR Cloud, Cong. Sub., 552.

22. CAPT Townsend, Cong. Sub., 520.

23. Firemen maintain and operate a ship's boilers and engineering equipment.

24. AOC Charles Johnson testimony, Haak Investigation, 61.

25. Johnson testimony, Haak Investigation, 61.

26. *Kitty Hawk* ship roster, Haak Investigation, Exhibit 1a.

27. CDR Cloud, Cong. Sub., 552.

28. SK1 Clifford Thompson testimony, Haak Investigation, 56.

29. Thompson testimony, Haak Investigation, 56.

30. Nonrated sailors are those ranked below the E-4 pay grade.

31. CAPT Townsend, Cong. Sub., 521.

32. *UCMJ* Article 115, Communicating Threats, and Article 117, Provoking Speeches and Gestures.

33. CAPT Townsend, Cong. Sub., 521.

34. Townsend, 521.

35. Townsend, 521.

36. LT David Combs statement, 7 November 1972, Haak Investigation, Exhibit 8.
37. Combs statement, Haak Investigation, Exhibit 8.
38. Fo'c'sle is the Navy term for forecastle, which on a carrier is a large compartment located farthest forward and on a deck level above the hangar deck.
39. LT Combs, Haak Investigation, Exhibit 8.
40. *Kitty Hawk* Ship Roster, Haak Investigation, Exhibit 1a.
41. AOC Charles Johnson testimony, Haak Investigation, 63.
42. CAPT Townsend, Cong. Sub., 514–515.
43. *Head* is the nautical term for a ship's toilet.
44. AOC Charles Johnson testimony, Haak Investigation, 63–65.
45. Johnson, Haak Investigation, 64.
46. Johnson, Haak Investigation, 65.
47. BMCS Virgil Enochs testimony, Haak Investigation, 53.
48. AOC Charles Johnson testimony, Haak Investigation, 65.
49. Report of captain's masts, Cong. Sub., 546.
50. Report of captain's masts, Cong. Sub., 546.
51. CAPT Townsend, Cong. Sub., 514.
52. Townsend, Cong. Sub., 508.
53. Townsend, Cong. Sub. 521.
54. Townsend, Cong. Sub. 537.
55. The *Kitty Litter* newspaper had no set schedule for publication or distribution.
56. CAPT Townsend, Cong. Sub., 529.
57. AOC Charles Johnson, Cong. Sub., 779.
58. *Kitty Litter*, vol. 1, issue 7, August 1972, Cong. Sub., 529.

3. Trouble in Subic Bay

1. Carriers typically tied up at the Naval air station because the planes in its onboard air squadrons were serviced there and had their weaponry loaded aboard the ship.
2. "Liberty" refers to a sailor's free time away from the ship or from his shore duty, usually granted for short periods such as overnight or for a weekend. "Leave," on the other hand, is granted for longer periods, and is earned at the rate of two and a half days per month. *The Bluejackets Manual*, US Navy, 25th ed., 18–19.
3. ADM B. A. Clarey, commander in chief of the Pacific Fleet (CINCPACFLT), written statement, Cong. Sub., 860.
4. Although seemingly derogatory, this term was used by all sailors, Black and white.

5. 1st Sgt. Willie Binkley, Cong. Sub., 740, and Capt. Carlucci, Cong. Sub., 608.

6. Capt Carlucci, Cong. Sub., 608.

7. Author interviews, Durward Davis.

8. Proclamation No. 1081, September 21, 1972. Marcos said that he had done so because of the "rebellion" of the sectarian Mindanao Independence Movement and the "communist threat" from the newly formed Communist Party of the Philippines. Martial law was not lifted until January 1981.

9. In the Philippines, Filipino citizens are often referred to as Nationals.

10. AN William Williams statement, 16 September 1972.

11. SA Michael Smith statement, 15 September 1972.

12. AOC Charles Johnson Investigative Report, 12 October 1972, Haak Investigation, Exhibit 4 (hereinafter Johnson Report). Allen Sickles was "striking" to become a radioman, hence his full rank of RMSA.

13. CAPT Townsend, Cong. Sub., 530.

14. Lino Marcelo statement, Johnson Report, 9 October 1972.

15. Rolando Palma statement, Johnson Report, 10 October 1972.

16. Johnson Report, Summary of Investigation, 2.

17. AOC Charles Johnson testimony, Haak Investigation, 66.

18. CAPT Townsend, Cong. Sub., 530.

19. Townsend, Cong. Sub., 496.

20. That commander's title was COMNAVPHIL.

21. CAPT Bobby Hatch Informal JAG Manual Investigation (hereinafter, Hatch Investigation).

22. CAPT Hatch testimony, Hatch Investigation, 132.

23. SN Dwight Horton statement, Hatch Investigation, 10 October 1972.

24. Horton, Hatch Investigation.

25. SA Roger Howard statement, Hatch Investigation, 9 October 1972. Howard was a USS *Niagara Falls* (AFS-3) crew member.

26. TM William McKean statement, Hatch Investigation, 11 October 1972, Exhibit 5r. He was a USS *Juneau* (UDT-11) crew member.

27. BMI John Gracio statement, Hatch Investigation, 10 October 1972, Exhibit 5t. He was also a USS *Juneau* crew member.

28. CAPT Hatch testimony, Hatch Investigation, 139.

29. Military Acknowledgement and Waiver of Rights, 13 October 1972.

30. SN Horton statement, Hatch Investigation, 13 October 1972.

31. Message from CAPT Townsend on the *Kitty Hawk* to COMUSNAVPHIL, 12 October 1972, Cong. Sub., 497.

32. The Naval Base investigator knew of the Horton incident from reports given to him, but also chose not to investigate and "didn't pursue the matter any further." CAPT Hatch testimony, Hatch Investigation, 139.

33. CAPT Hatch, Hatch Investigation, 141. The club was restricted to enlisted men E-1 through E-6.

34. Hatch, 132.

35. Hatch, 137.

36. Hatch, 132.

37. AMH2 Joseph Reeves statement, Hatch Investigation, 11 October 1972, Exhibit 5n.

38. CAPT Hatch testimony, Hatch Investigation, 133.

39. Hatch, Hatch Investigation, 134.

40. ABE2 Robert Pulley statement, Hatch Investigation, 14 October 1972, Exhibit 5l.

41. Pulley, Hatch Investigation.

42. BM2 Delacruz statement, Hatch Investigation, 14 October 1972, Exhibit 5m.

43. CAPT Hatch testimony, Hatch Investigation, 135.

44. Hatch, Hatch Investigation, 138.

45. Cpl James Lee statement, Hatch Investigation, 11 October 1972, Exhibit 5b.

46. LCpl Joseph Brock statement, Hatch Investigation, 24 October 1972, Exhibit 5y.

47. CAPT Hatch testimony, Hatch Investigation, 136.

48. CAPT Townsend, Cong. Sub., 497.

4. A Night to Remember

1. "Mess deck" is typically used on carriers to refer to the second deck, which contains the forward and aft mess compartments. Sometimes, however, the term is used to refer to the mess compartments themselves.

2. AN William Boone testimony, AR Coleman trial, 19 February 1973, 118–120.

3. AOC Charles Johnson testimony, ship's chief investigative officer, Haak Investigation, 68. This, and all other exhibits listed in the following citations were taken during, or were part of, the Haak onboard investigation.

4. Johnson, Cong. Sub., 787.

5. LCDR Allen Branch statement, 22 October 1972, Exhibit 106.

6. MM2 William McNeill statement, 24 October 1972, Exhibit 9.

7. AOC Charles Johnson testimony, Haak Investigation, 68–69.

8. Marine Force Report of Racial Turbulence Inquiry, 21 October 1971, Cong. Sub., 179, 182.

9. Sgt Danny Pringle, Cong. Sub., 755.

10. EN1 Jimmy Randolph testimony. Haak Investigation, 16–17.

11. CDR Cloud testimony, Haak Investigation, 123.

12. AA Ronald Glover, undated statement.

13. Ensign Joseph Edgerton testimony, Haak Investigation, 74–75.

14. AOC Charles Johnson testimony, Haak Investigation, 69–70.

15. Ensign Joseph Edgerton testimony, Haak Investigation, 75.

16. "Witness in Kitty Hawk Hearings," *New York Times*, December 27, 1972.

17. CPO Curtis Johnson, Cong. Sub., 681. Most sailors who first reported aboard *Kitty Hawk* were initially assigned menial tasks. In theory, they were eligible within a couple of months to move up to "real" Navy jobs they could be proud of. However, Black sailors often felt they were discriminated against in job advancement and promotions after those initial duty assignments. The Navy sometimes responded by stating it lowered its recruiting standards in 1972 in order to meet manpower requirements. Therefore, those with low scores on acceptance and placement tests had a limited chance for advancement. A senior official acknowledged, however, that those sailors had cause to complain. "One reason they are unhappy is because recruiters have not told them what type of job they can quality for. They go in [the Navy] with raised expectations." Roger Kelley, Asst. Secy. Manpower and Reserve Affairs, Department of Defense, Cong. Sub., 1112.

18. AOC Charles Johnson testimony, Haak Investigation, 71.

19. SA Bryan Hill statement, 13 October 1972, Exhibit 13.

20. Author interviews, Durward Davis.

21. CDR Cloud, Cong. Sub., 571.

22. Capt Carlucci statement, 14 October 1972, Exhibit 191, 1.

23. Capt Carlucci, Cong. Sub., 601.

24. Author interviews, Durward Davis.

25. Capt Carlucci, Cong. Sub., 600.

26. Capt Carlucci, Cong. Sub., 600.

27. AA Melvin Newson testimony, Haak Investigation, 83.

28. AA Dillard Hill testimony at AA Glover Article 39(a) hearing and special court-martial trial [herein Glover Hearing], 24 January 1973, 99–100.

29. AHS3 Charles Green, undated statement.

30. LCpl Josiah Wilson, Jr. Cong. Sub., 795.

31. Cpl Avina, Cong. Sub., 721.

32. Avina, Cong. Sub., 721.

33. Capt Carlucci, Cong. Sub., 601.

34. Cpl Avina statement, 13 October 1972, Exhibit 20.

35. LCpl Wilson, Cong. Sub., 795.

36. Cpl Avina, Cong. Sub., 728.

37. Avina, Cong. Sub., 727.

38. CDR Cloud, Cong. Sub., 570.

39. Cloud, Cong. Sub., 570.

40. Cloud, Cong. Sub., 571.

41. Deck plates are metal ramps set on the raised threshold of watertight doors to ease access.

42. CDR Cloud, Cong. Sub., 571.

43. AVCM Curtis Johnson testimony, Haak Investigation, 91.

44. AVCM Curtis Johnson statement, 23 October 1972, Exhibit 113. Corporal Avina was not transferred from the carrier.

45. Johnson statement, 1.

46. Navigator CDR Wayne House Jr. statement, 25 October 1972, 1, Exhibit 31. The "captain's bridge" is located high on the carrier's "island" on the starboard side. The island also contains the pilot house and helm.

47. CAPT Townsend, Cong. Sub., 526.

48. Townsend, Cong. Sub., 526.

49. AVCM Johnson statement, Exhibit 113.

50. CDR Cloud, Cong. Sub., 572.

51. CDR Cloud, Haak Investigation, 117.

52. CS1 Roland Clark testimony, Haak Investigation, 94–96.

53. AA Paul Selman testimony, SA Rowe Article 39(a) Pretrial Investigation Hearing, 21 October 1972, 19–20.

54. SN Malcolm Conyers testimony, Rowe PTI hearing, 22 October 1972, 18; quoting AA Selman.

55. Shortly after, a white sailor was assaulted by several Black sailors in an adjacent shower. RDSN John Callahan statement, 13 October 1972, Exhibit 47.

56. RMSA Mark Bornschein statement, 12 October 1972, Exhibit 16.

57. Capt Carlucci, Cong. Sub., 602.

58. LCpl Joseph Brock testimony, Cong. Sub., 733; LCpl David Reichle statement, 16 October 1972, Exhibit 29; and LCpl Daniel Jackson statement, 16 October 1972, Exhibit 30.

59. Some parts of the ship, such as berthing spaces, are occasionally muted to the 1-MC. AOC Charles Johnson, Cong. Sub., 783.

60. LCpl Brock, Rowe PTI hearing, 21 October 1972, 66.

61. Capt Carlucci, Cong. Sub., 603.

62. LCpl David Reichle statement, 16 October 1972, Exhibit 29.

63. AN Perry Mason statement, 13 October 1972, Exhibit 42.

64. Mason, Exhibit 42.

65. AA Ronald Glover, undated statement, Haak Investigation.

66. Glover, Haak Investigation.

67. SR Larry Williamson statement, 22 October 1972. Exhibit 43.

68. Williamson, Exhibit 43.

69. LT James Martin statement, 15 October 1972, Exhibit 108.

70. 1st Sgt Binkley, Cong. Sub., 739.

71. Binkley, Cong. Sub., 739.

72. LCpl Daniel Jackson statement, 16 October 1972, Exhibit 30.

73. LCpl Reichle statement, 16 October 1972, Exhibit 29.

74. ABH3 David Payne statement, 14 October 1972, Exhibit 78.

75. 1st Sgt Binkley statement, 13 October 1972, Exhibit 117.

76. 1st Sgt Binkley, Cong. Sub., 739.

77. LT Gary Fiske statement, 14 October 1972, Exhibit 38.

78. LCpl Jackson statement, Exhibit 30. Jackson identified the marine as Cpl Robert Anderson.

79. Jackson, Exhibit 30.

80. The Marine Detachment had five Black members. Capt Carlucci, Cong. Sub., 603.

81. AOC Charles Johnson testimony, Rowe PTI hearing, 75.

82. Johnson, Rowe PTI hearing, 75.

83. Author interviews, Perry Pettus.

84. Author interviews, Pettus.

85. CDR Cloud, Cong. Sub., 576.

86. AOC Charles Johnson testimony, Cong. Sub., 784.

87. CPO Virgil Ostberg statement, undated, Exhibit 194.

88. AOC Charles Johnson testimony, Cong. Sub., 785.

89. Capt Nicholas Carlucci, Cong. Sub., 602.

90. Cpl Robert Anderson testimony, AA Avinger Pretrial Hearing, 21 December 1972, 36.

91. Anderson, 37.

92. CDR Cloud testimony, Glover Hearing, 24 January 1973, 66, in response to questions by civilian defense attorney Dennis Kelly.
93. AVCM Curtis Johnson statement, Exhibit 113, 2.
94. CAPT Townsend, Cong. Sub., 533.
95. 1st Sgt Binkley statement, Exhibit 117, 2.
96. CDR Cloud testimony, Glover Hearing, 24 January 1973, 52.
97. ADJ3 Bennie Hall statement, 16 October 1972, Exhibit 88.
98. CDR Ben Cloud, Glover Hearing, 24 January 1973, 61–62.
99. CDR Ben Cloud, Cong. Sub., 575.
100. Cloud, Cong. Sub., 576.
101. CAPT Townsend, Cong. Sub., 533.
102. CDR Cloud, Cong. Sub., 576.
103. CAPT Townsend, Cong. Sub., 526.
104. LT Martin testimony, Glover Hearing, 24 January 1973, 181.
105. CAPT Townsend, Cong. Sub., 542.
106. Townsend, Cong. Sub., 526.
107. AVCM Curtis Johnson statement, Exhibit 113, 2.
108. Carlucci, Cong. Sub., 601.
109. "Kitty Hawk Officer Traces Riot to Marine Dispersal of Blacks," *New York Times*, January 25, 1973.

5. A Time to Remember

1. Cpl Robert Anderson statement, 13 October 1972, Haak Investigation, Exhibit 49. He was injured further while engaged in a later confrontation in sick bay. This, and all other exhibits listed in the subsequent citations were taken during, or were part of, the Haak onboard investigation.
2. SR Larry Williamson statement, 22 October 1972, Exhibit 43, and Williamson Medical Report Exhibit 165.
3. AN Perry Mason statement, 13 October 1972, Exhibit 42, and Mason Medical Report, Exhibit 174.
4. AA Ronald Glover Medical Report, Exhibit 144.
5. AN Jerry Parks Medical Report, Exhibit 137.
6. LCpl Joseph Brock statement, 16 October 1972, Exhibit 34.
7. Capt Carlucci statement, 14 October 1972, Exhibit 191, 3.
8. CDR Paul Salgado statement, 23 October 1972, Exhibit 109.
9. Salgado, Exhibit 109.
10. Capt Carlucci statement, Exhibit 191, 3.

11. Cpl Robert Anderson statement, 13 October 1972, Exhibit 49.
12. Author interviews, HM3 Arthur Duhon, 15 January and 2 February 1973; Duhon testimony, AA Avinger Article 39(a) hearing, 21 December 1972, 43 (hereinafter, Avinger Hearing).
13. HM3 Willliam McCain statement, 13 October 1972.
14. AA Ronald Glover letter requesting discharge from Navy, 20 October 1972.
15. Author interview, AN Glover, 15 February 1972.
16. HM3 Arthur Duhon testimony, Avinger Hearing, 43.
17. AA Glover, undated statement taken during Haak Investigation, 2.
18. CPL Anderson statement, Exhibit 49.
19. HM3 Arthur Duhon testimony, Avinger Hearing, 43.
20. CDR Frederick Deane statement, 22 October 1972, Exhibit 103.
21. CDR Cloud, Cong. Sub., 577.
22. Cloud, Cong. Sub., 578.
23. Cloud, Cong. Sub., 578.
24. CDR Cloud announcement as reported in a statement by CAPT Gerald Bell, COMCARDIV FIVE/CTF-77, Exhibit 91.
25. CDR Cloud, Cong. Sub., 578.
26. Cloud, Cong. Sub., 581.
27. CAPT Townsend, Cong. Sub., 534.
28. Townsend, Cong. Sub, 534.
29. CDR Cloud, Cong. Sub., 579.
30. As reported by CAPT Bell, Exhibit 91.
31. CAPT Townsend, Cong. Sub., 534.
32. CDR William Dunnam, Affidavit Amendment, 30 October 1972, Exhibit 192a, and Affidavit, 25 October 1972, Exhibit 192.
33. ABHC George Hill Jr. statement, 25 October 1972, Exhibit 116.
34. Author interview, CDR Cloud, December 1972.
35. Author interview, Durward Davis.
36. CAPT Townsend, Cong. Sub., 534–535.
37. AO1 Ralph Scott, Cong. Sub., 630.
38. RM3 Lynwood Patrick Medical Report, Exhibit 168.
39. SM3 Patrick Riggs statement, 13 October 1972, Exhibit 7.
40. CDR Frederick Deane testimony, Cong. Sub., 761.
41. SN Rodney Adair Medical Report, Exhibit 179.
42. CDR Deane testimony, Cong. Sub., 761–762.
43. AN James Radford testimony, Cong. Sub., 1004.

44. The applicator is a long aluminum tube with a metal nozzle at one end. In use, it hooks up to a water source and dispenses a broad spray mist to smother onboard fires.
45. AN Radford, Cong. Sub., 1005.
46. AN Radford Medical Report, Exhibit 186.
47. AN Radford Medical Case History, Cong. Sub., 1074.
48. CTO3 Ronald Lawson Medical Report, Exhibit 173, and Lawson statement, 13 October 1972, Exhibit 54.
49. AMS3 Kenneth Lewis statement, 13 October 1972, Exhibit 59, and Lewis Medical Report, Exhibit 161.
50. AOC Charles Johnson, Cong. Sub., 782.
51. Johnson, Cong. Sub., 782.
52. CDR Cloud, Cong. Sub., 582.
53. Cloud, Cong. Sub., 582–583.
54. Cloud, Cong. Sub., 583.
55. Cloud, Cong. Sub., 583.
56. Cloud, Cong. Sub., 584.
57. Cloud, Cong. Sub., 584.
58. AR Timothy Imes statement, 14 October 1972, Exhibit 80.
59. CDR Dunnam Affidavit, 25 October 1972, Exhibit 192, 1–2.
60. Dunham, Exhibit 192, 2.
61. AK1 James House statement, 14 October 1972, Exhibit 76.
62. House, Exhibit 76. The injured crew member was PH3 Michael Ward.
63. House, Exhibit 76.
64. Author interviews, Durward Davis.
65. AZAN James Toney statement, 13 October 1972, Exhibit 51, and Toney Medical Report, Exhibit 159.
66. AHS3 Charles Green, undated statement.
67. AHS3 Green Medical Report, Exhibit 145.
68. AA Nelson Mouton Medical Report, 13 October 1972.
69. AA Mouton, undated statement.
70. AA Lawrence Wommack Medical Reports, Exhibits 175 and 184.
71. SN Cleveland Mallory testimony at his trial, 4 January 1973, 285.
72. SN Mallory Medical Report, Exhibit 184.
73. AA Nelson Mouton, SR Larry Williamson, AA Ronald Glover, AN Jerry Parks, AA Lawrence Wommack, AN Perry Mason, AHS3 Michael Greene, AZAN James Toney, and SN Cleveland Mallory.

74. Only two of those nine injured Black sailors had their statements taken during the ship's onboard investigation. None of those nine unprovoked assaults was investigated, nor a single white crew member charged in connection with any of them.

75. HM3 Arthur Duhon, Avinger Hearing, 48.

76. Cloud testimony, Glover Hearing, 24 January 1973, 41–83.

77. Cloud, Glover Hearing, 44.

78. Cloud, Glover Hearing, 45.

79. Cloud, Cong. Sub., 588.

80. Cloud, Cong. Sub., 585.

81. Cloud, Cong. Sub., 587.

82. Cloud, Cong. Sub., 578.

83. AOC Charles Johnson, Cong. Sub., 787–788.

84. Johnson, Cong. Sub., 788.

85. Deane, Cong. Sub., 760.

86. Deane statement, 22 October 1972, Exhibit 103.

87. LT James Martin statement, 15 October 1972, Exhibit 108, 3.

88. Deane, Cong. Sub., 762.

89. Cloud, Cong. Sub., 585.

90. Cloud, Cong. Sub., 586.

91. Cloud, Cong. Sub, 586.

92. Cloud, Cong. Sub., 586.

93. Cloud, Cong. Sub., 587.

94. Cloud, Cong. Sub., 588.

95. Author interviews, Durward Davis.

96. "Armed Forces: Storm Warnings," *Time* magazine, December 11, 1972.

97. Townsend, Cong. Sub., 530.

98. "Armed Forces: Storm Warnings"; Cong. Sub., 530.

99. Townsend, Cong. Sub., 531.

6. Return to Subic Bay

1. CAPT Townsend, Cong. Sub., 540. ADM B. A. Clarey, commander in chief of the US Pacific Fleet; and VADM Cooper, commander of the Carrier Strike Force for the Seventh Fleet. *Kitty Hawk* was VADM Cooper's flagship.

2. "Navy Mum on Carrier Clash," *Honolulu Advertiser*, October 14, 1972.

3. Condition II is one step down from General Quarters. The crew is free to move about the ship, but with Condition Zebra also in place, they could move

only subject to severe restrictions. All "Z" marked closures (doors, hatches, porthole covers, and valves) are secured and can only be opened with special tools by designated crew members.

4. CAPT Townsend, Cong. Sub., 544.
5. SN William E. Boone, Cong. Sub., 944.
6. CAPT Townsend, Cong. Sub., 544.
7. Townsend, Cong. Sub., 544.
8. Townsend, Cong. Sub., 527.
9. Exhibit 1a, Haak Investigation, 20 October 1972. By comparison, the percentage of enlisted Black men in all the armed forces was 12.1 percent at the time. *Report of the Task Force on the Administration of Military Justice in the Armed Forces*, 30 November 1972, vol. 1, 10.
10. Townsend, Cong. Sub., 528.
11. Townsend, Cong. Sub., 528.
12. Cloud testimony, Haak Investigation, 128.
13. *UCMJ* Article 90, "Willfully Disobeying Superior Commissioned Officer," and Article 92, "Failure to Obey Order or Regulation."
14. Townsend, Cong. Sub., 519.
15. Zumwalt, Cong. Sub., 1082.
16. Townsend, Cong. Sub., 520.
17. Frank Haak was chief of staff to the commander of Carrier Division 5 serving the US Seventh Fleet.
18. LT James Martin, Glover Hearing, 23–26 January 1973, 174–175. Three agents from the Naval Investigative Service came aboard later, one of whom was a Black petty officer, 182.
19. LT Martin, Glover Hearing, 177.
20. Martin, Glover Hearing, 177.
21. In the military, courts-martial juries are called "panels."
22. Author interviews, former JAG Lieutenant Dick Smith.
23. Author interviews, Smith.
24. LT Martin, Glover Hearing, 185.
25. Priority Message from the Commander of Naval Forces, Philippines (COMNAVPHIL) to CINCPACFLT Makalapa Hawaii, 4 November 1972.
26. LT Martin, Glover Hearing, 198.
27. United States v. Airman Apprentice Ronald NMN Glover Chronology of Events, 1.
28. *UCMJ*, Punitive Articles 77–134.

29. *Manual for Courts-Martial*, Rule for Courts-Martial [R.C.M.] 307(c)(3).

30. *UCMJ*, Article 30(b)(1).

31. AA Glover Chronology of Events, 1.

32. AA Glover Charge Sheet, 16 October 1972.

33. Glover Charge Sheet.

34. So called because of the two same-width gold stripes on the dress blue uniform sleeve of a Navy lieutenant. Lieutenant junior grade officer uniforms also have two stripes, but one stripe is wider than the other.

35. Author interviews, Dick Smith.

36. Author interviews, Dick Smith.

37. *UCMJ*, Article 27(a)(1).

38. *Manual for Courts-Martial (MCM)*, Rule of Courts-Martial (R.C.M.) 506(b)(1).

39. *MCM*, R.C.M. 506(a)(1).

40. Glover Chronology of Events, 1. NAACP is the National Association for the Advancement of Colored People, and ACLU is the American Civil Liberties Union.

41. COMNAVPHIL Subic Bay Message, 4 November 1972, 5.

42. *Kitty Hawk* message to COMNAVAIRPAC, 18 October 1972, Glover Chronology of Events, 1.

43. *Kitty Hawk* message to CINCPACFLT, 22 October 1972.

44. Townsend, Cong. Sub., 546; author interviews with Alex Landon, San Diego civilian attorney and *Kitty Hawk* defense counsel.

45. Townsend, Cong. Sub., 546.

46. Author interviews, Dick Smith.

47. Author tape transcript, 13-1, and 21 February 1973 meeting with Lieutenant Dick Smith in San Diego.

48. Author interviews, Dick Smith.

49. *UCMJ*, Article 22–24.

50. *UCMJ*, Articles 26 and 27.

51. He was acting in that role when he directed the initial charges against the accused.

52. *UCMJ*, Article 1 (9).

53. *UCMJ*, Article 128(a)(1).

54. Author interviews, Dick Smith.

55. AA Glover Chronology of Events, 1.

56. CINCPACFLT Message to COMUSNAVPHIL SUBIC BAY RP, 27 October 1972.

57. Author interviews, Dick Smith.

58. CDR Cloud, Cong. Sub., 591.
59. Author interviews, Dick Smith.
60. A sailor appearing before a captain's mast is called an accused, not a defendant. Thereafter, if his case is referred to a courts-martial hearing, he becomes a defendant.
61. *UCMJ*, Article 29(b)(3).
62. *UCMJ*, Article 16(c)(1).
63. *UCMJ*, Article 52(a)(3).
64. *UCMJ*, Article 25(c)(2)(B), and (e)(1).
65. Author interviews, Dick Smith; author tape transcript, 13-7.
66. COMNAVPHIL Message, 4 November 1972, 4; Haak Investigation, Exhibit 188.
67. Haak Investigation, Exhibit 188, 6. The names of those tried on board are here kept confidential, as they were by the congressional subcommittee. See, CAPT Townsend, Cong. Sub., 545.
68. AOC Charles Johnson testimony, Haak Investigation, 64–65.
69. Author tape transcript, 13-7.
70. Author tape transcript, 13-7.
71. Haak Investigation, Exhibit 188, 6.
72. Author file notes and author tape transcript, 13-7.
73. Haak Investigation, Exhibit 188, 1.
74. Author tape transcript, 13-7.

7. Adding Insult to Injury

1. Author interviews, Durward Davis.
2. CINCPACFLT Message, 5 November 1972, 4, 5. Those three defendants had not requested civilian counsel, so their trials were not delayed,
3. Author interview, SN Cleveland Mallory, 22 November 1972.
4. Author interviews, Durward Davis.
5. COMUSNAVPHIL.
6. United States v. Airman Apprentice Ronald Glover, Chronology of Events, 1.
7. CINCPACFLT Message, 5 November 1972, 4.
8. Written statement of PNC John Simon, Chief Counselor of Subic Bay Naval Base Correctional Center, late November 1972.
9. Author tape transcript, 1-1.
10. Author interviews, Dick Smith.
11. Statement of Chief Counselor PNC Simon.
12. Simon statement.

13. In his statement, PNC Simon said, "I very strongly recommend that the Kitty Hawk group be placed in MAXIMUM security confinement until their trial."

14. As with virtually all convening authorities, CAPT McKenzie had no legal training; however, he had a JAG officer assigned to him as a Staff Judge Advocate. Convening authorities can accept Charge Sheets without change for cases transferred to them, or can amend the charges. CAPT McKenzie testimony, Cong. Sub., 448–449.

15. Author tape transcript, 1-1.

16. Author interview, SN Cleveland Mallory, 22 November 1972.

17. Stops were made at military airfields in Okinawa and Hawaii enroute to San Diego.

18. GySgt John Eveleth statement, 22 November 1972.

19. CAPT McKenzie testimony, Glover Hearing, 29 January 1973, 306.

20. NASNI had a storied aviation history of its own. In 1911, aviator Glenn Curtiss produced the world's first seaplane using the waters around the island. On May 12, 1927, Charles Lindberg flew off the island bound for New York in his San Diego built *Spirit of St. Louis,* enroute to Paris.

21. LCDR Caldwell testimony at AR Coleman special court-martial trial, 12 February 1973, 60.

22. Caldwell, 60.

23. CAPT McKenzie, Glover Hearing, 320.

24. The San Diego Naval Base is part of the Eleventh Naval District, which includes subdistricts in New Mexico, Nevada, Arizona, and California.

25. Author file notes, April 1973, 196.

26. Cpl Paul Willeford testimony at AR Coleman trial, 122.

27. Author file notes, April 1973, 192–194.

28. The Legal Center housed a legal team consisting of a military judge, non-JAG prosecutor, and two JAG defense counsel. It primarily dealt with UA cases. In fact, so many cases were processed daily it was often called the "UA mill." UA cases in other military branches are called Away Without Leave (AWOL).

29. Author interviews, Tom Phillips.

30. Author interviews, Phillips.

31. Author interviews, Phillips.

32. LT Phillips was prescient in his admonition, as some later trials proved.

33. JAG CDR Keiser, SN Mallory Article 39(a) hearing, 15 December 1972, 9.

34. Author tape transcripts, 1-1.

8. *Kitty Hawk* Lawyers

1. Accused right to individual military counsel. *MCM*, R.C.M. 506(b)(1).
2. Author tape transcripts, 1-3, 16-2.
3. List in author's case note files.
4. *UCMJ*, Article 128, Assault, and Article 116, Riot or Breach of Peace.
5. Faced with the impending prospect of likely infantry service in Vietnam, the number of law students nationwide applying for the program was overwhelming. We were told the Navy received more than sixty applicants for each opening.
6. LT Truhe testimony, Glover Hearing, 23 January 1973, 122–123.
7. Winner, South Dakota, current population about 2,800.
8. I received a Hardy Scholarship, which was offered to three first-year students.
9. I was a member of Northwestern's *Law Review* and in my final year, taught a first-year class on Legal Research and Writing.
10. Author interviews, Dick Smith.
11. The *UCMJ* had its origins in 1775 when the Second Continental Congress established Articles of War to govern the conduct of the Continental Army. The *UCMJ* is authorized by Article 1 of the US Constitution: "The Congress shall have power to make rules for the government and regulation of the land and naval forces."
12. *Miranda v. Arizona*, 384 U.S. 436 (1966).

9. *Kitty Hawk* Defendants

1. *Report by the Special Subcommittee on Disciplinary Problems in the US Navy*, 92nd Cong., 2nd sess., 1973, H.A.S.C. 92-81, Section II, B. 1.
2. LCDR Fred Canant, author case notes.
3. "Kitty Hawk Back in Home Port: Sailors Describe Racial Conflict," *New York Times*, November 28, 1972.
4. BM2 James Brown, Cong. Sub., 685.
5. Defendants' Service Record summaries, Haak Investigation, Exhibit 9.
6. Author interviews, Durward Davis.
7. Author interviews, Davis.
8. Author interviews, Vernell Robinson.
9. Author interviews, Perry Pettus.
10. I was later assigned to represent Seaman Willie Faison (E-3).
11. Author tape transcript, 1-6.
12. Author case note, November 1972; author tape transcript, 1-7.
13. LT Charles O'Neill, author case note, November 1972.

14. That officer was LT Dick Smith.
15. SN Mallory Service Record.
16. Author client interview, SN Mallory; author case notes, 22 November 1972.
17. Author case notes, December 1972.
18. Author tape transcripts, 1-6, 1-7.
19. Author tape transcripts, 1-7.

10. Pretrial Confinement

1. "Complaints Persist That Black Sailors Accused in Carrier Incidents Did Not Receive Equal Justice," *New York Times*, Earl Caldwell, April 1, 1973.
2. The last six defendants were released on 27 February 1973. *San Diego Evening Tribune*, Feb. 28, 1973; and author tape transcript, 15-4.
3. *Los Angeles Times*, December 14, 1972.
4. Author letter to JAG LT Dick Smith at Subic Bay Naval Base, 14 December 1972.
5. Author tape transcript, 5-1.
6. AR Coleman was tried on 12 February 1973.
7. Author notes of meeting, 28 November 1972, 4; author tape transcript, 1-2.
8. Author tape transcript, 3-1.
9. CAPT McKenzie testimony, Glover Hearing, 29 January 1973, 306.
10. McKenzie, Glover Hearing, 306.
11. That counsel was civilian attorney Dennis Kelly.
12. CAPT McKenzie testimony, Glover Hearing, 316–317.
13. McKenzie, Glover Hearing, 319–321.
14. McKenzie, Glover Hearing, 324.
15. LT Albert Larson testimony, Glover Hearing, 262–263.
16. CAPT McKenzie testimony, Glover Hearing, 316.
17. Milton Silverman Affidavit, November 30, 1972.
18. CAPT McKenzie testimony, Glover Hearing, 305.
19. *MCM*, R.C.M. 305(h)(2)(B).
20. *MCM*, R.C.M. 304 (c).
21. *Navy Corrections Manual* as cited in NAACP legal brief to COMFAIR, 30 November 1972, 19.
22. *MCM*, R.C.M. 304 (a).
23. LCDR Caldwell, at 12 February 1973 AR Coleman special court-martial trial, 62.
24. *MCM*, R.C.M. 305 (g).

25. Defense counsel Dennis Kelly statement at Glover Hearing, 313–314.

26. "Witness in Kitty Hawk Hearings . . ." *New York Times*, December 27, 1972.

27. Author interviews, Durward Davis.

28. Cpl Paul Willeford testimony at SR Coleman special court-martial trial, 12 September 1973, 122–123.

29. Testimony of SR Coleman at his trial, 126–128.

30. Clinical Record, LCDR MC Dennis Kottke, Report of Psychiatric Evaluation, 5 February 1973.

31. "Kitty Hawk's Black Exec Denies Friction with Captain on Riot," *San Diego Independent Post Telegraph*, December 7, 1972.

32. Author tape transcript, 11-5.

33. Clinical Record, LCDR MC Dennis Kottke, Report of Psychiatric Evaluation, 30 November 1972.

34. Kottke, Report of Psychiatric Evaluation.

35. "Kitty Hawk's Black Exec Denies Friction," *San Diego Independent Post Telegraph*.

36. COMFAIR's headquarters were also at the North Island Naval Air Station.

37. Milt Silverman letter and legal brief to COMFAIR, 30 November 1972.

38. Author letter to LT Dick Smith in Subic Bay, 14 December 1972, 3.

39. Report of the Task Force on the Administration of Military Justice in the Armed Forces, November 30, 1972.

40. Report, Vol. I, 7.

41. Author conversation with Nathaniel Jones in San Diego, 2 March 1973. Author tape transcript, 1-3.

42. Author tape transcript, 1-3.

43. Author tape transcript, 1-4.

44. In 1994 this court was renamed the United States Court of Appeals for the Armed Forces.

45. *Newsome v. McKenzie*, 22 C.M.A. 92, 46 C.M.R. 91, 94 (1973).

46. Author tape transcript, 10-6, 29 January 1973.

47. Stipulation in Glover Hearing, Defense Exhibit K, and author file notes.

11. Command Threat

1. LT Glenn Haase and I each represented six *Kitty Hawk* defendants.

2. Author tape transcript, 1-4.

3. LT Truhe testimony, SN Cleveland Mallory Article 39(a) hearing, 15 December 1972, 11–12 (hereinafter, Mallory Hearing).

4. CDR Krenke was the pilot of the COD plane. Author case notes, 28 November 1972, 10.

5. Author tape transcript, 1-4. A detailed Navy account of the episode of Silverman's flight to *Kitty Hawk* is in a report submitted to the Congressional Subcommittee. "Report from Commander, Naval Air Force, U.S. Pacific Fleet, to Commander, U.S. Pacific Fleet, 27 November 1972," Cong. Sub., 895–897.

6. Author case notes, 28 November, and author tape transcript, 6-1, 6-2.

7. ADM Clarey, Cong. Sub., 900.

8. Author interviews, Milt Silverman.

9. CAPT Townsend testimony, Cong. Sub., 545.

10. Townsend, Cong. Sub., 543.

11. That commander was CAPT Dee Douglass.

12. LT Truhe testimony, Mallory Hearing, 12–13.

13. Henry Giler, Larry Williams, and Hank deSuvero. Author case notes, 28 November 1972, and Complaint 73-63-7, US District Court for the Southern District of California, 23 February, 1973, 10.

14. LT Truhe testimony, Mallory Hearing, 13.

15. Truhe, Mallory Hearing, 14.

16. Truhe, Mallory Hearing, 15.

17. Sworn Affidavit of LT Marvin D. Truhe, JAGC, USNR. early December, 1972.

18. LT Truhe testimony, Mallory Hearing, 17–18.

19. CAPT Lazar H. Benrubi, who was stationed at the Eleventh Naval District Headquarters in downtown San Diego.

20. LT Truhe testimony, Mallory Hearing, 19.

21. ADM Clarey, Cong. Sub., 900.

22. Message introduced at Subcommittee hearing, Cong. Sub., 543.

23. Author case notes, 28 November 1972, and author tape transcript, 1-6.

24. SECNAV letter to congressional subcommittee, 9 December 1972, Cong. Sub., 893.

25. ADM Clarey report to Commander in Chief, U.S. Pacific Fleet, Cong. Sub., 896.

26. Clarey, Cong. Sub., 895.

27. CAPT Townsend, Cong. Sub., 543–544.

28. Townsend, Cong. Sub., 543.

29. Townsend, Cong. Sub., 543.

30. In fact, the staff judge advocate to the convening authority sent a message to *Kitty Hawk*'s legal officer stating, "There was [sic] no unusual incidents aboard ship involving Mr. Silverman." Cong. Sub., 896.

31. CAPT McKenzie testimony, Glover Hearing, 29 January 1973, 310–311.

32. CAPT McKenzie's Staff Judge Advocate's report, Cong. Sub., 896–897.

33. *Manual for Courts-Martial*, Rule for Courts-Martial 601(c), Disqualification.

34. *MCM*, R.C.M. 104(a)(1), Unlawful Command Influence.

35. *UCMJ*, Article 138, Complaints of wrongs. LT Glenn Haase and I hand delivered a copy of our motion to CAPT McKenzie on 2 December 1972. Author's tape transcript, 1-6.

36. My cocounsel was civilian attorney Dennis Kelly.

37. LT Truhe testimony, Mallory Hearing, 14–16.

38. Truhe, Mallory Hearing, 19.

39. Truhe, Mallory Hearing, 20.

40. Truhe, Mallory Hearing, 26–29. CAPT McKenzie suggested I misrepresented myself by not telling the pilot I was a JAG officer from the law center. However, the pilot CDR Krenke said he knew I was attached to the law center when I called. He made that statement during a meeting that included all Navy personnel involved in the flight incident. Author file notes of 28 November 1972 meeting at Naval Air Station North Island, 5.

41. LT Truhe testimony, Mallory Hearing, 33–34.

42. CAPT McKenzie testimony, Mallory Hearing, 48–50.

43. McKenzie, Mallory Hearing, 51–52.

44. McKenzie, Mallory Hearing, 52.

45. LT Thomas Grogan was the Assistant Judge Advocate on CAPT Mckenzie's staff.

46. Grogan, Glover Hearing, 287.

47. CAPT McKenzie testimony, Glover Hearing, 309–310.

48. CAPT Benrubi testimony, Mallory Hearing, 89.

49. CAPT McKenzie testimony, Mallory Hearing, 80–81.

50. ADM Zumwalt, Cong. Sub., 1088.

51. CAPT McKenzie testimony, Mallory Hearing, 55–56.

52. ADM Zumwalt, Cong. Sub., 1088.

53. Attorney Milt Silverman, Mallory Hearing, 92–95, 101.

54. Judge Bryant statement, Mallory Hearing, 108.

55. Author interviews with Milton Silverman and former JAG Lieutenant Harry Carter.

56. *UCMJ*, Article 133.

57. *Manual for Courts Martial*, §90(b(2).

12. Justice on Trial

1. "Court-Martial Opens for First of 21 Blacks on Carrier," *New York Times*, December 29, 1972.
2. Author tape transcript, 3-2.
3. Navy or Marine personnel who escort prisoners are called chasers.
4. The Service Dress Blue enlisted uniform is sometimes called the "Crackerjack," because that uniform is worn by the sailor appearing on the cover of Cracker Jack boxes.
5. 1972 and 1973 author file and interview notes of SN Cleveland Mallory case.
6. Author tape transcript, 3-3.
7. Author tape transcript, 13-1.
8. TC Lieutenant Bob Pearson and ATC Lieutenant Harry Carter.
9. *UCMJ*, Article 39.
10. Trial transcript of United States v. SN Cleveland Mallory special court-martial, SPCM Convening Order No. 6-72, as amended, 115–116 (hereinafter, Transcript).
11. AO3 Walter Unland, Transcript, 117–119.
12. Unland, Transcript, 119–120.
13. Unland, Transcript, 124–125. Dogging wrenches are seven-inch metal tools used for leverage in opening and closing watertight doors and hatches.
14. Unland, Transcript, 133.
15. Unland, Transcript, 125–128.
16. Unland, Transcript, 130.
17. Unland, Transcript, 133.
18. Unland, Transcript, 133.
19. Unland, Transcript, 134.
20. AN Charles Webber, Transcript, 138.
21. Webber, Transcript, 140.
22. Webber, Transcript, 143.
23. Webber, Transcript, 143.
24. Webber, Transcript, 143, 147.
25. Webber, Transcript, 148.
26. AA Edgar Murphy, Transcript, 180.
27. SA Alfred Weber, Transcript, 187–188; and AA Murphy, Transcript, 173.
28. AN Laurie, Transcript, 191–192.
29. Laurie, Transcript, 195.
30. Laurie, Transcript, 196–198.

31. Laurie, Transcript, 198–199.

32. Laurie, Transcript, 199.

33. Laurie, Transcript, 202.

34. Transcript, 210.

35. LT Truhe testimony, AN Michael Laurie special court-martial, 20 September 1973, 53.

36. Ogden Taylor, Transcript, 206–207.

37. Taylor, Transcript, 208.

38. LTJG Beassie, Transcript, 212.

39. Beassie, Transcript, 213. Mallory's mast record indicated "Unauthorized absence from 0600, 72 July 07 until 0730, 72 July 07."

40. Beassie, Transcript, 211–213.

41. Beassie, Transcript, 214–215.

42. Transcript, 215.

43. Author trial notes, quoting CAPT Newsome.

44. BTFN Francis Tucker, Transcript, 218.

45. LT Martin statement to Naval Investigative Service, 6 April 1973.

46. BTFN Francis Tucker, Transcript, 219–220.

47. The trial counsel was LT Bob Pearson.

48. Tucker, Transcript, 220–221.

49. Tucker, Transcript, 222.

50. Tucker, Transcript, 224.

51. Tucker, Transcript, 226.

52. Tucker, Transcript, 227–228.

53. Tucker, Transcript, 228–229.

54. Tucker, Transcript, 230.

55. Tucker, Transcript, 232.

56. Tucker, Transcript, 232.

57. Tucker, Transcript, 235.

58. Tucker, Transcript, 238–239.

59. Tucker, Transcript, 240–241.

60. Tucker, Transcript, 239.

61. Tucker, Transcript, 243.

62. SA Alfred Weber, Transcript, 247–251; and AN Edgar Murphy, Transcript, 251–256.

63. LT Truhe, Transcript, 259–262.

64. Truhe, 267–268.

65. Transcript, 272.

66. Author tape transcript, 7-3.

67. Reporter Bob Meyers, author tape transcript, 7-3.

68. LT Bob Pearson, author tape transcript, 7-3.

69. Author tape transcript, 7-3.

70. *Manual for Courts-Martial*, Rule for Courts-Martial 1001(a)(1)(A)(iv).

71. *MCM*, Rule for Courts-Martial 1001(a)(1)(C).

72. Transcript, 272–273.

73. SN Cleveland Mallory, Transcript, 284–285.

74. Mallory, Transcript, 286.

75. Mallory, Transcript, 285.

76. GMM2 George Smith Jr., 275–276.

77. CS1 Roland Clark, 282.

78. SH1 Gerald Henry, 289–292.

79. Mallory, Transcript, 286–287.

80. CAPT Bryant, Transcript, 305.

13. Undercover

1. Author tape transcript, 7-5.

2. "Court-Martial Opens for First of 21 Blacks on Carrier," *New York Times*, December 29, 1972.

3. See further discussion in chapter 19.

4. Author tape transcript, 7-4.

5. Tape, 7-4.

6. Tape, 7-6, 7-7.

7. Tape, 7-5, 8-4.

8. Author interviews, Milt Silverman who said he received $10,000 for that purpose.

9. My wife and I had since moved from Chula Vista to Linda Vista.

10. Author tape transcript, 7-6.

11. Affidavit of B. L. Hicks, 19 February 1973, submitted in Cleveland Mallory Appellate Brief. Author tape transcript, 8-4.

12. Author tape transcript, 7-7.

13. Tape, 7-7.

14. Tape, 7-7.

15. Address list document in author's personal files.

16. Coronado Island is the name most civilians give to what military personnel typically refer to as North Island.
17. Author tape transcript, 8.4.
18. Tape, 15-8.
19. Tape, 15-9. The recorder had receiver wires extending down inside both arms of Hicks's long-sleeved shirt.

14. Withholding Evidence

1. Motion filed in Glover Hearing, 23 January 1973.
2. *Brady v. Maryland,* 373 U.S. 83, 87 (1963). This case gave rise to the "Brady Rule."
3. *Manual for Courts Martial,* Rule for Courts-Martial 701(a)(1) (C).
4. *MCM,* R.C.M.701(a)(1).
5. *MCM,* R.C.M. 701(a)(1), Discussion.
6. *MCM,* R.C.M. 701(a)(6)(A).
7. As referenced in a letter from CAPT McKenzie to Milt Silverman, 2 January 1973 and as referenced in Western Union Telegram from Milt Silverman to CAPT McKenzie, 26 December 1972.
8. LT M. D. Truhe letters to *Kitty Hawk* Trial Counsel, 11 and 14 December 1972. Additional letter discovery requests were made to CAPT McKenzie by attorneys Ben James and Dennis Kelly on 15 and 16 January 1973.
9. Milton J. Silverman letter to Commanding Officer, San Diego Naval Air Station, December 15, 1972.
10. *Manual for Courts-Martial,* R.C.M. 701(d).
11. AN Laurie testimony at AA John Rowe Pretrial Investigation Hearing, 21 October 1972, 54.
12. LT Martin testimony, Glover Hearing, 24 January 1973, 201.
13. LCDR Fred Canant, author case notes.
14. *Military Rules of Evidence,* 505(h)(2)(A)(i).
15. Attorney Milt Silverman, author's file notes. See, also, Complaint 73-63-7, US District Court for the Southern District of California, February 23, 1973, 8–9.
16. Author tape transcript, 11 February 1973, 11-6. See, also, 25 January 173 letter from CAPT McKenzie's Staff Judge Advocate to *Kitty Hawk* Trial Counsel forwarding "all known *relevant* [emphasis added] material."
17. *MCM,* R.C.M. 701(a)(1) (C).
18. Author tape transcript, 13-7.
19. Glover Hearing, 23 January 1973.

20. LT Truhe, Glover Hearing, 23 January 1973, 109.

21. Truhe, Glover Hearing, 112–113.

22. Truhe, Glover Hearing, 115.

23. Truhe, Glover Hearing, 114.

24. Truhe, Glover Hearing, 118–119.

25. Truhe, Glover Hearing, 121.

26. Truhe, Glover Hearing, 111.

27. Truhe, Glover Hearing, 111–112.

28. Truhe, Glover Hearing, 114–115.

29. LT Martin testimony, Glover Hearing, 222.

30. LT Truhe question to the court, Glover Hearing, 222.

31. Memo from Head Trial Counsel to Defense Counsel, 18 December 1972.

32. Silverman letter to CAPT McKenzie, December 15, 1972.

33. *MCM*, R.C.M. 703(d)(1).

34. CAPT McKenzie testimony, Mallory Hearing, 54.

35. CAPT McKenzie letter to Milton J. Silverman, 4 January 1973.

36. *UCMJ*, Article 38(b)(3)(B).

37. Silverman letter to CAPT McKenzie, December 15, 1972.

38. Lieutenants Dick Smith, Bruce Locke, and Ernie Lindberg.

39. CAPT McKenzie letter to LCDR Fred Canant, 15 January 1973.

40. *Manual for Courts-Martial*, R.C.M. 703(a) and (b).

41. LT. M. D. Truhe letters to Commanding Officer, Naval Air Station, 7 and 16 January 1973, requesting JAG LT Richard Philpott.

42. CAPT McKenzie letter to LT. M. D. Truhe, 17 January 1973.

43. Glover Hearing, 26 January 1973, 35.

44. Glover Hearing, 231.

45. Author tape transcript, 13-7.

46. LT Truhe testimony, Glover Hearing, 26 January 1973, 237.

47. "Prejudice and Perjury Charged in Investigation of Carrier Riot," *New York Times*, February 23, 1973.

48. "Navy Accused of Injustice," *San Diego Union*, February 10, 1973.

49. Author tape transcript, 17-4, 17-6.

50. Tape, 10-7, 10-10, 11-3, 12-4.

51. Fortunately, that tension subsided after the *Kitty Hawk* trials concluded, and our friendships resumed as strongly as before.

52. NAACP attorney Clifton Blevins, 23 February 1973, author tape transcript, 14-5.

15. Undercover Triumph

1. Billy Hicks tape transcript of Laurie statements [hereinafter Hicks Tapes], Doc. 1, February 1, 1973, 1, 4.
2. Hicks Tapes, Doc. 2, February 7, 1973, 12, 19. Author tape transcript, 11-3.
3. Author tape transcript, 12-4.
4. Tape, 12-7.
5. Tape, 12-7.
6. Tape, 12-7.
7. Document 1: January 31, 1973 (Hicks and Laurie present) and February 1, 1973 (Hicks, Laurie and his wife, and AN Chuck Weber present); Doc. 2: February 4 and 7, 1973 (Hicks and Laurie present); Doc. 3: February 8, 1973 (Hicks, Laurie, and Laurie's wife present); and Doc. 4: February 9, 1973 (Hicks, Laurie, and Laurie's wife present).
8. Hicks Tapes, Doc. 1, February 1, 1973, 4–5.
9. Hicks Tapes, Doc. 2, February 7, 1973, 12.
10. Hicks Tapes, Doc. 2, 12–13.
11. Hicks Tapes, Doc. 2, 15.
12. Hicks Tapes, Doc. 2, 17–18.
13. Hicks Tapes, Doc. 2, February 4, 1973, 1–2.
14. Hicks Tapes, Doc. 4, February 9, 1973, 4.
15. Hicks Tapes, Doc. 1, February 1, 1973, 5–6.
16. Hicks Tapes, Doc. 1, 7–8.
17. Hicks Tapes, Doc. 1, 10.
18. Hicks Tapes, Doc. 2, February 7, 1973, 18–19.
19. Author tape transcript, 13-2.
20. LT Harry Carter.
21. Author tape transcript, 13-2.
22. LT Bob Pearson.
23. Tape, 13-2.
24. Tape, 13-3.
25. Tape, 13-3.
26. Tape, 13-3, 13-4.
27. Tape, 13-4.
28. Tape, 13-4.
29. Tape, 13-4.
30. Tape, 13-4.

31. Tape, 14-3. Neither Hicks nor his wife were ever threatened, nor did any harm come to them.

32. Tape, 14-1.

33. Complaint 73-63-7, US District Court for the Southern District of California, 23 February, 1973. No further litigation followed the filing of that lawsuit, but four days later the Navy released the defendants who still remained in the brig.

34. "Prejudice and Perjury Charged in Investigation of Carrier Riot," *New York Times*, February 23, 1973.

35. Earl Caldwell, "Kitty Hawk Back at Home Port; Sailors Describe Racial Conflict," *New York Times*, November 29, 1972.

36. Caldwell, "Navy's Racial Trouble Persists Despite Long Effort to Dispel It," *New York Times*, May 28, 1973.

37. Author tape transcript, 19 March 1973, 16-8.

38. Tape, 15-1.

39. Special Court-Martial Order No. 2-5-73, 26 February 1973.

40. "Conviction of Black Overturned by Navy," *New York Times*, February 27, 1973.

41. Earl Caldwell, "Complaints Persist that Black Sailors Accused in Carrier Incidents Did Not Receive Equal Justice," *New York Times*, April 1, 1973.

42. Author tape transcripts, March 1, 1973, 16-1, 16-2.

43. San Diego Channel 8 News, February 27, 1973; author tape transcripts, 15-2, 15-3.

44. Ben James, author tape transcript, 15-3.

45. Tape, 15-3, 15-4.

46. Tape, 15-5.

47. Reporter Judith Hillman, Channel 10 News, 28 February 1973; author tape transcripts, 15-5, 15-6.

48. Author tape transcript, 15-8. Two weeks later, Cleveland Mallory accepted an early out from the Navy with an honorable discharge, and returned home to Pittsburgh. Author tape transcript, 16-8.

49. Tape, 12-5, 15-4; "Six Former Kitty Hawk," *San Diego Evening Tribune*, February 28, 1973.

50. Tape, 15-4.

51. That defendant was SA James Allen.

52. Author tape transcript, 15-4.

53. Tape, 16-4.

16. Unequal Justice

1. *Nation*, "Some Very Unhappy Ships," November 12, 1972.
2. Amendment XIV, §1, U.S. Constitution, adopted in 1868; and it also applied to military law.
3. Billy Hicks tape transcript, Doc. 2, February 7, 1973, 14.
4. Hicks Tapes, Doc. 3, February 8, 1973, 3.
5. "Navy Man Loses Dismissal Plea," *San Diego Evening Tribune*, January 27, 1973.
6. *United States v. Armstrong*, 517 U.S. 456 (1996), 464.
7. *United States v. Armstrong*, 457.
8. Glover Hearing, 23–27 January 1973.
9. CDR Frederick Deane.
10. CAPT Townsend, Cong. Sub., 531.
11. CDR Cloud testimony, Glover Hearing, 73.
12. LT Truhe testimony, Glover Hearing, 108–109.
13. PO1C Andrew Woodridge, *San Diego Evening Tribune*, "Ex-crewman tells of disarming sailors," March 13, 1973, B-3.
14. CDR Cloud testimony, Glover Hearing, 73–74.
15. LT Truhe, Glover Hearing, 111.
16. AMH3 Hiram Davis, *Los Angeles Times*, "Others Started Carrier Fight, Blacks Declare," December 28, 1972.
17. Hicks Tapes, Doc. 4, 4.
18. Benjamin D. James Jr. letter to CAPT Robert McKenzie, January 15, 1973.
19. CAPT Robert P. McKenzie letter to Benjamin D. James Jr., 22 January 1973, 1.
20. LT Truhe, Glover Hearing, 109.
21. *UCMJ*, Article 31(b).
22. Author tape transcript, 28 February 1973, 15-7, 15-8.
23. Mallory statement, 13 October 1973, Haak Investigation, Exhibit 86.
24. That "interview" was conducted by Petty Officer Second Class McNealy.
25. AN Mallory testimony, Glover Hearing, 89.
26. Glover Hearing, 88–90.
27. CDR Cloud testimony, Glover Hearing, 77.
28. LT James Martin testimony, Glover Hearing, 211–212. As noted, one investigator spoke to Mallory for five minutes.
29. Martin, SN Mallory trial, 296.
30. *The Bluejackets Manual*, 135.

31. Martin, Glover Hearing, 212.

32. Letter to Ben James from CAPT McKenzie, with copy to LT M. D. Truhe, 22 January 1973.

33. Martin, SN Mallory trial, 3–4 January 1973, 298.

34. Martin, Glover Hearing, 213–214.

35. Martin, Glover Hearing, 181.

36. Martin, Glover Hearing, 215.

37. Martin, Glover Hearing, 195.

38. ADH3 Charles Green.

39. AOC Charles Johnson testimony, Cong. Sub., 782.

40. CDR Cloud testimony, Cong. Sub., 586.

41. LT James Martin, Glover Hearing, 205.

42. Martin, Glover Hearing, 205.

43. Martin, Glover Hearing, 206.

44. Martin, Glover Hearing, 219–220.

45. CDR Cloud, Glover Hearing, 61–62.

46. Cloud, Glover Hearing, 52.

47. Article 116, *UCMJ*, and §54(b)(1)(c) of the *Manual for Courts-Martial*.

48. Judge Bryant statement, Glover Hearing, 220.

49. LT Martin testimony, Glover Hearing, 217.

50. *UCMJ*, Article 117, Provoking Speeches or Gestures.

51. Charge II, Specifications 2 and 3 of ADJ3 Bennie Hall Charge Sheet.

52. LT Martin testimony, Glover Hearing, 217.

53. Stipulation in Glover Hearing, Defense Exhibit N.

54. LT Martin testimony, SN Mallory trial, 4 January 1973, 299.

55. *Manual for Courts-Martial*, R.C.M. 615.

56. AA Paul Selman testimony, Glover Hearing, 140–141.

57. AA Selman, author interview notes, January 1973.

58. AA Selman testimony, Glover Hearing, 143.

59. Selman, Glover Hearing, 144–145.

60. Selman, Glover Hearing, 145.

61. Selman, Glover Hearing, 146.

62. Selman, Glover Hearing, 48.

63. AN Don Gossner, author interview notes, 15 January 1973.

64. LT Martin testimony, Glover Hearing, 227–228.

65. Martin, Glover Hearing, 228.

66. Martin, Glover Hearing, 228–229.

67. Martin, Glover Hearing, 224–226.

68. Glover Hearing, 226.

69. AN Laurie testimony at his special court-martial trial, 20 September 1973, 80.

70. Stipulation, Defense Exhibit O at selective prosecution motion hearing.

71. LT Glenn Haase testimony, Glover Hearing, 154.

72. Haase, Glover Hearing, 154.

73. Haase, Glover Hearing, 154.

74. Haase, Glover Hearing, 158.

75. Glover Hearing, 158.

76. CAPT Bryant, Glover Hearing, 158–159.

77. *Manual for Courts-Martial*, R.C.M. 502(d)(3),

78. LT Martin testimony, Glover Hearing, 209–210.

79. LT Truhe closing argument, Glover Hearing, 245–247. My statement of "no rights ever being given" refers to the fact that the witnesses were never advised they could remain silent during questioning, had the right to counsel, etc.

80. CAPT Bryant, Glover Hearing, 247. He was also quoted in a *San Diego Union* article, "Lack of Professionalism Claimed in Navy Probe," January 27, 1973.

17. Finding Justice

1. "Navy Closes Book on Racial 'Mutiny' Aboard Kitty Hawk," *Los Angeles Times*, April 11, 1973.

2. "Witness in Kitty Hawk Hearing Charges," *New York Times*, December 27, 1972.

3. Author tape transcript, 14-3, 14-4.

4. Author tape transcript, 14-1.

5. AN Laurie testimony at his special courts-martial trial, 20 September 1973, 67.

6. "Armed Forces: Storm Warning," *Time* magazine, December 11, 1972.

7. CAPT Townsend later submitted a lengthy rebuttal to the *Time* magazine article. Cong. Sub., 530–531.

8. "Kitty Hawk Back at Home Port: Sailors Describe Racial Conflict," *New York Times*, November 29, 1972.

9. LT Martin testimony, Glover Hearing, 25 January 1973, 205.

10. "Kitty Hawk Violence Related at Hearing," *Santa Cruz Sentinel*, December 22, 1972, 9.

11. "Quiet Crackdown by Navy Aimed at Dissident Blacks," *New York Times*, December 24, 1972.

12. "Quiet Crackdown."

13. LT Martin, Glover Hearing, 205.

14. *New York Times*, December 27, 1972; author tape transcript, 12-5.

15. CDR Cloud, Cong. Sub., 588.

16. Martin, Glover Hearing, 205.

17. Mike Pancer was a San Diego civilian attorney, active in the ACLU, and was asked by the NAACP to help represent the *Kitty Hawk* defendants. He agreed to do so, but declined any compensation.

18. Author tape transcript, 12-7.

19. Tape, 14-2. The witness was AN L. McCauley.

20. Tape, 14-2.

21. Tape, 14-2.

22. Tape, 7, March 1973, 16-4.

23. Tape, 14-4.

24. Tape, 16-8.

25. Tape, 1 March 1973, 16-1.

26. Author case notes.

27. NAACP attorney Ben James, *San Diego Union-Tribune*, 10 February 1973.

28. Author interviews with SA Davis's JAG Defense Counsel, Bruce Locke.

29. Civilian attorneys Dennis Kelly and Cecil McGriff.

30. Author interviews, Bruce Locke, and author tape transcript, 14-1.

31. Author interviews, Durward Davis.

32. Author interviews, Durward Davis.

33. ADJ3 Bennie Hall.

34. Author tape transcript, 16-8, and author case notes.

35. AR Robert Coleman.

36. *San Diego Union*, February 14, 1973, and author case notes.

37. Author tape transcripts, 12-4, 16-8, and author case notes.

38. Not to be confused with SA Durward Davis.

39. Author interviews, Alex Landon.

40. Author tape transcript, 13 December 1972, 3-1,

41. *UCMJ*, Article 97.

42. Alex Landon, in interview by Jim Gordon of San Diego Channel 8 TV News, January 2, 1973; author tape transcript, 7-1.

43. Author file notes, 11 January 1973.

44. Milt Silverman, author tape transcript, 13-8.

45. Author tape transcript, 14-5.

46. Author interviews, Vernell Robinson.

47. JAG LT Cliff Hapgood, civilian attorney Clifton Blevins, and LT Phillips.

48. Author interviews, Tom Phillips.

49. LtCol William Eleazer, "Carrier Trial Told of Witness Threat," *San Diego Union*, April 4, 1973.

50. "Jury Clears Sailor of All Riot Charges," *San Diego Tribune*, April 7, 1973.

51. Eleazer, "Carrier Trial Told of Witness Threat."

52. Author interviews, Vernell Robinson.

53. "Jury Clears Sailor of All Riot Charges."

54. *San Diego Tribune*, April 7, 1973; author interviews, Tom Phillips.

55. Author interviews, Vernell Robinson.

56. Cpl Robert Anderson statement, Haak Investigation, 13 October 1972.

57. AA Glover statement, 20 October 1972.

58. Glover statement.

59. CAPT McKenzie Endorsement Letter to COMFAIR, 11 January 1973.

60. COMFAIR letter to AA Glover, 12 January 1973.

61. Author interview, AA Oscar Martin, 15 February 1973.

62. Author interview, RMSN Ronnie Palmer, 7 February 1973.

63. Author interview, AA Malcolm McCreary, 15 February, 1973.

64. Following the trial, a Glover juror said they believed he acted in self-defense when he struck the marine corporal who bit him. Author tape transcript, 15-10.

65. Report of Result of Trial, AN Glover, 1 March 1973.

66. Author tape transcript, 16-8.

67. Tape, 11-3. His defense counsel included civilian attorney Cecil McGriff and JAG LT Albert Larsen.

68. LT Bradley prosecuted seven *Kitty Hawk* cases, and two other prosecutors, LT Harry Carter and LCDR Dan Closser, were also each assigned seven *Kitty Hawk* cases. Author tape transcript, 2-4, and author interviews, Jim Bradley.

69. BM3 Anthony Feeola statement, 18 October 1972.

70. SA Brian Broomhead, undated statement.

71. *UCMJ*, Article 89.

72. Author file notes.

73. Author interview, William Boone, 13 February 1973. Author tape transcript, 12-3. Boone is the white sailor who was charged several months after the incident, and only after my cross-examination of the ship's legal officer during the hearing on our selective prosecution motion.

74. Author interviews, Mike Sheehy.
75. Author interviews, Mike Sheehy.
76. "Sailor Faces Trial in Clash," *New York Times*, February 4, 1973.
77. Author interviews, Mike Sheehy.
78. Two others, as noted, pled guilty to rioting to get out of the brig and go home with early outs and honorable discharges.
79. Author case notes.
80. The jury also sentenced him to a reduction in rank and additional brig time but with a recommendation that both be suspended, which they were. Author case notes.
81. *UCMJ*, Article 116 and *Manual for Courts-Martial*, §54(b()1).
82. LT Dick Smith, AA John Rowe Article 39(a) hearing aboard *Kitty Hawk*, 21 October 1972, 82–83.
83. Naval History and Heritage Command, 7 October 2016.
84. Z-Gram #66, "Equal Opportunity," 17 December 1970.
85. "A Sort of Mutiny: The Constellation Incident," *New York Times*, February 18, 1973. That so-called "sit-down protest" occurred on 4 November 1972.
86. "Sort of Mutiny."
87. "Navy Receives Ultimatum on Race Relations," *Los Angeles Times*, November 5, 1972.
88. "Text of Zumwalt's Remarks," *New York Times*, November 10, 1972.
89. "Racial rifts, sabotage have Navy concerned," *Minneapolis Tribune*, November 8, 1972.
90. "Navy Receives Ultimatum."

18. Perjury on Trial

1. The telegram was sent by Leonard H. Carter, the West Coast regional director of the NAACP. Author tape transcript, 14-3.
2. Tape, 14-3.
3. Tape, 14-3.
4. Tape, 14-4.
5. Tape, 14-5.
6. Tape, 14-7, 15-2.
7. *Manual for Courts-Martial*, §81(c)(2)(c).
8. Author tape transcript, 14-7.
9. Tape, 14-3.
10. Now the Naval Criminal Investigative Service (NCIS).

11. NIS statements of TC LT Bob Pearson and ATC LT Harry Carter, 13 March 1973.

12. NIS statement of LT James Martin, 6 April 1973, 1.

13. AN Laurie, NIS statement, 0941H, 16 May 1973.

14. Laurie, NIS statement, 0823H, 16 May 1973.

15. AN Laurie testimony at his special court-martial trial, 20 September 1973, 76–77 (hereinafter, Laurie Trial).

16. AN Laurie NIS statement, 18 June 1973.

17. Laurie, 18 June 1973.

18. Laurie, 18 June 1973.

19. CAPT Richard E. Case, Laurie Trial, Amendment to SPCM Convening Order NO. 1-73, 21 September 1973.

20. AN Laurie Charge Sheet, 23 July 1973, Article 131, *UCMJ.*

21. Laurie Charge Sheet, Article 134, *UCMJ.*

22. Laurie Trial, 99.

23. JAG CDR Alvern D. Christian, Laurie Trial, 2, 118.

24. LT Truhe testimony, Laurie Trial, 53–54.

25. AN Laurie testimony, Laurie Trial, 68.

26. Laurie, Laurie Trial, 70–72.

27. Trial counsel, JAG LT Jay Kenoff, Laurie Trial, 99.

28. Defense counsel, JAG LT Dale Reed, Laurie Trial, 101.

29. Laurie Trial, 28–29. The jury included two lieutenant commanders, a lieutenant junior grade, and two chief warrant officers.

30. Laurie Trial, 116, 118.

31. Laurie Trial, 118.

32. *San Diego Evening Tribune*, September 21, 1973.

33. In response to a question by his defense counsel, Laurie testified he would be willing to accept "whatever punishment" the jury gave him. Laurie Trial, 73. In fact, he well knew his pretrial agreement would negate, for example, a BCD sentence by the jury.

19. Reflections

1. *The Bluejackets Manual*, 313–314, 349.

2. CPO Virgil Enochs, Cong. Sub., 664.

3. 1st Sgt Willie Binkley, Cong. Sub., 746.

4. ADM B. A. Clarey, Cong. Sub., 874.

5. CAPT Townsend, Cong. Sub., 519.

6. Townsend, Cong. Sub., 518.

7. Townsend, Cong. Sub., 527.

8. Michael Dokosi, "Did You Know a White Cook's Refusal to Serve Sandwich Triggered Racial Violence on the USS Kitty Hawk In 1972?," Face2FaceAfrica .com, January 10, 2020, https://face2faceafrica.com/article/did-you-know-a -white-cooks-refusal-to-serve-sandwich-triggered-racial-violence-on-the-uss -kitty-hawk-in-1972.

9. *New York Times*, April 1, 1973, quoting an unnamed Navy captain.

10. *Los Angeles Times*, December 11, 1972, part 1, 3.

11. CAPT Townsend, Cong. Sub., 520.

12. Townsend, Cong. Sub., 538.

13. AOC Charles Johnson, Cong. Sub., 783.

14. CAPT Townsend, Cong. Sub., 520.

15. CDR Wayne House Statement, Haak Investigation, 22 October 1972, Exhibit 115.

16. CDR William Dunnam statement, Haak Investigation, 25 October 1972, Exhibit 192.

17. CDR Malcolm Guess statement, Haak Investigation, 22 October 1972, Exhibit 112.

18. CDR House, Haak Investigation, Exhibit 115. Some critics said CAPT Townsend should have remained on the bridge to direct control efforts against the upheaval, instead of roaming the ship to face individual groups of sailors.

19. CDR James McKenzie statement, CO Attack Carrier Air Wing Eleven, Haak Investigation, 23 October 1972, Exhibit 101.

20. CDR Jack Wilbern statement, CO VAW-114, Haak Investigation, 23 October 1972, Exhibit 93.

21. CDR Mason Gilfrey statement, CO VA-195, Haak Investigation, 23 October 1972, Exhibit 97.

22. CDR Cloud report of 7 November 1972, Haak Investigation, Exhibit 195.

23. CAPT Townsend, Cong. Sub., 518.

24. Townsend, Cong. Sub., 518.

25. Cpl Anthony Avina testimony, Cong. Sub., 723.

26. AN James Radford, Cong. Sub., 1013.

27. CAPT Townsend, Cong. Sub., 520.

28. CDR Cloud, Cong. Sub., 587–588.

29. CDR Dunnam statement, Haak Investigation, Exhibit 192, 2.

30. CAPT Carlucci, Cong. Sub., 605.

31. LCDR Robert Riley, Cong. Sub., 645.

32. *Manual for Courts-Martial,* Article 94(a)(2).

33. *UCMJ,* Article 94(b).

34. LCpl David Reichle statement, 16 October 1972, Haak Investigation, Exhibit 27.

35. AOC Charles Johnson, Cong. Sub., 786.

36. CDR Cloud, Cong. Sub., 572.

37. Cloud, Cong. Sub., 580.

38. Cloud, Cong. Sub., 580.

39. CAPT Townsend, Cong. Sub., 533.

40. Townsend, Cong. Sub., 533.

41. Townsend, Cong. Sub., 545.

42. AN James Allen, "Others Started Carrier Fight, Blacks Declare," *Los Angeles Times,* December 28, 1972.

43. Townsend, Cong. Sub., 526.

44. Townsend, Cong. Sub., 520.

45. Townsend, Cong. Sub., 534.

46. Townsend, Cong. Sub., 521.

47. Townsend, Cong. Sub., 531.

48. "Kitty Hawk Back at Home Port; Sailors Describe Racial Conflict," *New York Times,* November 29, 1972.

49. CAPT Townsend, Cong. Sub., 517.

50. Townsend, Cong. Sub., 530.

51. Findings of Cong. Sub., II A. 3.

52. ADM Zumwalt, Cong. Sub., 10–11.

53. Zumwalt, Cong. Sub., 15.

54. CDR Cloud, Cong. Sub., 567.

55. CDR Cloud, Haak Investigation, 123.

56. CAPT Townsend, Cong. Sub., 517.

57. Townsend, 530.

58. Townsend, 526.

59. CDR Cloud testimony, Glover Hearing, 24 January 1973, 66.

60. CDR Cloud, Cong. Sub., 567.

61. CDR Frederick Deane testimony, Cong. Sub., 771–772.

62. ADM Zumwalt, Cong. Sub., 15–16.

63. AN William Boone testimony at AR Coleman special court-martial trial, 12 February 1973, 120.

64. Boone, 120.

65. "Court-Martial Opens for First of 21 Blacks on Carrier," *New York Times*, December 29, 1972.

66. AOC Charles Johnson, Cong. Sub., 788.

67. CAPT Townsend, Cong. Sub., 508.

68. Townsend, Cong. Sub., 521.

69. Secretary of Defense Melvin Laird, *Los Angeles Times*, November 30, 1972.

70. *Report of the Task Force on the Administration of Military Justice in the Armed Forces*," November 30, 1972, Volume I, 3.

71. Nathaniel R. Jones, "Discrimination in the Military," *Crisis*, January 1973.

72. Jones, "Discrimination."

73. Jones, "Discrimination."

74. ADM Zumwalt, Cong. Sub., 15.

75. Earl Caldwell, "Complaints Persist That Black Sailors Accused in Carrier Incidents Did Not Receive Equal Justice," *New York Times*, April 1, 1973.

20. Where Are They Now?

1. Author interviews, Durward Davis.

2. Author interviews, Vernell Robinson.

3. Author interviews, Perry Pettus.

4. Author interviews with Donna Mallory-Coleman, sister of Cleveland Mallory.

5. Marland Townsend obituary, *Stars and Stripes*, July 2020.

6. "Benjamin Cloud Personal Papers," San Diego Air & Space Museum, accessed April 25, 2022, https://sandiegoairandspace.org/collection/item/benjamin-cloud -personal-papers; Obituary for Benjamin W. Cloud, *San Diego Union-Tribune*, September 5, 2021. https://www.legacy.com/us/obituaries/sandiegouniontribune /name/benjamin-cloud-obituary?id=16817148.

7. Obituary for Benjamin W. Cloud, *San Diego Union-Tribune*.

8. *Coronado Eagle and Journal*, "Six Area Captains chosen for flag," April 19, 1973.

9. "GEN David C. Jones, chairman, Joint CHIEF of STAFF, U.S. Armed Forces (2nd from left), is accompanied . . ." photo archived in Public Domain Media, NARA & DVIDS Public Domain Archive, February 2, 1982, https://nara .getarchive.net/media/gen-david-c-jones-chairman-joint-chief-of-staff-us-armed -forces-2nd-from-left-095035.

10. Robert P. McKenzie obituary, Together We Served, https://navy.togetherweserved .com/usn/servlet/tws.webapp.WebApp?cmd=ShadowBoxProfile&type=Assign mentExt&ID=1720215.

11. Bobby Day Bryant obituary, PeopleLegacy, accessed June 14, https://peoplelegacy .com/bobby_day_bryant-5.7D6v.

12. Billy Lee Hicks obituary, *Daily Courier*, Prescott, AZ, June 2, 2010.

13. Author interviews, Alex Landon.

14. Author interviews, Milt Silverman.

15. Author interviews, Dennis Kelly.

16. Author interviews, Gayle Lash, sister of Glenn Haase, August 19, 2021.

17. Author interviews, Bruce Locke.

18. Author interviews, Tom "TJ" Phillips.

19. Author interviews, Dick Smith.

20. My clients were protesting conditions aboard the *USS Ogden* (*LPD*-5) while it was engaged in Operation End Sweep, clearing mines in Haiphong Harbor.

21. Author interviews, Jim Bradley.

22. Author interviews, Mike Sheehy.

23. *US Naval Institute News*, "Sale of Last Conventional Supercarriers Deals Final Blow to Museum Hopes," October 13, 2021.

INDEX

Page numbers in *italics* refer to photographs.